Cultural Memory
in
the
Present

Mieke Bal and Hent de Vries, Editors

NAMING THE WITCH

James Siegel

STANFORD UNIVERSITY PRESS

STANFORD, CALIFORNIA

Stanford University Press
Stanford, California

Printed in the United States of America
on acid-free, archival-quality paper

Library of Congress Cataloging-in-Publication Data

Siegel, James T., 1937–
    Naming the witch / James Siegel.
        p.   cm. — (Cultural memory in the present)
    Includes bibliographical references.
    ISBN 0-8047-5194-3 (cloth : alk. paper)
    ISBN 0-8047-5195-1 (pbk. : alk. paper)
      1. Witchcraft.   2. Sorcery.   3. Witchcraft—Indonesia.   4. Indonesia—
Social conditions.   5. Lévi-Strauss, Claude—Criticism and interpretation.
6. Evans-Pritchard, E. E. (Edward Evan), 1902–1973—Criticism and
interpretation.   I. Title.   II. Series.
GR530.S54 2005
398'.4'09598—dc22

                                                                2005013566

Original Printing 2006

Last figure below indicates year of this printing:

15   14   13   12   11

In memory of Bernard J. Siegel

Prologue

In Banyuwangi, East Java, Indonesia, about 120 people accused of witchcraft were killed between December 1998 and the end of February 1999, just after President Suharto left office. Witch hunts continued in other parts of the country, notably in South Malang, East Java. Here are the photographs of some of the survivors, along with their statements.

~

A woman with her mother and her niece from the Banyuwangi countryside. Here is part of her statement:

Dad was accused of being a witch by the neighbors. He was a farmer and went to the fields every day. He wasn't a witch. He was just ordinary. Every day he would take part in the neighborhood gatherings [*arisan*], he would be with his friends [*silaturahmin,* a word popular in the New Order, which means something like "forging the bonds of friendship"], and so on.

Then the house was stoned. My brother was in Bali working. I waited till midnight for Dad to come home. Next morning, I went to where they had the neighborhood gathering. I saw blood. I followed the traces. I just followed them. Then I looked for him in the gardens and in the fields. Then, at five in the morning, on the edge of the road, covered with banana leaves, there he was. His leg was cut off. He was crushed in all over. His neck had a rope around it and his trunk was cut almost all the way through. [She weeps.]

I waited till nine to report to the village headman to tell the police, the doctor, and so on. Then he was brought home. He was bathed like an ordinary corpse. Why not; he was already a corpse.

He was tortured. If you saw him, Mister, if you saw him, you would be afraid to look. There was no proof. What was the proof? The real proof. Where was it?

Everyone has to die, Mister. But not tortured like that, Mister.

They arrested four people. In fact, there were lots and lots of people who came to the house. I couldn't see them all. I was afraid. I couldn't look at them one by one. In fact, they threatened to whip me. They wouldn't believe Dad wasn't here. Really. They came into the house armed with whips, looking for Dad. They took lots. On top of everything else, they were thieves, too.

Please have something to drink.

They cut him up. Just cut him up.

~

This boy's brother was arrested for the murder of three "witches." The boy himself lives in a village a few kilometers from the killings. He told us he regretted he was not there that night since he surely would have joined in. His own mother was ensorcelled by "Muki," one of the three accused sorcerers (the other two were Muki's wife and son; his daughter escaped). It was a sign of Muki's power that he was able to make this boy's mother ill at such a distance.

~

This woman's daughter married Muki's son. Neither she nor her daughter wanted the marriage, but they were convinced that if they did not comply with Muki's wish they would fall ill. After the marriage, she fell ill in any case. Her legs swelled to such an extent that she could not urinate. The rest of her body was also swollen, to the point where she had to sleep sitting up. Her husband was also afflicted. After Muki was killed, she got well. "Proof" [that Muki was a witch], she said.

~

One of the men arrested for the killing of Muki. His father, he told us, had to urinate the whole day long and finally died dried out, a victim of Muki. He was released until his trial.

~

This man's father and brother, who were also his neighbors, were killed as witches. The village headman asked them to move, anticipating the attack. They refused. The man in the picture said it was because "they had to guard their good name. If someone is a witch, its better to kill them. But really, truly, they were not witches."

When the mob came to get them, he tried to rush out of his house to protect them, but his wife and daughter sat on him to keep him safe.

Contents

Introduction   I

PART ONE: THE MAGIC WORD

1   The Truth of Sorcery   29

2   Voodoo Death   53

3   Institutionalizing Accident   70

PART TWO: WITCHES RESURRECTED

4   Suharto, Witches   III

5   Menace from All Directions   171

6   No Witch Appears   193

7   Naming the Witch   210

    Acknowledgments   233

    Notes   235

NAMING THE WITCH

Introduction

Certain historians have studied the European witch hunts of the six-teenth century to show their destructive violence. For them, the witch hunt shows how some individuals and even groups can be placed outside the community, and how therefore they can be slain with the consent and the participation of the community to which they had belonged. By con-trast, anthropologists have tended to minimize the violence of witchcraft, instead focusing on social tensions and their resolution through witchcraft accusations. Alternatively, witchcraft beliefs are shown as an effect of the force of beliefs. In the most striking of these cases, the bewitched person wastes away and dies. This, according to W. Lloyd Warner, is the result of the operation of social norms themselves. It displays the strength of society as that strength is directed against one of its members who acquiesces in its judgment. By contrast, one could, as I try to show, see this as an example of the inability of socially determined thinking (not to use the word "rea-son") to comprehend certain situations.

In anthropological views, the social itself explains witchcraft. The opposing view looks for sources of violence that serves no social purpose and stem not from social realities but from points where no definition of social reality can take place—where, therefore, phantasms and, often, violence occur, a violence that does not serve to construct new social forms or restore old ones. I will argue it is a violence that inheres in the social and that turns against it. I begin by looking at the formative anthropological studies of witchcraft, those that took the first point of view, to show that within them there is evidence of the second. My ambition is to contribute to the question of destructive violence and its provenance within anthropological study.

One might grant that witchcraft resolves no issues and still believe that it contributes to the myth of the community. One might think that the murder of the witch, even if another soon takes his or her place, aids, perhaps even founds, the coherence of the community as it bases itself against an enemy—a structural precursor of the enemy as conceived by Carl Schmitt, but only a precursor since it exists before the political as the latter understood it. But I will claim that this is not the case. In the examples we look at, no political hierarchy forms itself against the witch. Were one to do so, one would have to ask if the word "witch" has changed its reference. Instead of referring to something sensed or suspected rather than known, "witch" would have a determined, locatable sense. Perhaps if one looked at witchcraft after reading Heidegger's *Being and Time* one might be helped to understand its nature, associated as it so often is with death and being as indefinable as the death that Heidegger describes. But the immersion of the community in everyday life as Heidegger describes it, holding onto normality and thus denying the menace of death and of the uncanny, draws a line between life and death that in many cultures is not clearly evident. The witch can be a part of normality, something one anticipates and even accepts. His identification can be the route to his acceptance. Here, however, acceptance, as I understand it, is incomplete and certainly reluctant. It can also happen that the definitions generated of the witch fail, and yet something occurs which seems to deserve the name, leaving "witch" as a concept without a content, producing consternation and instability.

Moreover, an existential approach which sees the division between life and death as fundamental is difficult to apply to societies where the line between the two is fluid. Furthermore, when one approaches witchcraft from a quasi-linguistic point of view, as did Lévi-Strauss when he analyzed witchcraft as an attempt to make expressible something which ordinarily could only be suspected, what it is that is suspected remains undetermined, or so we shall argue. The menace of death in this context is itself an effect of naming the witch, rather than death being the reality counterposed against normality.

Furthermore, the opposition between "death" and "normality" will not do once one sees, as anthropologists studying Africa in particular have seen, that witchcraft is not necessarily a local matter and thus to be explained in terms of the community against a force that threatens its coherence. When witchcraft is set in the state, in the nation and in the international economy, one needs to account for complex exogenous factors. Still, witchcraft precedes the state and the international economy and has to be first examined in its local settings because it is there that the ideas of witchcraft took shape. I will thus look at the studies where the basic ideas of witchcraft were formulated before I describe a contemporary witch hunt in Indonesia.

I. The Gift, Witches

On what basis can an anthropologist justify a view of witchcraft that within the discipline has been set aside if not exactly disavowed? In the first place because there is evidence for this view in the classic anthropological studies. But also because it is possible to think about the relation between the social and witchcraft by looking at the latter from the perspective of the well-examined idea of the gift as it was formulated by Marcel Mauss and passed through the thinking of Georges Bataille and, most recently, of Jacques Derrida.

For Bataille, in "archaic" societies (we would today call them societies based on gift exchange), exchange had a characteristic lost in later historical evolution. Bataille took Mauss's description of the potlatch and noted that the economies of the societies who practiced it were based on consumption and therefore on loss. In the potlatch, as Mauss has noted, hierarchy is established through the ostentatious giving of gifts, challenging the receiver to reply in kind. This "nonproductive expenditure" is nonetheless useful since it establishes a social structure. The person who gives is superior to the one who receives. He noted also, again following Mauss, that sometimes, in place of gifts, goods were destroyed. Display of loss alone was enough to open a form of communication that in bourgeois society in particular has been lost. Eventually, nonproductive expenditure becomes ruled out, to the point that even "the most lucid man" no longer imagines "that a human society can have . . . an *interest* in considerable losses, in catastrophes that, *while conforming to well-defined needs,* provoke tumultuous depressions, crises of dread, and, in the final analysis, a certain orgiastic state." "But," Bataille added, "this exclusion is superficial." He wavered on the question of whether such negativity would always be incorporated into social structure or not.[1]

The negativity of the potlatch, the willingness to risk everything, is easily assimilated to the risk of death in the Hegelian duel. The duel is preceded by entities which oscillate, each taking the place of the other, and ends with defined positions, the master and the slave, the master being the one who risks everything and the slave the one who prefers life and who therefore consents to slavery. The destruction of valuables and the risk of death in the Hegelian duel have in common that a negativity, through the risk of oneself as a social being, results in structure.[2] Bataille understood the potlatch as "a kind of deliriously formed ritual poker. But the players can never retire from the game, their fortunes made; they remain at the mercy of provocation."[3] Without the ever present possibility of provocation, there could be no challenge and hence no response. Somehow, in the moments of giving or destruction there is the opening of a fundamental sort of communication which cannot be ignored. Jean-Luc Nancy characterizes it: "Bataille communicates to me that pain and that pleasure which result from the impossibility of communicating anything at all without touching the limit where all meaning spills out of itself like a simple ink stain on a word."[4]

Precisely because there is communication, it seems to follow that there is also community. But there remains the possibility of a negativity that not only fails to reach full expression but also produces no community and yet has effects. "What would it take . . . to think the logic of the gift in its most rigorous form? To think a giving so 'pure' it would tolerate no return . . . a giving which would exceed every circuit of compensation and challenge every measure of exchange?" asks Rebecca Comay.[5] Could one still speak of "communication"? If so, socially constructed entities would neither constitute its recipients or its agents, nor would they be its result.

Is it necessary that a gift beget a return, that there always be a discourse that would make the possibility of a gift without the waking of obligation, hence return, impossible?

The gift demands a return gift, said Mauss in his famous essay on the subject. In certain societies exchange primarily takes the form of gifts. "In theory these are voluntary, in reality they are given and reciprocated obligatorily."[6] But, said Jacques Derrida, a true gift must be disinterested. Such a gift is hard to imagine in practice. "For there to be a gift, *it is necessary* [*il faut*] that the donee not give back, . . . and that he never have contracted a debt."[7] He adds, "A true gift has to be given without thought of recompense. One could go so far as to say that a work as monumental as Marcel Mauss's *The Gift* speaks of everything but the gift."[8] Mauss, said Derrida, did not understand what a gift is, "*if there is any.*"[9] Not only should the giver not expect a return, he should not even recognize what he gives as a gift. "This simple recognition suffices to annul the gift. Why? Because it gives back, in the place . . . of the thing itself, a symbolic equivalent."[10] Recognizing something as a gift, one thinks of another object which would match it. The conventional gift appears as a gesture, a symbol, addressed to us. And with that there is the possibility of response. Recognizing the object as a gift brings with it gratitude. And thus there is no more gift.[11] Receiving whatever is given destroys the possibility of the gift. Perhaps the most social of objects, one on which, one can argue, the social bond rests, is never achieved in social life.

There may be no pure gift, but there are gifts that seem purer than others. We feel most strongly indebted when a gift comes to us without any previous sense that the donor was obligated to us. The less he was obligated, the more we are grateful. Nothing about ourselves that we are aware of made it necessary that we be given something; we may come to feel that we have previously unknown attractive attributes. The gift that approaches the true gift is thus always a surprise.

It is possible that surprise is present even in the most conventional forms of the gift. There is a well-known passage in Mauss's *The Gift*, in which Mauss cites the ethnographer Elsdon Best quoting a Maori about a concept central to formalized Maori gift exchange, the *hau*.

The *hau* is not the wind that blows—not at all. Let us suppose that you possess a certain article (*taonga*) and that you give me this article. You give it to me without setting a price on it. We strike no bargain about it. Now, I give this article to a third person who, after a certain lapse of time, decides to give me something as payment in return (*utu*). He makes a present to me of something (*taonga*). Now, this *taonga* that he give me is the spirit (*hau*) of the *taonga* that I had received from you and that I had given to *him*. The *taonga* that I received for these *taonga* (which came from you must be returned to you).[12]

The *hau* is the spirit that makes the gift circulate. When a Maori gets "a certain article" as a gift, he knows both who gave it to him and why it circulates if not why he himself received the gift. This, despite the complicated triangular trajectory. You give me something; I do not give back to you. I give to someone else, a third person, and it is another person again who gives something back to me. This last person gives me something in return because the thing is animated by something that also animated the gift I received from you. If it were not for this spirit, there would be no return. The gift, as in other places where gifts circulate, is not dyadic. It owes its power to a force which later Mauss will interpret in a Durkheimian manner: the power to circulate is a social force, an expression of society itself.

No matter where the gift is at any moment, it always comes indirectly from a third party. There is no original giver; the person who first gave me the gift got it from someone else. I did not get the gift because the donor wanted to give it to me. Rather, he was obliged to give it to me. The source of the obligation is seen through the string of third parties. Each time I get a gift, it comes from "elsewhere." The name of this "elsewhere" is a force that transcends any particular individual, meaning that the gift always embodies something strange. It cannot be reduced to the volition of any particular giver. It rather contains in itself an element foreign to any particular giver and receiver. No one who holds the object can ever claim complete ownership; the foreign element obliges him to put the object back in circulation. This foreignness is given a name, *hau*.

Mauss found this text "of capital importance." His account of how he came across it is unusual for an author who ordinarily avoids the superfluous. He introduces the text referring to "our much regretted friend Hertz."[13] Robert Hertz was one of the group around Durkheim who was killed in World War I. Mauss took on the task of completing the work of his fallen colleagues. The "much regretted Hertz" was, according to Mauss, aware of the facts of the *taonga*. "With his touching disinterestedness he had noted down 'For Davy and Mauss,' on the card recording the following fact."[14] The fact on the card is merely that Maori had an exchange system. "But Hertz had also noted—and I found it among his records—a text whose importance had escaped the notice of both of us, for I was equally unaware of it."[15] Mauss here refers to the text quoted above. This text was "capital" because it illustrated the Durkheimian notion of exchange. His lengthy exposition of his indebtedness to Hertz for his understanding of exchange, which starts with this text, is finally ambiguous. He and Hertz both knew of the text, but neither had seen its importance. Even though both had overlooked its importance, somehow without Hertz he would neither have come across it nor understood it.

Mauss feels obligated to Hertz for a gift. One that comes to him only after Hertz's death. It is this that accounts for the convoluted tracking of Hertz's influence, which is both acknowledged and denied. Both had missed the significance of the text; nonetheless, Mauss saw it due to Hertz, in his, Mauss's opinion. The regretted Hertz is still effective. His effects are felt after his death in the stimulation they gave Mauss to look carefully at the Maori passage. What he regarded as his discovery—the nature of gift exchange, its obligatory and voluntary character—he feels came to him from the dead. He is obliged to Hertz and he acknowledges his obligation for something which he got from Hertz but which was not Hertz's but which somehow is attributed to him after his death. It is now his, Mauss's, but he is obliged to pass it on to others. We in turn acknowledge our debt to him in elaborating his discovery.

Mauss's discovery is a gift from beyond, just as Maori gifts come from a distant and inhuman source. In both cases one can name the immediate giver and this does not suffice to account for the obligation one feels. It is necessary to look further; in one case to the *hau*, in the other to death. The gift comes from nowhere. It is truly a gift when one cannot account for its origins; when one knows only that the parties who exchange are not responsible. As in the potlatch, the giver must be possessed by a spirit, with the result that the recipient is also. In the case of Mauss and Hertz, we can substitute "inspired" for "possessed." A chief involved in the potlatch, says Mauss, "can only preserve his authority over his tribe and village, and even over his family, he can only maintain his rank among the chiefs . . . if he can prove he is haunted and favoured both by the spirits and by good fortune, that he is possessed, and also possesses it."[16] Only those haunted by spirits can convert the gift into hierarchical position. In the same way, the value of Mauss's discovery, the possibility of his being known as the one who understands the gift, is, in his mind, enhanced when it comes to him through the inspiration of Hertz. He made the discovery, but it was not he himself who was responsible. It possesses a value which he did not create but which came from beyond him. He possesses and is possessed by his discovery; he must pass it on to others.

We can understand the naming of this possession as the domestication of the pure gift. It is a way of saying that what I received came from somewhere; that it has an origin, even if that origin is always a third party. It thus claims the gift as social against the possibility that what one receives comes somehow from outside that realm. A pure gift would go unnoticed by the very definition of the gift. Once noticed, the possibility of something having arrived that entirely exceeds recognition is denied. In place of a lack of origin, there is instead, "*hau*," "death," "inspiration," and other crucial ideas as well, which institute the social in the place where otherwise we recognize nothing.

The pure gift would not be recognized as such. Whatever we received "for no reason" would seem to come to us accidentally. The roll of $50 bills we find on the street comes to us by chance. It is an accident, not a gift, unless we think that luck, a word similar to *hau*, is with us. What happens to us accidentally could be considered a gift, though not necessarily one we enjoy receiving. It is in the accident, in this sense, that the major interpretation of witchcraft, one which still stands in anthropological thinking and practice, was founded. E. E. Evans-Pritchard, explaining the nature of witchcraft among the Azande of the southern Sudan, began with the example of a granary which, one day while people were sitting beneath it, collapsed. We shall treat this famous example at length later. Suffice it to say here that Azande who know about termites gnawing through the supports are not satisfied with this as a reason for the calamity. They ask rather about the particularities of the event. Why did the granary collapse at that moment, and with certain people beneath it. In looking for their answer, they find the witch to whom the event is attributed.

Where ideas of witchcraft prevail, "the notion of witchcraft explains unfortunate events," said E. E. Evans-Pritchard in a famous phrase. Evans-Pritchard even went further: "The concept of witchcraft . . . provides [Azande] with a natural philosophy . . . " Western philosophical tradition depends on banishing magic and on basing knowledge on what reason can comprehend. Witchcraft makes comprehensible what is beyond reason. Evans-Pritchard's sentence continues, " . . . by which the relations between men and unfortunate events are explained and a ready and stereotyped means of reacting to such events."[17] This cheerful understanding of the witch follows (or perhaps established) the anthropological tendency to avoid thinking both the violence of witchcraft and the fear it inspires. Witch killings among the Azande were rare at the time Evans-Pritchard lived with them. But Azande believed that death was caused by witches and were accordingly terrified of them. Explanations of the cause of death ameliorated its sting in the assumption of Evans-Pritchard, but as we will see, Azande society was permeated by suspicion. One could equally well argue that belief in witchcraft kept the fear of death more present than otherwise it might have been.

The accident which occurs "for no reason" and affects my life, comes, like the gift that it is, from nowhere. "Witch" names the accident and asserts that it has a source. What happens "for no reason" and therefore proceeds from no place namable is possibly recovered for the social, if only in ambiguously contributing to a myth in which death is extraneous to life. But it is not always possible to establish this myth, with the result that "witch" does not work as an explanation even though the word continues to be used.

The murderers of witches whom I know were certain that they were fully justified in their acts, even when the court found them guilty. Their defense, indeed, was to admit to murder. Doing so en masse hampered the police in finding the individuals who had dealt the fatal blows. They acted, they said, out of necessity. They were obliged to kill the witch in order to protect the community from death. They did not understand why the police did not support them. The witch killers feared their own deaths and acted to prevent it from happening in the next instant. They thought of their violence as restoring normal life. Indirectly, their fear mediated a gift whose content, identical to its source, "death," once named was impossible to make part of social life and which therefore had to be eliminated. Everything depended, for them, on giving this gift a name. Its correct identification and the action that resulted would restore their normal bonds with each other. But their understanding was never accepted by the society in which they lived. They were possessed by something they could not make known to anyone outside their circle and even, it is possible to argue, to themselves.

Precisely this non-meaning would be the indication of something else at work. There would be an effect of the negative which would remain behind any possibility of signification and yet still somehow announce itself. The name they gave to what they knew, "witch," meant to them, "bearer of death." But "death" here was a word arising from the attempt to name something unnamable. One does not dare to say it was only a word. These murderers were obsessed with the communication of nothing at all, Jean-Luc Nancy's "a simple ink stain on a word," a signifier with indefinite, infinite references.

When it concerns writing, we are likely to call this sort of communication "literature," of course. It builds a community in a way that Bataille and many others felt had been lost in bourgeois society. It binds those who read, creating a community in that limited sense, but remains, too often, outside the usefulness of society as we know it today. Yet in societies without the "strange institution" [Derrida's term] of literature, what place is there for such a communication? (Which is not to say that literature guarantees peace in those places where literature exists.) What then occurs? Sometimes witchcraft is itself made into a strange institution, as among the Azande. And sometimes it is not institutionalized. Outside the institution it rages and calls for recognition, but it does not achieve it.

When one finds events magically linked together, it is partly because the conventions of magic allow one to do so. But sometimes it is because no conventions account for such linkage and yet one makes them anyway. One must somehow be prepared to do so. This preparation occurs in conditions which are historically given. Yet the description of historical circumstances cannot account for accusations of witchcraft; the same conditions produce accusations in some and not in others. Witchcraft brings people to the limit of their understanding of others in regard to themselves. One wants to describe these circumstances without using them to explain away the negative. To do so, one must change perspective in order to hold accident and the strange sort of communication that occurs in some cases of witchcraft in view. One needs to undo explanation by the description of naming the witch itself. The second half of this book describes a case of witchcraft using this double perspective. The first half looks at early anthropological studies which did so much to indicate the nature of witchcraft, out of which comes the problems and the outlook that govern the second half.

II. Studying Witchcraft

The British social anthropologist Lucy Mair, in a book written in 1969 that summed up the state of the study, defined "witch" in a way that anthropologists today still find acceptable:

> In many parts of the world people believe that it is possible for human beings to cause harm to their fellows by the exercise of powers not possessed by ordinary folk, powers which operate in a manner that cannot be detected, so that the cause can only be recognized when the damage comes to light. The persons who are supposed to have these powers are commonly called witches.[18]

One notes the "supposed" in this definition. Witchcraft is assumed by Mair to be fantasy because it tries to answer questions that have no answer: "The question always remains, 'Why me? Why just then?'"[19] That witchcraft is phantasmatic does not make it necessarily violent. And that it is violent does not necessarily mean that its violence is socially useless. But it seems as if from the time it began to be analyzed the power associated with witchcraft has been suspected of lying outside ordinary categories of power, not merely because it is "mystical," to use the term Mair used, but also because it is a sort of violence that exceeds legitimacy. Jean Bodin, for instance, the inventor of the idea of sovereignty, wrote a long treatise on witchcraft in 1580 in order to deny that it had an autonomous source of power which would have conflicted with that of the sovereign. The power of both was from God. Bodin believed in witches, but witchcraft has few defenders, though it does have some, as we will see. It is usually considered to be a source, if not "the" source, of trouble and is therefore if possible eliminated but certainly opposed and its force attributed to extraordinary sources.

The malevolence of witchcraft makes it from time to time the object of study of those who want to know about the extreme events of the twentieth century. Is there such a thing as a power which cannot be assimilated to social structure, which is socially useless and, worse, merely destructive? This question, of course, was forced on us again by Nazism. The historian H. R. Trevor-Roper studied the witch hunts of the sixteenth and seventeenth centuries in order to explain the extraordinary violence of the Nazi period. He concluded that at a certain moment some groups were unassimilable for reasons that had to do with the state of the society in which they lived.[20] Unbeknownst to Trevor-Roper, the sources he used were forgeries, and his findings were dismissed. But the idea that witchcraft depends on unassimilability, or at least on the refusal to accept "the other" remains. The questions of how the other is formed and the generation of power that issues in their elimination still press.[21]

Anthropologists, especially those working in Africa, have been less concerned with its violence than with its social functions. At the same time, the formative studies of witchcraft in particular did not neglect violence. They found its origins in local social structures. Today, anthropological investigations have taken a new direction. The global economy and the state, rather than, or, sometimes, as much as, local considerations are seen as the setting for witchcraft. In Cameroon people accused of witchcraft can be brought before the courts and judged. Usually they are convicted on the evidence of an expert considered to have supernatural powers, not at all the same powers that, for instance, authorize the judge.[22] The state recognizes the power of witchcraft, leading to further complications. The crux of the problem was formulated in the eighteenth century. The citizen of a civil state, according to Rousseau, was obliged to rise above private interests and instinctual behavior:

The passage from the state of nature to the civil state produces a very remarkable change in man, by substituting justice for instinct in his conduct, and giving his actions the morality they formerly lacked. Then only, when the voice of duty takes the place of physical impulses and right of appetite, does man, who so far had considered only himself, find that he is forced to act on different principles, and to consult his reason before listening to his inclinations.[23]

Witchcraft, following this formulation, might be considered instinctual or natural, a giving in to spontaneous feelings of hatred. The defenders of witchcraft, however, do not necessarily defend hatred. Steve Biko of the African National Congress, said this:

> We [the black consciousness movement] do not reject it [witchcraft]. We regard it as part of the mystery of our cultural heritage. . . . Whites are not superstitious; whites do not have witches and witch doctors. We are the people who have this.[24]

Biko defends witchcraft as superstition. But this particular superstition is traditional. This changes its nature. It is not natural but cultural, an inherited form which is valuable enough to defend. Biko understands that whites reject superstition. They cannot assimilate it into their thinking. Africans have done so. Whites are incapable of doing so so long as they cling to reason, which is the opposite of superstition and incompatible with it. For a white to do so would alienate him from himself and his kind. That is not the case for Africans. Africans, defending witchcraft, defend something they have in common. If, then, an African state endorses witchcraft, it is understandable.[25]

Understandable, but still not acceptable to those outside the tradition, if for no other reason than justice. "Witch hunt," in English, is used metaphorically as a label for the persecution of innocent people charged with crimes they did not commit and prosecuted with evidence either insufficient or manufactured. For Rousseau, accession to the state implies also accession to reason, which assures proper procedures. The state, as Rousseau understood it, would be opposed to witchcraft as incompatible with the conduct of public life.

Biko implicitly answers Rousseau. Witchcraft can and even should form a part of public life, at least in Africa. In his defense of sorcery he speaks not only of witches but also of witch doctors. By the latter, I take it he means curers and those who protect against witchcraft. Witchcraft should be part of public life in order to defend against the fears that it brings. To whites, superstition brings fear; to eliminate it is to eliminate fear. To Biko, "witchcraft," as superstition and as an element of tradition, means bringing fear to light. Not to acknowledge witchcraft would be not to acknowledge secret activities that one would have to deal with in private ways or without established procedures. He implies not that he advocates witchcraft, but rather the recognition of its "mystery," a possibility not open to those who refuse to recognize the irrational as having a part in public life. With its recognition comes the possibility of defense against what issues from enigmatic traditional belief.

The relation he makes between fear and traditional forms makes one ask about the nature of these forms. Can there be an institution established on the basis of fear which is not merely the defense against that fear but also the assertion, and many would say, the production of it? Lévi-Strauss, for instance, in an article I shall deal with at length, describes a Zuni man who, accused of sorcery, Lévi-Strauss claims, was pardoned. Admitting he was a sorcerer, he displayed truth and this was more important than justice. This is akin to the widespread African practice in which the admission of witchcraft is also its neutralization. But it is more than that, and Biko's statement also goes beyond the assertion that to admit to witchcraft is to tame it. Witchcraft is a fact in his statement, and therefore to acknowledge it is necessary. One cannot help but assert that there are witches when they exist. "We" have always done so. Thus the witch comes into being: nothing is proof against him, he is never entirely eliminated, and he becomes part of African traditions.

Witchcraft moreover displays a violence which remains socially untamed. Isak Neuhaus shows how during the battle against apartheid in South Africa there were many accusations of witchcraft accompanied not by pardon but by execution of those accused of witchcraft who supported the regime. But it was impossible to keep witchcraft accusations and political affiliations aligned. Similarly, in Cameroon analysts first asserted that the recognition of witchcraft by the state, the bringing to trial of accused witches, was a tactic of new elites who saw accusations of witchcraft against them as political maneuvers. These elites, it was said, were trying to eliminate witchcraft. Peter Geschiere, however, has shown that witchcraft in Cameroon is more ambiguous than that. Those who make accusations of witchcraft attribute occult power to others who succeed where they do not; they are jealous. But this power, for which Geschiere cannot find an adequate adjective in French or English, exceeds even malevolence. What we call witchcraft makes for success and success is itself ambivalent. There is more than jealousy involved; to perceive witchcraft at work is to become excited at being close to power. This power, however, remains outside the constitution of state institutions. But instead of the political class acting to eliminate witchcraft, witchcraft becomes built into the understanding of the operations of politics and commerce. However, as I understand Geschiere, it does not furnish the authority by which a policeman arrests you. It may be that the policeman came across you, however, because you were cursed.

The African state is not Rousseau's. In its recognition of irrational factors, it might be considered by some as in advance of the liberal West. But even were the African state to be Rousseauist and still, by some magic, able to recognize witchcraft, we would have to know whether or not it is at the cost of obscuring its nature. Its genesis in accident remains. We would be faced with either generating a mystery of another sort or of overlooking the way in which accident produces effects while at the same time concealing its nature as accident and therefore as singularity. The problem is to describe the nexus of singular events, their effects on thinking and the violence that accompanies them, while at the same time seeing the complex role of political, social, and cultural factors in any given incident.

But before we can began to do so we are faced with the difficulty of knowing whether we are studying anything at all. Witchcraft has articulate defenders whose criticism of anthropologists is that they leave out the essential of witchcraft and do not allow those who believe in witchcraft to reply to anthropological descriptions of their beliefs.[26] Steve Biko's comments were recorded in the 1970s. He emphasized the difference between Africans and whites. Some today defend witchcraft from another standpoint. They contend that anthropological explanations, and even Evans-Pritchard's in particular, a founder of modern anthropological study, leave them out by emphasizing the difference between Africans and Westerners.[27] Viewed from the outside, from a post-Enlightenment perspective, witchcraft is delusion, even if it has its uses, as anthropologists show it to have. Viewed from the inside, by its believers, witchcraft has a reality whose denial puts them at peril. The discourse of anthropologists reinforces that denial by reducing witchcraft to causes located in social tensions, for instance, thus missing what its victims are saying.

And what do they say? A statement frequently reported, not merely in Cameroon but elsewhere in Africa, is, "The colonial state [which prohibited the prosecution of witches] did not protect us," with the implication that the independent state ought to do so.[28] They mean by this that colonial states often forbade the prosecution of witches and thus left sorcerers free to do their work. The Cameroon state recognizes witchcraft because citizens of Cameroon demand protection from witches by the state. The very formulation of a demand by "the people," the subjects of the state, and its response enters witchcraft into a discourse of modernity. But what makes its modernity questionable is that it does not accept the line between public and private which regulates the relation of the liberal state to its subjects. It is not that witchcraft is unthinkable, but that it is understandable only as the subjective beliefs and fears which the liberal state can regulate merely in their external manifestations. Thus, a zoning law might say where a church can be located, but the state cannot say what the worshippers in that church should believe. There are self-proclaimed witches in America, Britain, France, and other places today. Their practices are tolerated by the state as the personal beliefs of individuals. But the liberal state does not and cannot recognize a power intrinsic to witchcraft itself. When accusations of witchcraft broke out recently in the United States, certain people were convicted of child abuse, but no one was convicted of witchcraft. How could they be? Nowadays in the United States one cannot convict people of believing in the devil (not at all a necessary part of witchcraft, particularly outside Europe and America), only of causing harm while carrying out their beliefs. Today, in the West, the power thought intrinsic to sorcery by its believers is unintelligible in a court of law. There is no such power in the eyes of the law; there is only the behavior of individuals, each comparable with the other by the same standards.

If the state acts otherwise, it recognizes as a reality what is unrecognizable as such by the cannons of evidence, both legal and philosophical, current in the West.[29] Furthermore, were it to do so, liberal ideas of toleration which depend on leaving unjudged the beliefs of others are put into question. In Cameroon, a person can be sentenced to ten years in jail on the testimony of experts who see signs of witchcraft by virtue of powers unique to themselves and who assess the qualities of the person—"He is a witch."[30]

The anthropology of colonial times saw the positive functions of witchcraft; the conflict that went with it was benign and even helped to maintain social structures. The content of beliefs might also be described, as it is today. To do so meant to decode what was said in an idiom that was strange but whose content could be accepted as the beliefs of others—beliefs which responded to social tensions and ambiguities. But as I have said, some Africans today feel they exist only as subjects of a discourse which does not allow them the possibility of reply.[31] Faced with this, contem- ← porary anthropologists assert, "We must listen to what they are saying," and showing that they have listened, they explicate the categories through which the phenomenon called "witchcraft" is conceptualized, and show at the same time that such thinking is compatible with the life of a modern state. There is nothing incompatible for most anthropologists, or, for that matter, historians, in analyzing the substantive ideas of witchcraft while also treating the political contexts in which it is found. This still, however, leaves those who claim the validity of witchcraft on the other side of a divide. "They" are left out of our discourse and "we" are left out of theirs. The editors of an anthology that takes up this question find the solution by considering witchcraft as part of a "generalized form of thought" which takes different shapes in different places but is found everywhere.[32] This, it seems to me, makes witchcraft seem more easily retrievable than it is. As we will see, no matter how eager we may be to close it, the gap between anthropological investigator and subject remains, and even structures the study, as it must if we accept Biko's formulation that witchcraft is a "mystery," belief in which marks the difference between cultural traditions.

Without the frisson that comes to the anthropologist, and that, in my experience, is one of the pleasures of ethnography, when one has to take seriously that which one cannot accept, anthropology, as the study of the other, would change its nature. It may already have done so, but without, in my opinion, studying the consequences. There is no question that an analysis of the idioms of witchcraft is possible but whether this makes it part of a "generalized form of thought" that allows the sort of communication between its believers and its analysts rather than simply making the gap apparent is not clear. I should add that it is not only in situations of cultural difference, but of difference of any kind, that this gap occurs.

The anthropological predilection, which I share, to explain in local terms risks losing sight of certain aspects of witchcraft. The contextualizing of it risks its denaturing. One glides over the killings that often enough accompany witch hunts and the extreme fear they can produce as one unravels the logic of the beliefs and the reasons one might have to murder. Furthermore, this logic, unacceptable to the anthropologist himself or herself—we do not ordinarily end up practicing witchcraft or protecting ourselves against it—becomes merely the beliefs of others in a place where everyone, it seems, believes in witches.

On the other hand, for historians of the West, the injustice of witchcraft accusations and the violence that followed has often prompted its study. The developments in witchcraft, on the one hand, and the interesting recent analyses of witchcraft by historians make it seem, at least to me, more important than ever to understand its violence. Studies of historians of Europe, for instance, indicate that witch hunts were instigated from outside the village and that they were part of the movement by which the state established itself. Christina Larner, for instance, in her important work on witch hunts in Scotland, located the persecution of witches in the breakdown of the feudal order and the beginning of the centralized state. There were witches before, but they were contained within the village. The notion of the witch was reformulated. Instead of a village figure from whom one could demand restitution for harm suffered, the witch now seen by jurists and theologians was in league with the devil.[33] In effect, witchcraft was seen as a power not only alternative to that of the state, but one which menaced it, with the result that instead of sporadic individual persecutions, there was the continuous routing of witches on a large scale.

In studies of witchcraft on the continent, Robert Muchembled showed how witch hunts were the attempt of the state, in the process of its formation, to do away with the authority that passed from women to their children in favor of the authority of schools. He thus explains why European witches were mainly women, which is not the case in most other places. Larner saw Christianity as the first ideology of the state. It became important to peasants of Scotland, whereas it had not been before, and it became a means to try to enforce obedience to the state. Muchembled's explanation runs on similar lines. He, too, sees the witch hunts as a way to form the subject of the state. The violence involved in doing so indicates the resistance encountered as well as the fears of the interrogators.[34]

The explanations of European witchcraft posit a complex interaction between village and state. The educated persons of the nascent state feared the witches that they invented. Indeed, if they did not, there would probably have been no witch hunts. They thus reflected the attitudes of villagers, but they also inflected the latter. The question of the fear, without which witchcraft as we know it does not exist, is located in a certain contagion which begins in the village, even as the witch is re-formulated by those connected to the state. One then has to ask what instigates this fear. The explanations of historians rest on the unsettled political situation. However correct such explanations might be, they do not account for the fact that fear expressed itself through witchcraft accusations.

The idea that fear of witches was an effect of the workings of power was formulated by Michel Foucault. Foucault would have disagreed with Trevor-Roper. One cannot account for social exclusion by the qualities of the excluded or the temporary state of a society. In twice discussing the book of the psychoanalyst Thomas Szasz which linked the witch of earlier times with the psychoanalytic patient of today, Foucault accepted the connection, but not because the two had qualities in common. One should look instead at the genealogy of exclusion that runs through European history. Foucault remarks:

The book of Szasz does not say . . . the mad person was the sorcerer of another era, or that the sorcerer from another time is the mad person of today. It says something else, historically and politically more important: the practices by which one marks a certain number of people, and through which one suspects them, isolates them, interrogates them and by which one "recognizes" them as witches are techniques of power, begun under the Inquisition which one finds today (after being transformed) as psychiatric practice.[35]

Foucault's view of witchcraft is thus a version of his view of madness. The advantage of his approach is that it does not assume a constant meaning of madness which merely takes different forms. Rather, it thinks of madness and its equivalents as produced by the thinking of those in power, which changes through time. Here is a theory of social exclusion which does not take for granted the qualities of the excluded as the cause of their exclusion.

The African case, however, casts doubt on Foucault's suggestion, as it exemplifies a historical trend quite different from that which prevailed in Europe. It is clear that Cameroon, for instance, is not the Rousseauist state. In the latter, the rationality posited as necessary to belong to the state is implicitly directed against traditional feudal social relations. The formation of the Western state at the time of the breakup of the feudal order contrasts with the genesis of many African and Asian states formed by colonial authorities and which, responding to the demands of their inhabitants after independence, embody elements of traditional beliefs, adapting them to current situations. It is true that an argument has been made which would make them comparable. It has been claimed that African witchcraft was a threat to the centralizing tendencies of the state, as has been said also of Europe, and that the courts were interested in eradicating it for that reason.[36] But Fisiy and Geschiere point out that the Cameroon court's use of mystical experts implies official recognition of witchcraft. "One can wonder whether the new persecutions do not confirm the belief in witchcraft instead of eradicating it."[37] The state tries witches, but not in order to banish alternative sources of power incompatible with those of the state. Rather the opposite. Witches are tried because of popular demand. (In some African states, such as South Africa, where the same demand has been made, the state has refused to do so.)

Evans-Pritchard is included in the objections of Africans who find themselves mere subjects of his study. Evans-Pritchard's first studies of magic were devoted to showing that one need not posit a difference in mentality, as had Lévy-Bruhl, to see the reasonableness of magic. Looking at its logic, once one sees its premises, and looking at its practice, one can understand it. His contemporary critics, however, say, somewhat bewilderingly to me, that the premise of the argument of Lévy-Bruhl continues in the minds of readers of Evans-Pritchard's major book on witchcraft, *Witchcraft, Oracles, and Magic among the Azande*.[38] But if one reads Evans-Pritchard's study in a certain way, it may be that we can approach what those Africans who asked for the protection of the state are trying to express. We might pay more attention not merely to the misfortune but to the trajectory which leads from an accident to an accusation of witchcraft. The difficulty comes when we see that between accident and misfortune there is a gap. Accident, as Evans-Pritchard explained it, is singular. It happens once, "to me." The problem in explanation is not to account for the collapse of the granary physically, as the work of termites, for instance, but to explain "Why was I there just at that moment?" Between the singularity of the event and the explanation there is necessarily a discrepancy. One can say, "It was the work of a witch," but in effect this means, "There is no explanation." One has recourse to an account of events which can not be validated by ordinary means. African insistence on protection from witches and anthropological insistence on explaining the "real" cause of their fears are necessarily at odds since the latter reduce the fears of the bewitched to more general categories, whereas Africans who insist on the word "witch" say, in effect, that singularity has its own category, a category that cannot be transformed into others. Not to be able to transform a category of knowledge into another is a way of saying, "We agree that the event contained within this category is unknowable." If we hold on to this quality of witchcraft, I contend, we will see something Lévi-Strauss later postulated, namely that it is not explanation that is at stake but rather the possibility of bringing to expression something otherwise only suspected and incapable of being signified in the normal way. As Lévi-Strauss expressed it, and as this problem has been taken up by others, it is scarcely one limited to Africa, rooted as it is in the nature of signification itself. The question is to account for the effects of this failed attempt at signification.

The difficulty of studying witchcraft, then, is that it remains inaccessible, not only to the anthropologist, but, it often seems, to those who believe in it. Peter Geschiere, author of *The Modernity of Witchcraft*, the excellent study of Cameroon from which I have drawn much of my material about that place, wrote that he began to take witchcraft seriously when he realized that, interested as he was in the modernity of life in Cameroon, he had to understand that witchcraft was linked to power and that "discourses on sorcery or witchcraft are intertwined, often in surprising ways, with modern changes."[39] Consequently, he had to find the ideas that governed witchcraft. Indeed, without trying to explain the other in his own terms, anthropology would not exist. The question is how to do so. The preface to the English-language edition, by a colleague of Geschiere, Wyatt MacGaffey, points out that educated and influential Africans are now disregarding Western opinions. "It is time we listened to them [Africans], but to do so it is first necessary to be able to hear in indigenous languages, to liberate ourselves from what Geschiere calls the 'moralizing terminology' of 'witchcraft' and 'sorcery,' so that we may begin to understand [their] concepts."[40] Because, after all, there may be no such thing as witchcraft, only a series of local practices which Westerners perhaps wrongly group together.

Perhaps it is always important to understand what pe⌐ ˙ especially so in the study of witchcraft since the latt⌐ ˙

on what is said, unlike, for instance, a study of the economy. In order to understand witchcraft, it is necessary to listen, not only to be sure that we have an integral object of study, but, in the first place, to comprehend the attempt to signify. This rests on the ability to hear tonality as opposed to content. And, indeed, it is through a question of tonality that Geschiere himself says he began to take witchcraft seriously. He reports how his car broke down in the forest. Geschiere felt "ill at ease," but his assistant, Meke, felt excited. Geschiere, the perfect field worker, since he recorded the statement of his assistant at this random moment, quotes Meke:

"Oh, if Mendonga was with us. We are like innocent kids. But she would see the witches that fly around here. She has the second sight. She can see what mischief they are plotting."[41]

Mendonga was a woman from a neighboring village, the greatest witch doctor of the area. Hearing this, Geschiere realized that, whereas he felt anxious, his assistant felt excited to be close to power. When he saw this, he began to investigate witchcraft as the explanation of the success of people in the national arena.

Geschiere's study begins, then, by taking seriously what he had not paid sufficient attention to earlier. He had not seen how a certain notion of power, one to which he had no direct access, could explain events to the point where witchcraft and modernity, at least by certain definitions, could go together. Not that Geschiere became a believer, or even that he approved of what he saw. He says of his study, that

it stems from an effort to take distance from the vicious circles of witchcraft and sorcery: from the hope, no doubt naïve, that showing how these discourses are linked to specific historical and cultural contexts might relativize their self evidence and weaken their hold over people's minds.[42]

It apparently is not enough to know in advance that one must understand the other in his own terms and his own language and that one should study the concepts that govern witchcraft wherever it is to be found. It takes something more. In this case, it is a matter of Geschiere seeing that his assistant knows there is something present which he, the assistant, cannot see but which someone else could:

I was . . . struck by the clear note of excitement and regret in his voice. Apparently, he regretted—at least at this moment—that he was an "innocent" without special powers. For the first time I understood that *la sorcellerie* (witchcraft/sorcery) was not just something evil to the people among whom I lived but that it also meant thrill, excitement, and the possibility of access to unknown powers.[43]

Geschiere describes a critical moment in his study, but it is also a strange one. He understands something about sorcery precisely when he hears his assistant say that he, Meke, does not have access to sorcery. He does not learn about sorcery as such. He learns, instead, that something inaccessible excites people in ways he had not suspected before. His understanding of the subjects of his study depends on a moment when they reveal that they have no access to what he wants to study. At that moment, he finds himself on the track to understanding. The next sentence continues, "I realized also that I risked overlooking an essential dimension of my research if I continued to neglect the close conceptual link for these people between witchcraft and power."[44]

Geschiere turns to sorcery at the moment when he sees that it captivates people. But that captivation seems to have something to do with not being able to grasp it ("If only . . . "). Geschiere himself feels at the same time an imperative need to understand. He says, "One must listen to them." He finds himself listening and still not understanding. He knows he is in the presence of something. The imperative is to bring that "thing," in whose presence he feels and in which he does not believe, to the understanding of himself and of others. Just at the moment he feels excluded from something and that something is unbelievable, he finds a gap between himself and . . . The rest of the sentence is hard to fill in. Is it Africans, Cameroonians, the people of the area, his friend and assistant? He sees that he does not understand, and he must have known that he was not understood. How can he be when he does not believe in what they believe, even if he can speak of the "modernity of witchcraft." He can take the stance of the ethnologist, but if he does, he simply consolidates the criticism of Africans: they are excluded. And he is excluded, at least by himself, from their point of view.

This argument might be reframed. From the point of view of its practice, belief in witches can be seem as a form of the sublime. Kant spoke of the sublime as a feature of a reaction to nature. In nature there exists an objective quality which we cannot cognize, or at least have not yet ever done so. Faced with such, we feel overcome. Our mental powers fail us.

But we recuperate ourselves because even if we cannot define whatever it is that is in front of us, in taking in its objectivity we realize that we do in fact have powers of cognition; we understand the objectivity of something that before did not exist for us. To recognize the limitation of our powers of cognition is thus to confirm that we really do have certain capacities. We find ourselves again apart from this objectivity, separating ourselves from it as we escape its influence over us by separating out what belongs to us and what to it. After having felt fragmented by our experience, we thus consolidate ourselves. We then better understand the difference between it and our powers of knowing. To feel fragmented and overwhelmed in confronting what we do not know thus ends in a strengthened definition of ourselves.

A condition for the sublime to operate is that we do not try to say what it is that is beyond our cognitive powers to determine. To do so would, no doubt, be called superstition. Whoever saw something unidentifiable at night in the middle of the jungle and called that "a witch" would be guilty of superstition from this point of view. But whoever said it was impossible to say what it was that frightened would be strengthened in his mental powers by his restraint. These, I believe, are the positions of those arguing about African witchcraft.

This impasse is defined by an eighteenth-century idea which still has considerable relevance for life today both in the West and elsewhere. But it is possible today to see that such an experience has other possible outcomes, not foreseen earlier. The sublime is something known in retrospect. After the event we see what we went through using our powers of memory and analysis. But suppose that we had not recovered such abilities. If so, the experience would still work through us. We would then suspect, rather than know, that something was affecting us. Would the result not be fear? And would we not call that fear the fear of the uncanny? That is, fear of something whose source we cannot account for; something whose source was definitively neither subjective nor objective. For Kant this seems not to have been a possibility. The sublime was a moral category. He spoke of soldiers in battle, for instance, who stood up to danger. One could, and should, be educated to have the possibility of sublime experience. Not to have it would be a moral or a cultural failure. But we know from at least the time that trauma became a topic after the First World War that such recovery may not be possible, regardless of one's preparation. For any one at all, it seems, it is possible to have an experience that brings one close to death, to be able to recount it, and yet not to have this recounting reestablish one's own capacities. One relives the event as one retells it, leaving one's powers conflated with one's experience.

It is in the face of the uncanny that Geschiere's friend had another sort of reaction. He called up witches rather than assuming that he was *en face* of something he could not explain. The belief in witches might seem to make the uncanny explicable and therefore no longer uncanny. But the excitement of Geschiere's friend does not indicate that the uncanny has been put to rest. This points to the ambiguous nature of witchcraft beliefs in Cameroon. They are said to explain, but what they explain can also be thought to be inexplicable and potent. Such beliefs, then, are not reasonable; they insist on the continued presence of an unknown that ideas of the sublime would seal off. It is for this reason that witchcraft beliefs both depend on suspicion—one suspects a power is at work—and at the same time keep suspicion alive by introducing a term—"witch"—that is incapable of doing more than designating that something is at work which is not understood, which is identified only to the extent that it remains not only unknown, but also continues to have unpredictable consequences. In the face of this situation Geschiere's friend turned to someone else, an expert who, were she only present, would have understood. Someone understands somewhere, but it is not me. I was overwhelmed and I remain so.

The sublime did not operate and the unreasonable was at large, a judgment that might have been shared in the eighteenth century. But today we give a place to the unreasonable nonetheless. Phantasms occur not necessarily out of a moral or cultural failure to separate oneself with one's rational powers from what it is that cannot be known, but rather when such separation cannot be made. Witchcraft accusations can be one example among others.

Beyond that, we can postulate from within gift exchange the possibility of exchange which never takes place. This would be the indescribable experience of the pure gift, the non-event which, though it never happens, leaves a trace. Geschiere eventually could explain the interest in the power of witchcraft, but he could not explain the experience of hi: not his fault. The trace of the pure gift would not be identifia' would not be knowable, but it could be hypothesized from certain states, such as a fear which would have no verifiable explanation. No historical account could lead to the basis of such fear. It would only be in the baring of a situation in which the identification of something fails and it remains unknown that we might be *en face* of the pure gift. We would still have to account for the "objectivity," as Kant had it, of what we failed to recognize. We will explain the logic of such identification in the final chapter. For the moment, we say only that it is not the objectivity that already exists in nature, but a construction that occurs with the uncanny.

The questions that follow are how uncanny moments arise, a historical question as well as a cultural matter, and what paths of reaction follows. Accounts of the circumstances of witch accusations are necessary, but they do not by themselves explain how the accusations are made. In the places where people believe in witches some people call them up and others in the same circumstances do not. Thus, belief in witches and determination of the uncanny are separate questions. We follow the trail of the uncanny rather than that of beliefs in hypothesizing the process that follows from experience of it. A certain trajectory ensues; at its end the witch is named. Our discussion of cases of witchcraft will give us the materials for such an account. But it will stand apart from historical description to a certain degree. Precisely in this gap we will see the contingency of witchcraft accusations.

PART ONE

THE MAGIC WORD

1

The Truth of Sorcery

Lévi-Strauss in his famous essay "The Sorcerer and His Magic" retells a case from Zuni pueblo. A young man accused of witchcraft confesses to the accusation after first denying it. Zuni regularly put witches to death. In this case, Lévi-Strauss tells us, the man is let go because he gives his accusers "the satisfaction of truth which they prefer to justice." With his confession, witchcraft and associated ideas "cease to exist as a diffuse complex of poorly formulated sentiments and representations and become embodied in real experience."[1] Lévi-Strauss's assumption is that witchcraft beliefs are not ideas. They are vague assumptions impossible to articulate under ordinary circumstances. When there is suspicion of sorcery, the accused makes evident by his confession what otherwise was only vaguely sensed. It is a question of articulation, of bringing into language, and particularly into speech, something that until that time was merely guess, sentiment, and suspicion. It is equally a question of restoring coherence to social life that has been upset by feeling a general malaise or threat.

From a certain perspective the possibility of speaking itself would be reaffirmed by sorcery trials. When one is haunted by whatever it is that needs articulation but cannot be said convincingly, all of speech risks sounding hollow. The "truth" of sorcery presumably lies in the transformation between inchoate feelings and the delimitation of these in such a way that they are tellable.

Sorcery in this view is no longer superstition. Not that it is justified by its social functions, as it has been in anthropology since the 1930s at least. Rather, as a place from which articulation takes shape, it is a source of truth. Of course, this is Zuni truth, but since it concerns articulation of ideas via communal action it has general implications. Without sorcerers there would not only be no one to blame, there would be no way to bring into consciousness whatever it is that unconsciously presses for expression. Sorcery becomes the lifting of the barriers to expression. It furnishes both a means of locating truth—in the sorcerer via his confession—and an instrument of articulation as he, the sorcerer, speaks what not merely the victim of his sorcery but the community cannot say.

The expression of truth is satisfying, guilt is secondary, thus rational discussion of the causes of whatever misfortune is involved, necessarily with the expression of different opinions, has no place. Lévi-Strauss describes the operations of what, thanks to Jacques Derrida, we know as phallogocentrism. Although it seems at first our notions of justice are upset—a man is about to be executed on the basis of suspicion alone—Lévi-Strauss validates these operations by showing that the giving of a voice to the community gives a coherence to social life that, in the end, results in the forgetting of the man's crime.

There is never any doubt about the "facts" in the minds of the youth's accusers. He certainly bewitched the girl. However, "proof" is necessary. "Proof" of what? The boy confesses twice. The first time is insufficient. His accusers do not accept his statement. They require more detail. He must "validate a system of which they possess only a fragment," says Lévi-Strauss. When, finally, the youth says that his powers are due to magical plumes, they require him to produce them. He rips out a portion of the walls of his mother's house before he finds one. Lévi-Strauss used the account of Matilda Coxe Stevenson for his analysis. He quotes Mrs. Stevenson to describe this moment:

"There was consternation among the warriors, who exclaimed in one voice: 'What does this mean?' Now they felt assured that the youth had spoken the truth."[2]

Here is the moment of "truth." What they already believed is confirmed. But, as Lévi-Strauss says, the confirmation produces consternation rather than triumph. They did not mean "proof of a crime" but rather "witness to the reality of the system which had made the crime possible." This they get by "validating its objective basis through an appropriate emotional expression." The "truth," then is not confirmation that an act was performed—that, in particular, the girl was ensorcelled. It is rather an "expression," in fact, "an appropriate emotional expression." Usually, we are astonished by finding out what we do not know. They look for evidence of what they believe, and they are astonished at getting it. This is because they are unsure of its meaning: "What does this mean?" are their words. When they find what they are looking for, it is a fact so large, so incomprehensible, that they are upset. It is a truth that they know but do not have the ability to say; for that they need a sorcerer and so they manufacture one themselves.[3]

Why are they speechless? What are they defending themselves against? What is so horrible to say? Pain, of course, produces speechlessness. We know this, for instance, in our notion of trauma. The traumatized person can say what happened to him, but saying it does nothing for him. It does not put the event behind him, in a past defined as prior to the moment of speaking. Lévi-Strauss deals with this in the companion essay to the piece we are discussing, "The Efficacy of Symbols."[4] There, he describes a woman in childbirth who can only suffer her pain. A shaman recites an epic that describes a passage through the woman's body. When he finishes, she gives birth. "The cure would consist . . . in making explicit a situation originally existing on the emotional level and in rendering acceptable to the mind pains which the body refuses to tolerate." "The shaman," says Lévi-Strauss,

provides the sick woman with a *language* [his emphasis], by means of which unexpressed, and otherwise inexpressible, psychic states can be immediately expressed. And it is this transition to this verbal expression—at the same time making it possible to undergo in an ordered and intelligible form a real experience that would otherwise be chaotic and inexpressible—which induces the release of the physiological process."[5]

"Language" (the French is *langage*[6]) here marks "a transition to . . . verbal expression." In "The Sorcerer and His Magic," Lévi-Strauss has an equivalent formulation. He says that

the patient is all passivity and self-alienation, just as inexpressibility is the disease of the mind. The sorcerer is activity and self—projection, just as affectivity is the source of symbolism. The cure interrelates these opposite poles.[7]

So, out of "chaos," his word, comes "the coherence of the psychic universe," again his words. The central element of both curing as well as sorcery in Lévi-Strauss's accounts, is the ability to form speech.[8]

Lévi-Strauss in making his analysis draws on the work of Marcel Mauss on magic. "Imagine for a moment—if you possibly can," Mauss asks of his readers,

a sick Australian aborigine who calls in a sorcerer. . . . [The sorcerer dances, "falls into a cataleptic fit," and when he returns, extracts a pebble from the sick person.] Obviously there are two subjective experiences involved in these facts. And between the dreams of one and the desires of the other there is a discordant factor. Apart from the sleight of hand at the end, the magician makes no effort to make his ideas coincide with the ideas and need of his client.[9]

Nonetheless, "Magic consists in uniting the two."[10] Lévi-Strauss, in "The Efficacy of Symbols," elaborated and modified this idea, showing how the curer supplies the speech lacking in the suffering patient. Lévi-Strauss explicates the logic of this union in psychoanalytic terms. He explains how the curer becomes the voice of the patient and thus ultimately restores her voice. Mauss himself put his argument in Durkheimian terms (it is a question of social belief), but he also relied on Kant[11] and on grammatical categories:

The magician, they say, reasons from like to like by applying the law of sympathy, thinking in terms of his powers or his auxiliary spirits. The rite causes the spirits to work, by definition.[12]

The "they" of the first sentence refers to Frazer and his famous laws of magic. (Mauss argues against Frazer off and on throughout the book without naming him. He was always subtle in his opposition, preferring not to engage directly. Thus, his criticisms of Durkheim usually come in the middle of the paragraph, the conclusion sustaining Durkheim, his uncle.) Mauss sees Frazer as describing magical laws as Kantian analytic judgments. Analytic judgments are true by definition. (They are, Kant tells us, judgments in which "the predicate B belongs to the subject A as something which is [covertly] contained in this concept A"[13]; thus, for example, the explication "All bachelors are unmarried.") Mauss sees Frazer not through the vast collection of cases which fill the twelve volumes of *The Golden Bough* but through the structure of the two proposals which the very numerous examples illustrate. Thus, things once in touch remain in touch—a law for Frazer, true by definition—is not really a law, Mauss says. If Frazer were correct, everything that bears resemblance to something else would be thought to be the same, and everything that was once in touch would be thought to remain in touch. But this is not so. It is not a matter of analytic judgments but of social conventions. These conventions pick out only certain objects which remain in touch with or resemble others which they influence. If they are not analytic judgments, they must be synthetic judgments. Synthetic judgments are all those where the predicate is not contained in the subject. "Judgments of experience, as such, are one and all synthetic," Kant says.[14] For Mauss, magical judgments are expressions of social conventions applied to experience. As synthetic judgments they are dependent on testing in the world.

This testing is problematic because it is prejudicial.[15] Still, testing is necessary because of the nature of synthetic judgments. To be known to be true they have to be demonstrated, and the demonstration has recourse to the world. Thus, for instance, that $7 + 5 = 12$ appears to many to be an analytic judgment, but, says Kant, the principle that unites $7 + 5$ to make 12 can never be shown without recourse to the world: "We have to go outside these concepts, and call in the aide of the intuition which corresponds to one of them, our five fingers."[16] Whatever makes people believe in the truth of arithmetic and yet count on their fingers to make sure is the same as what makes them believe in magic and yet want it demonstrated in the world.

Mauss moves from his allusions to Kant to the objectivization of experience. If people can objectivize their experience, which in particular includes the ability to relate it, it is because society gives them terms outside of themselves with which to do so.

It is this belief (the universal belief in magic) which allows people to objectivize their subjective ideas and generalize individual illusions. Again, it is this belief which gives magical judgments their affirmative, inevitable and absolute character. In brief, while they exist in the minds of individuals, magical judgments, even from the outset, are—as we have pointed out—well nigh perfect, a priori, synthetic judgments. The terms are connected before any kind of testing.[17]

Mauss says that magical beliefs are founded on the world, not on thought or definition; they are synthetic judgments in that sense, but they are special ones because they are embedded in belief. No experience is likely to change them.

All over the world, magical judgments existed prior to magical experience. . . . Experiences occur only in order to confirm them and almost never succeed in refuting them."[18]

Still, he adds, they need testing of a certain sort.

However, it must be made clear that we have no wish to imply that magic does not demand analysis or testing. We are only saying that it is poorly analytical, poorly experiential and almost entirely a priori.[19]

Thus the transformation of suffering into coherent expression comes via belief. But this does not mean that the connection is in any way automatic.

"What, then, operates this synthesis?" Mauss asks. It can not be done by the individual. There has to be "collective confirmation," and this has to be supported by "at least two persons—the magician performing the rite and the individual who believes in it," or in the case of folk magic the single person who practices it and the one who taught him to do so. Social belief in magic thus furnishes the terms in which suffering can be externalized; communal participation more or less follows from this as the means to confirm the validity of the terms of judgment. The "testing" that is called for does not have the aim of seeing whether the terms are valid or not. It "tests" only to confirm. Magical judgments, which Mauss terms "prejudicial," are rarely contradicted by evidence. Such evidence is ignored, as with all prejudice. Testing is called for merely because the terms apply to the world and are thought to be founded in it.[20] We are not yet at the point made by Lévi-Strauss where testing is the point where articulation occurs.

In Mauss, the "operation" of magic has to take place. There must be a rite, but it is not clear just why. Indeed, if magical judgments were analytic, the need for ritual would be even less obvious. At one point, Mauss says that "there has never been, in fact, any need to operate it. Magical judgments arise in the form of prejudice and prescription."[21] He means that it is strange, the prejudice of magical belief being so firmly established that evidence can rarely contradict it, that there is nonetheless testing and ritual. In *A General Theory of Magic* Mauss considers many kinds of magical rituals. But in the conclusion it is curing rites that implicitly sum up the power of magic. We imagine the sorcerer returning from trance and the passive sick person. The paradigmatic "synthesis" occurs between the two of them. "Obviously there are two subjective experiences involved in these facts. And between the dreams of one and the desires of the other there is a discordant factor," to quote these two important lines again. The conjunction comes magically and Mauss perceives this magic in the mind of the magician. "His judgments always involve a heterogeneous term, which is irreducible to any logical analysis. This term is force or power, . . . or mana."[22] We will come back to the nature of this force and what it has to do with articulation. First, we must return to the Zuni incident.

Lévi-Strauss, we have said, drew on the account of Matilda Coxe Stevenson for his Zuni example. Mrs. Stevenson was the wife of the leader of the Bureau of American Ethnology expedition to Zuni and the rival of her colleague on this expedition, Frank Cushing. Cushing stayed on when the expedition left and is sometimes named as the inventor of participant-observation. Stevenson's report was published in 1902. Her description of sorcery begins by saying that "these people are in constant terror of being conjured." She names the sorts of people likely to be involved in sorcery. They are infants, the impoverished, and the physically deformed, along with those who challenge "a prominent member of the tribe."[23] Neither the ensorcelled girl nor the accused sorcerer fit these categories, so far as we are told. The girl was twelve, the boy, at most, seventeen. The accusation, thus somewhat outside the usual, is made because, according to Mrs. Stevenson, "the girl's illness must be accounted for" (398). According to Mrs. Stevenson, she was "hysterical." "A beautiful young girl, about 12 years of age, had suffered for five weeks, the cause being suppression of the menses" (388). "She rolled and tossed, pulled at her hair and throat, and threw her arms wildly about, her legs moving as violently as her arms. Her head was never quiet for a moment" (389). According to Mrs. Stevenson, the patient suffered for thirteen days, during which time the girl's family made inquiries and "learned that on the morning before the attack she was seen romping with a young man, who held her hands, and this was sufficient evidence to bring him before the court for trial" (398).

It seems from the family's information that there was a sexual advance and that this precipitated the girl's convulsions. The boy, accused because he was seen holding hands with the girl, "earnestly denied the accusation, declaring that he knew nothing of witchcraft." He was accused, one notes, not of a sexual gesture but of sorcery. The girl, meanwhile, also refused to speak, or perhaps was incapable of doing so. "The grandfather appealed to the invalid, begging her to tell all she knew, to talk without fear: 'Hota (granddaughter), tell us.'" These appeals have an effect. "The child, held up by her grandfather told her story with great difficulty in broken sentences. . . . The spasms made it almost impossible for her to articulate, and her head was not still for an instant." She manages to say only a little, but it is enough to incriminate the boy. "'When a short distance from my house, this boy wanted me to go with him, and when I refused, he grabbed my hand. As soon as he touched me, I began to tremble, and I ran home.'" Her parents are certain the boy is at fault. They follow the girl's statement by saying, "'And in a short time our child was crazy, as you see her now'" (400).

Her parents think the girl is insane, but Mrs. Stevenson has a different opinion. "The fact is, the child was perfectly rational, but her nervous condition induced them to think her mind was not right" (400). That the girl's parents say she is "crazy" and "think that her mind is not right" in no way makes them believe the girl's account less. This is because what is at stake is not sexual assault, whether it happened or not, but sorcery. If the problem were sexual assault, the girl's coherence would be essential to establish what happened to her. But if the girl is "crazy," it is the effect of sorcery and sexual assault is forgotten. Their minds go directly to the latter possibility and pause not a moment at the girl's experience. "Sorcery," here, is not a code word for something sexual. No code word is needed. The sexual dimension is admitted to. The boy, in his first confession, says that he got "love philters." Just as Lévi-Strauss says, the issue is making clear the nature of sorcery, the "truth" of sorcery.

The girl's experience, and, in fact, her condition, are neglected. The boy confesses that he went to a magician and got love potions. His hearers demand "proof." He produces two roots, presumably given him by the sorcerer. One he claims he used to drive the girl insane; the other will cure her, again according to the boy. He first uses the sort that will drive her insane. It does.

Taking a bite from the root . . . , he chewed it, ejected it upon his hands, and rubbed his body. In a moment he distorted his face, spun around, and jumped about; then, shaking his body violently, rushed to the invalid, pulling at her arms and running his hands over them. The spectacle was so harassing that it was with difficulty the writer retained her composure. The child's efforts to scream as she endeavored to release herself from the grasp of her father and brother who held her, her terror each time the boy approached her, the cries of the women, and the tears of the men, except the warriors, who were absorbed in what was going on before them, presented a scene never to be forgotten. (402)

The boy then chews on the second root. This root, instead of restoring the girl to normality, has the same effect as the first.

He swallowed a small quantity of the other medicine and became perfectly rational in his demeanor. He now touched the girl's lips with his own and pretended to draw disease from her heart, while she was almost thrown into convulsions by his touch. (402)

The boy clearly does not cure the girl, and even makes her worse. At this point, Mrs. Stevenson intervened: "The child was in such an alarming condition of nervousness that the writer decided that the farce must end" (402).

Compare this to Lévi-Strauss's statement: "The girl recovers after he [the accused sorcerer] performs his curing ritual." Lévi-Strauss's assertion is true only in the sense that later (apparently about ten days after the event described) the girl begins to recover. This occurs, according to Mrs. Stevenson, after she has her period, which happened thirteen days after her first onset of trembling. "The patient continued gradually to improve until her health was fully restored" (389). There is no indication that the cure is attributed to the sorcerer. Rather the contrary. Mrs. Stevenson's says that the girl was given "fetishistic medicines," by whom is not said; but that the failure of the girl to get well led her parents to appeal to Mrs. Stevenson to help their child. There is no clear sense of a cure at all, nor whether if there had been it would have been attributed to Mrs. Stevenson or to "fetishistic medicines," but it certainly seems unlikely to have been attributed to the accused sorcerer.

Mrs. Stevenson intervenes also on behalf of the accused sorcerer. She speaks to the warriors who are acting as judges and they agree to release the boy on the understanding that the next morning two of them will go with him to Mrs. Stevenson's camp. The boy, however, runs away, "news which was most gratifying," she tells us. But they chase after him, bring him back, and retry him.

The renewed trial is the occasion for a new story. The chief judge, Nau'ichi, himself a prominent curer, rejects the accused's first story saying it is not true. Mrs. Stevenson does not report why he thinks so. He simply tells the boy, "'I am here to see that you speak the truth. I shall keep you talking until you do speak the truth'" (403). The judge evidently is not in search of the boy's innocence or guilt. The boy has confessed already; what remains is to make a more convincing confession. Lévi-Strauss does not discuss the trials in detail. His explanation, that the judges want to know the nature of sorcery in particular, that they are in search of the "truth" of sorcery, seems to me to be right. But it leaves unanswered the nature of this truth. What is it that is not shown by one story that requires another?

The boy is disheartened. He no longer believes his story is credible. "Losing all faith in winning belief for his story, the wretched boy invented another, which he hoped would satisfy his judge: 'Yes, I lied,'" he tells them. He adds that he did so to protect his parents and his sister who are also witches. "'I lied because I loved my father and mother and sister, and did not wish to speak of them.'" But he gives no sign that he thinks he has now betrayed them. On the contrary, acknowledging their involvement sets off a series of boasts in which he identifies himself with them and in which they are made to seem practically omnipotent. He strives for effects to convince the judges of his power. "'All my grandfathers were wizards,'" he says. To clinch this, he adds, "'I have the plume offerings brought to this world by my witch ancestors.'" And he tells them that at the winter solstice witches gather at his mother's house to prevent the rain and snow.

One of the warrior judges challenge him. "'You lie,'" he says. If it were true, they would have the witches gather. But the boy has an answer, one that relies again on a delirium of the possession of power:

"Ancient plume offerings held to our hearts and yucca strings crossed over our breasts, while we jump through a hoop made of yucca, empower us to make ourselves into dogs, cats, coyotes, hawks, crows, and owls, so that we pass quickly and unknown about the country. We gather in an inner room of my mother's house where four ancient lamps hang, one on each wall, and by this light we sit and talk and make the rain-makers angry, so that they will not work. I can assume the form of a cat and pass through the smallest hole to enter a house. I can fill my mouth with cactus needles and shoot them through windows and destroy life. I have killed two infants, three girls, and two boys. I have ancient prayer plumes, and I have two others that are used to convert us into other forms than our own." (403)

He boasts of murdering seven people; he lays his parents and his sister open to accusations of the same. If the judges are skeptical, it is not because they want the sort of truth that pertains in our courts. It is not a question of evidence of acts. It is a matter of showing that there actually is a certain power. The answer to the judges' refusal of his confession is not to make it more plausible (and certainly not to say that he was completely uninvolved or that sorcery is implausible) but to invent more power.

At that point, they adjourn to find the plumes. Two walls of the boy's mother's house are torn apart before a plume is found. The first story is designed to fit the facts of the patient's condition. Mrs. Stevenson notes that before his first confession, "the writer observed that he was closely watching every movement of the girl" (400). And, "It was evident to the writer that the boy had made use of his observations of the girl in weaving his story, and it was a clever thought which prompted him to claim to possess a medicine which would counteract the effect of the other" (401). Thus, his story fits hers: he indeed wanted to possess her and she did indeed tremble after he shook her hand just as she did during the séance. The second story leaves the girl out almost entirely. It is only about sorcery. Sorcery, it is no surprise by now, is power, and power fascinates the warrior judges. During the first confession, "the warriors had become so absorbed by their interest in the narrative of the boy that they seemed entirely to have forgotten the cause of his appearance before them" (401). The girl's experience does not interest them. The obtaining of magical power fascinates them. "In one voice they demanded a manifestation." And this they get as he shows how he made her tremble. We are not told that his failure to cure disappoints them. Only the intervention of Mrs. Stevenson, trying to prevent further suffering of the girl, puts an end to the first session. Everyone else seems to have forgotten her in favor of wanting to see the sorcerer's power.

It would be premature to conclude that the truth of sorcery is ever satisfactorily revealed. The boy is taken to his mother's house, the lock is opened by the warriors despite the protest of the boy. The boy is set to work. He knocks off the plaster in the first room and finds nothing. The warriors accuse him of lying. He leads them to another room and there finds two packets of ritual plumes. The warriors demand an explanation. He tells them that these plumes are used to destroy the corn crops. "There was consternation among the warriors who exclaimed with one voice, 'What does this mean?' Now they felt assured that the youth had spoken the truth. . . . But the warriors were not to be satisfied until the prayer plumes used to transform the witch into beast form were produced. In despair the boy declared they must be in a room below" (404). After an hour's search, another plume is found in the plaster. This is the feather used to convert witches into animals. The warriors "rejoice." However, "they were not to be satisfied with the one prayer plume; they must have the other" (405). Finally they leave because of the cold and the dust from the shattered plaster.

Then Mrs. Stevenson intervenes again. Referring to herself as usual in the third person, she says, "She was not sure what Na'uichi[24] [the chief judge] intended to do with the boy, but was determined that the poor fellow should not be hanged. The boy was seated with a warrior on either side of him, and the writer talked to him and doctored him a little, and finally convinced Na'uichi that the boy would never again be able to practice his diabolical art, and that therefore it was not necessary to hang him" (405).

The boy is led to the plaza, where there is a crowd. There is silence when they learn the boy is about to speak: "The appetite of the warriors for marvels was not yet satisfied." And the powerful curer, Na'uichi, tells the boy to confess to the assembled people. He talks on till midnight. The magical objects are placed in front of him." The people moved in a great wave toward the spot to peer at the mysteries" (405). "The longer the boy talked the more absorbed he became in his subject. He added many wonderful statements to those made during the day. At times his face became radiant with satisfaction at his power over his listeners" (406). The truth of sorcery, then, rests in the demonstration of its miraculous power. Not, of course, in the actual workings of it since this is at best a failure, but in the fabrication of its story with its accompanying artifacts. The boy declares he has lost his power and they are thus powerless too. But as he tells his final story, "his face became radiant with satisfaction at his power over his listeners" (406). The equation, or the substitutability of linguistic for phallic power, is evident. Here is, or, rather, should be, the moment of truth; the moment when his speech puts his experience into the past, or, one could say, makes sorcery into something relatable, taking it out of the deep but vague mystery in which it was assumed to have been embedded.

The boy is increasingly absorbed by his own story. And this story incriminates him. Remember that sorcery earns the death penalty. He would be putting himself to death under ordinary circumstances. Mrs. Stevenson thought that the boy invented the story of the feathers in order to frighten his accusers with his power. The boy did not confide his intentions to her; she guessed them. But whether she was right or not, it is evident that there is a mutual interest in power by accusers and accused which begins before this, with the first confession. Once the boy confesses for the first time he already is set on the path to the display of magical force, and he tries to use it in his defense when he attempts to cure the girl. Mrs. Stevenson herself did not think that this strategy would work, judging by what she does later. In any case, it is evident that, as Lévi-Strauss says, the boy's interest in his story puts his interest in saving his life to the side, as all parties find themselves fascinated with power. It remains to be seen, however, if there was an exchange of justice for truth.

In Lévi-Strauss's account, the Zuni love for the truth of sorcery makes them soft-hearted and they allow the boy his freedom. But in Mrs. Stevenson's story it is different. Mrs. Stevenson was well known to her rival and co-member of the Bureau of American Ethnology expedition to the Zuni, Frank Cushing, for her interference and for calling in the militia, particularly when the Zuni threatened to put a witch to death.[25] Once, before our incident took place, Na'uichi, the curer and chief judge of the second trial of our sorcerer, was "obdurate" about putting a witch to death. Mrs. Stevenson tells us:

He [Na'uichi] was told that the United States government would certainly punish him. He retorted: "I am your friend. Friends do not betray one another. Would you betray me to the soldiers?" "I have not said I would inform upon you," was the reply; "I am too much your friend to wish to see you suffer." "I shall hang this wizard, even though I displease you," he declared. "I shall hang him though the United States Government put me in prison for one month, six months, a year, or forever. He has killed my child, and he must die." (397)

Mrs. Stevenson finds herself in a dilemma. "The position of the writer was a delicate one. The man must be saved, but she must not make an enemy of a tried friend and one of the men most important to her in her studies" (397). So she arranges a trial of her own, with a warrior judge present. Na'uichi, the obdurate, the same man who wants to kill our sorcerer, is also present. "The result was that the unfortunate was released. This was brought about by a declaration on the part of the writer that she had deprived the man of his power of sorcery" (398). Very much the same occurs in our case. She takes the boy to her camp, along with Na'uichi. It is after this that the boy is led to the plaza and speaks to the crowd. The boy concludes his oration, saying:

> While with my mother [this seems to refer to Mrs. Stevenson], and while she talked to me, I felt my eyes change from black to blue, and then turn from blue to black, and then I felt that all my power of witchcraft was gone, not only for a little while, but for all time. Alas! No more shall I be great among my people. I shall be one of them no more. My power is all gone! all gone forever! (406)[26]

He is then cheered by the crowd. Mrs. Stevenson concludes: "This incident is mentioned simply to show that it is possible, if these people are managed in the right way, to overcome their miserable superstitions" (406). Management prevails only while the formidable Mrs. Stevenson remains in Zuni as the manager. It is, she says, only after her departure that the militia actually comes to Zuni. Na'uichi is arrested for hanging a woman accused of witchcraft (406). It seems clear that Na'uichi agreed to let the accused go because of Mrs. Stevenson's threats of force made acceptable by a face-saving device.

The boy incriminates himself, and he does so before he knows that he will be set free and not, in my opinion, in the hope of being let go. He speaks out of fascination with the story he makes up; his confession is the generation of a conception of power. With it he captivates his audience. There is a real power of sorcery, in that sense. It remains, unlike the power of curing, unmanageable; he himself is equally captivated. The killing of the sorcerer, which would have been the result in the youth's case without Mrs. Stevenson, is a futile attempt to bring this power under control. But after one witch is killed, others emerge.

Mauss says that magic is a form of prejudice. He means that evidence seldom can invalidate magical judgments. The belief in magic is too firm to allow that. But we see here that the prejudice of magic is not located in belief but in fascination with power. No doubt there must be communal belief for this fascination to occur. In our example, however, we see communal belief generated in the reflection of the boy's story in the minds of his interlocutors and their subsequent insistence that he tell more. At the foundation of the story is indeed something communal, but preceding that there is the heightened sense that the boy knows something and that they do not know quite what it is. The interlocutors function not as judges who examine evidence by standards they have already in mind but as people convinced that there is something to know, that they know who it is that knows it and that they must find it out themselves. This is the strange prejudice of magic that forbids the finding of innocence, that is, that there is no magic at work, thus nothing to find out. It is a prejudice stemming not from prior belief but from unbearable curiosity and desire that there be a mighty and uncontrollable power available for them to be witness to.

We ask again, what is the power of sorcery? The power of curing is the capacity to form a composite voice; the curer speaks for the patient, suffering turns into experience. As Lévi-Strauss explains it, the witch hunt results in the formation of a composite voice as well, the confessing sorcerer speaking for the community, the vague ideas of sorcery turning into explicit and therefore manageable notions. In the end, the community presumably speaks of sorcery as the patient speaks of her suffering: as something gone through and forgettable, at least in the sense that it is no longer remembered involuntarily. But as described by Mrs. Stevenson there is no mastery of this truth. The boy is as fascinated with his story as his accusers. Moreover, as we have seen, this occurs before Mrs. Stevenson has arranged to save him from hanging. He accuses himself not simply out of desire to please his accusers, but to associate himself with the power that has been attributed to him even if it means that he will be executed. In that sense, he is in its power.

In having a double persona, the sorcerer is like the curer. But the curer, when successful, reintegrates the once-ill person into the community. He thus seems to say that magical power is also social p
persona of the curer raises no difficulty; in one incarnati
bridge to a world of inspiration drawn on for the good.
version of this world, but not merely that. As mere invers
cery would show that the power to cure is also the powe

the sorcerer, power, whether to harm or to cure, is also power out of the control of individuals. This goes unnoticed in curing because of its desirable effects. When, in our story, a person incriminates himself and when the injured party is forgotten, and, in particular, when one sees the process by which stories are fabricated, one sees the nearly autonomous force of language as it merely uses the voice of the accused and as it inhabits the judges, causing them to forget the victim and making them eager to see more and more. The sorcerer, presumably responsible for his deeds, is in fact possessed by language, as are his interlocutors. It remains, then, to show where in language this power is located.

For Lévi-Strauss's own explanation we have to turn to his *Introduction to the Works of Marcel Mauss.*[27] Lévi-Strauss comments on this passage from Mauss's study of magic:

The magician, they say, reasons from like to like by applying the law of sympathy, thinking in terms of his powers or his auxiliary spirits. The rite causes the spirits to work, by definition. The magician conjures up his astral body because this body is himself. The smoking of the aquatic plant brings a cloud because it is a cloud.[28]

Lévi-Strauss:

Magical reasoning, implied in the action of producing smoke to elicit clouds and rain, is not grounded in a primordial distinction between smoke and cloud, with an appeal to mana to weld the one to the other, but in the fact that a deeper level of thinking identifies smoke with cloud; that the one is, at least in a certain respect, the same thing as the other: that identification is what justifies the subsequent association, and not the other way round.[29]

Lévi-Strauss modifies Mauss by turning to Saussure. By which I mean not that he cites Saussure, but that he relies on assumptions which are found in Saussure's notion of language. Saussure conceived language as coming into being at a single stroke. The material out of which thought is produced comes together with analogous sound material. All distinctions appear simultaneously when signs with their two parts, signifier and signified, take shape. Lévi-Strauss postulated the existence of one signifier, however, which lacks a corresponding signified. He called this the floating signifier; without definite reference, the floating signifier takes on the import of all signification before the latter registers as distinctions. The magical word is the prototypical floating signifier. The original moments of indistinction alluded to above are reached through it. Thus Lévi-Strauss thought that magical thinking simply makes apparent what people already know but know unconsciously or without lucidity.[30]

Lévi-Strauss's interpretation is bold. Here, however, I want to go back to Mauss's own words. The passage from Mauss, above, continues:

> However we have clearly shown that this reduction to analytical terms is quite theoretical and that things really happen otherwise in the magician's mind. His judgments always involve a heterogeneous term, which is irreducible to any logical analysis. (122)

Mauss here refers to the fact he has established that magical judgments are not analytic and in fact function outside logic. The function of magical terms is to conjoin. Specifically, they put together objects that either resemble each other or were once in touch with each other. It is not an error in thinking, as Frazer said, that allows them to do so. Rather, the magical term has a power to do so that stems from social belief.

> The term is force or power, . . . or *mana*. The idea of magical efficacy is ever present and plays far from an accessory part, since it enjoys the same status which the copula plays in a grammatical clause. It is this which presents the magical idea and gives it being, reality, truth. (122; translation modified)

It is illogical to think that one can act on a red object to affect someone wearing a red shirt. Nonetheless, the belief in magical efficacity allows one to assume it is possible.

As with Lévi-Strauss, for Mauss, language was at the center of the analysis of magic. There was, for him, no magic without language. "Every ritual action . . . has a corresponding phrase, since there is always a minimal representation through which the nature and object of the ritual is expressed, even if this is achieved only through an interior language. It is for this reason that there is no such thing as a wordless ritual."[31] This language was of a specific nature: "The fact that all spells are formulas and that virtually all non-verbal rites also have their formulas shows at once to what degree all magic is formalistic."[32] He goes on to say that "spells are composed in special languages," always foreign to the magicians and their clients.[33]

Formalistic language is close to language without content and thus brings him near to Lévi-Strauss. However, it is not by reference to signifiers which say everything by their very lack of definite reference that Mauss proceeds. He finds his path through his comparison between magical words and the function of the copula. What is at stake is the way in which associations are made. Usually we think of them as resulting from suggestions that arise out of similarity. But in language we conjoin, or associate, simply by the power of certain words, in particular, copulas. The prime example of the copula in grammar is the word "is." "Is" of course simply asserts that one thing "is" the other. A statement of this sort seems to state the very terms of an analytical judgment, one in which the attribute of the thing is already contained in the subject: "All bachelors are unmarried." This, one says, is true by definition. The power of definition, however, is first of all linguistic. After that, when we doubt, we subject a sentence with the word "is" to the test of worldly experience. We thus have a synthetic judgment. But in magic, where the word "is" is magical, such a test has no consequences except to confirm the terms of judgment. For that reason, Mauss speaks of "prejudice." Instead of resisting the illogical and the unnatural, in making magical judgments we validate them. In doing so, we of course confirm the "truth" of the magical word "is" and reject evidence. Such is Mauss's view of magic. For him, the force of magic, in the last analysis, stems as much from language as it does from social belief.[34]

The "truth" of magic is the power inherent in language to conjoin. But this power is not simply present in words; recall that there must be a rite and a rite is always, in Mauss's thinking, composed of words. The power of magic, then, is a performative power. It is the power to make something true by saying particular words, those that, at least sometimes, are thought to create truth via their enunciation.

Lévi-Strauss posited the source of power of magical signifiers in his notion of the source of signification. He thus was able to show the relation between magic and the restoration of the ability to represent and, in particular, to speak. For him, the social side of magic consists not only in shared belief in magical signifiers but in the capacity of magic to restore language to the community. In the face of a traumatic event, one that makes it impossible for the sufferer to meaningfully relate what happened to him, the power to speak is attenuated to the point where language seems without force. The Cuna woman who suffers a difficult childbirth can perhaps say what the trouble is, just as the Zuni girl can tell her grandfather what happened to her. But each continues to suffer and everyone finds the accounts inadequate. It is the moment in which the magician is summoned. He demonstrates the "truth" of sorcery, which is to say, the magical power to make appear something hidden. The community believes in magic and so he does not demonstrate anything they do not know. But he has a performative ability they lack at that moment. He becomes their voice; they speak through him and finally are able to do so themselves. Thus, the capacity to speak is restored to the community as a whole.

Magical power, performative power, is located first in certain words and secondly in their proper enunciation by magicians. It is contained in the magician's ability to link together the suffering of the sick woman and the conception of her body contained in the long chant the shaman recites, for instance. The shaman sutures together the painful feelings of the woman and the images of the text. He says, in effect, that "this" (the spirits mentioned in the epic) is "that" (the body of the woman), though this is grossly overly simplified, the chant itself, in the case Lévi-Strauss cites, containing various kinds of spirits and entities. But as both Mauss and Lévi-Strauss assert, the cure consists in this articulation of two states that results in changing an amorphous state (pain) into one that is relatable.

The capacity of language to say something without regard to the actual state of the world to which it nonetheless refers is essential to magic. The "prejudice" of believers makes it impossible to contradict the statements made by magical articulation. In magic, language "says" and no reference to fact invalidates what it says. Prejudice here is not a disability. On the contrary, it is essential to the power of language to overcome reference. Without prejudice, there is no magic, only disputable fact. Without this prejudice, this refusal to look hard at the world, magic would not disappear; it would be transformed into fiction. One might revise this to say that magic is fiction with power superior to that which language has in places where the institution of literature exists. The institution of literature keeps magical language in a bounded place, at least under ordinary circumstances. The prejudice of magic is an effect of the abnormally forceful capacity of magical language to forge connections. Magical prejudice is not prejudice in the first degree; it is, rather, the effect of a certain superior linguistic power to articulate.

One sees how extreme this power is in the example Lévi-Strauss uses to begin "The Sorcerer and His Magic." So-called "voodoo death" occurs in various parts of the world. A person is told that he is bewitched. He then suffers and dies. In Australia, aborigines point a bone at the victim in laying this magical curse. Here is an account from Dr. Herbert Basedow, who witnessed several cases:

The man who discovers that he is being boned by an enemy is, indeed, a pitiable sight. He stands aghast, with his eyes staring at the treacherous pointer, and with his hands lifted as though to ward off the lethal medium, which he imagines is pouring into his body. His cheeks blanch and his eyes become glassy and the expression of his face becomes horribly distorted. . . . He attempts to shriek but usually the sound chokes in his throat, and all that one might see is froth at his mouth. His body begins to tremble and the muscles twist involuntarily. He sways backwards and falls to the ground, and after a short time appears to be in a swoon; but soon after he writhes as if in mortal agony, and, covering his face with his hands, begins to moan. After a while he becomes very composed and crawls to his wurley. From this time onwards he sickens and frets, refusing to eat and keeping aloof from the daily affairs of the tribe. Unless help is forth coming in the shape of a counter charm administered by the hands of the nangarri, or medicine man, his death is only a matter of a comparatively short time. If the coming of the medicine man is opportune he might be saved.[35]

Belief causes his death. Belief and not trauma. The person who suffers from trauma repeats the traumatic event in his dreams or in his speech precisely because he cannot believe it. He cannot understand what happened to him, even though he can say what it is that occurred. In voodoo death, either trauma is not at work or there is a paradox: the man believes what has happened to him and for that reason we might say he is traumatized. "Belief," here, would be used in the sense of "I know there is a catastrophe coming because the magical beliefs of my people say so." Were he traumatized, he might repeat the story of the threat without being about to put himself, the speaker, fully into his own picture. But this is not the case. There is a problem of speech, as we will see, but it is not one of the difference between the person who utters a sentence and himself as the subject of that sentence. Quite the opposite. He believes he will die. He, the speaker, and he, the subject of the sentence, coincide. Or would coincide if only he could bring himself to utter the words that describe his condition.

The man, we are forced to say, anticipates his death. He is certain of it and therefore he is in the process of dying. This is all that language allows us to say. It would be paradoxical to say, "The man is dead." He is clinically alive, but he is in a condition analogous to people on life support, around whom there are arguments about whether they are "really" dead even if their hearts still beat. His death has arrived, but he is still present.

A bone has been pointed at this man. Mauss, we repeat, says that magical objects are congealed words, that each rite is a verbal formula, even if it is not pronounced. We can reconstruct the sentence attached to the pointed bone: it is "You will die," or even "You are dead." Belief here consists in accepting the truth of this sentence. The sick man in the case above cannot speak: "He attempts to shriek but usually the sound chokes in his throat, and all that one might see is froth at his mouth." Were he able to articulate, he would say either "I will die" or "I am dead." That is, his murder is effected by a logical impossibility, if we accept the latter version. Here, belief consists in the first place of accepting the word "is" as the magical copula. It links "I," the speaker as the subject, with the predicate, "dead." This is, of course, heterogeneous, not at all to the rules of grammar, but to both analytical and synthetic judgments.[36]

Voodoo death, in that sense, is the contrary of the examples of curing Lévi-Strauss gives, even when, in the English, these are referred to as "sorcery." The truth of magic here is still the power to conjoin. It is not, however, a curative power which enables the sufferer to formulate her experience and thus to leave it behind and find a voice again through the voice of the medium or curer. In voodoo death, the voice of the victim issues from the dead. It does not formulate suffering, changing it into experience. The victim, if he speaks at all, speaks proleptically, anticipating biological death and making death already his own. Though at that point one might more accurately say "it" rather than "he." The social person is gone, shunned by his fellows. The cursed man, convinced of his death, exists only in anticipating it. "I am dead" in its magical form gives such force to "to be" that its very sense is superceded. The result, according to the testimony above, is that the ensorcelled person cannot speak at all. He cannot pronounce the magical word either because he is already dead from the perspective of the living and so incapable of speech or because, were he to do so, he would be beyond "death" altogether. By this I mean that he would surpass the cultural constructions, particularly ghosts, that are often made to represent the return of the dead. Only a ghost can say, and believe, "I am dead." A ghost here would be a cultural form made to accommodate a belief in life after death. The cursed person who says "I am dead" finds no such construction to put on himself. "I am dead" thus remains for him an impossible sentence. And yet it is linguistically possible and it is culturally possible once there is the power of magic that ensures that comparison with reality does not avail. The most powerful of all magical words is thus, qua magical word, under certain circumstances, unspeakable.

The magical signifier bends reality. It links what cannot conceivably be conjoined. The signifier that cures conjoins and is speakable. It brings about the possibility of speech. The magical signifier that kills remains unspeakable. It fascinates and is coveted, but finally those in whom it is lodged are shunned, expelled, murdered. It is why the sorcerer's confession is inadequate to the needs of his accuser. He gets no reprieve (in the Zuni case he was, we have seen, rescued by Mrs. Stevenson, backed by the U.S. cavalry). There is, in this case, no coherence. What produces speech also produces delirium. There is no complete control of this element. Therefore, once the witch is killed, another one is hunted.

Demonic possession, said Freud, was hysteria before it was interiorized in neurosis.[37] Indeed, witchcraft resembles hysteria in that something is said that under ordinary circumstances would not be said. More accurately, witchcraft is a failure of hysteria since hysteria is a compromise formation in which a symptom is formed that allows a forbidden wish to surface without being recognized. It is hidden under another form except for a point of resemblance. Magic, by contrast, knows no compromise. It links anything with anything even if the result is catastrophe. From this point of view, the man cursed in voodoo death dies of anxiety that knows no compromise and therefore surpasses all forms of expression.

There is excessive power in sorcery. It articulates, but "articulate" has at least two senses. One is "to conjoin"; the other is "to speak." In curing, both are present. In sorcery, only the first. There is conjunction or association without speech being in the control of the speaker. The origin of the power of sorcery is not the person. It is, if one can speak in the singular at all, neither language as such, in the Sausurrian sense, nor speech, but a place suggested by the string of articulations that never end and thus suggest a source without ever being able to represent it. Finally, one can never say, "This is what he meant" or "This is what he did" in a definitive way. Thus, the admission of sorcery by the Zuni youth required another; and the finding of magical objects meant more had to be found. No story, no object, adequately expressed magical power.

It is exactly this lack of a single place of origin that makes social and political authority interested. Their own claims to religious or supernatural valorization are challenged. Such claims depend on a fixed pantheon of supernatural beings, each definable and associated with particular tales and powers of intervention in human life. By contrast, in sorcery there is something they cannot grasp themselves and cannot grasp even with the help of all the witches they hang. But it is something whose force they recognize.

Absolute power of articulation is intolerable and turns against itself. Lévi-Strauss would like to say that in the process of the witch's confession he discovers the social origins of communication, its truth—that is, the possibility of communicating at all. But, in fact, it displays the contrary. The sorcerer addresses the community, is executed and later replaced by another, also to be executed. He shows how the full power of speech does not ensure social acceptance in exchange for "truth" but exceeds the social, finds its source in forbidden places, and remains, if not outside communication altogether, certainly on its margins.

Sorcery, then, is not an example of enormous phallic power filling in a fixed lack that, once established, assures normal speech. It is, rather, a matter of an excessive power pointing not to a place but to places from which nothing acceptable can issue. That such a power fascinates and is phallic is certain. But it is not phallocentric; the power of sorcery is not under centralized control; the sorcerer's magic arises not in a fixed center but in obscure and seldom visited places. The words of sorcery are thus eccentric by comparison both to normal speech and to those of magical curing.[38] This is not to say that language may not be organized in a phallic manner in most if not all human societies. But that does not mean that all possibilities are exhausted. The witch hunt is the attempt to close these possibilities.

" . . . The youth, who at first was a threat to the physi

his group, became the guardian of its spiritual coherence."[39] It would only be true if, first of all, there had been an exchange of truth for justice. This was not the case. It would be true if occult power were transformed into literature and narrative satisfied the fascination with the production of all possibilities. But literature never replaced sorcery in the Zuni world of the time of Mrs. Stevenson, and witches continued to be hanged. In the end, however, this particular youth did communicate. Mrs. Stevenson recorded his words, Lévi-Strauss read them, and we read them today. Does this show that he was at the source of communication? Or only *a* source? If the Zuni sorcerer continues to speak to us, it is, finally, because, like the Zuni, we too want to know the possible sources of articulation outside those already established. This might be the "truth" of sorcery, if there is one. We moderns cannot deny such sources exist, but in our theories, like Lévi-Strauss, we unjustly try to unify them. Finally, we can say, there is no "finally"; we only add our stories to others that travel across borders of all sorts.

The "truth" of the exchange of truth for justice is, we have seen, a sort of slight of hand. Not because there is no referent, but because if there were one it would not be recoverable. The boy, as he boasts of sorcery, manufactures fantasies. At the same time, Zuni suspicion is not baseless. There is a source of fantasies, and these fantasies are not only about power; they confer power on those capable of conjuring them up. But, contrary to Lévi-Strauss, this power remains unrecoverable by the warriors who are so eager to have it. It remains outside the grasp of the community, never fully a part of discourse, and for that reason, without Mrs. Stevenson, the boy was certainly at risk of being killed.

Voodoo Death

> "No one knows with regard to death whether it is not really the greatest blessing that can happen to a man but people dread it as through they were certain that it is the greatest evil; and this ignorance, which thinks that it knows what it does not, must surely be ignorance most culpable."
>
> —SOCRATES, ANNOUNCING HIS ADVANTAGE OVER THE REST OF MANKIND

When, in the 1960s, Lévi-Strauss wrote his important article on witchcraft, he asserted that bringing something to expression that can only be suspected and that is by the standards of that society and perhaps by universal standards inexpressible is the function of witchcraft. By articulating what others could only suspect, a magical power that Zuni somehow knew to exist but which they found unimaginable, he confirmed, in effect, that there is nothing that escapes signification. There is nothing that exists necessarily outside of discourse.

Lévi-Strauss began his article with voodoo death. Voodoo death is the phenomenon in which a person is bewitched, that is to say, effected only by words, and for no other apparent reason dies. Voodoo death would thus be the hyperbolic form of Lévi-Strauss's argument. Even words that kill can be part of discourse. He did not, however, elaborate. To have done so, he would have had to assert not only that words could kill, but that these words would be pronounceable and would circulate despite their effects. "Death," however it is understood or even merely pronounced, would be part of social life, incorporated into it rather than separated from it.

Of course, the line between life and death is drawn differently in different cultures. But everywhere there are funeral rites, at least so far as I know, which means that everywhere there is the attempt to separate life from death and thus to define one in terms of the other. An institution that attempts to bring death back into society would thus contradict what would seem to be a fundamental, universal principle: life and death must be kept apart. Is this the case, and if so, how is it possible?

The study of W. Lloyd Warner called *A Black Civilization* contains extended description and analysis of magically inflicted death. Warner did field work in Arnhem Land in northern Australia in the late 1920s. Warner was a Durkheimian, and he explained voodoo death as Durkheimian suicide: killing of the self as an expression of the social. A man is confronted with a sorcerer who points what is a called a "killing stick" at him; he sickens and dies. This stick is said to drip with the souls of those the sorcerer has killed—souls that have not yet returned to the proper realm of the dead, the totemic well. No one can help a man thus affected. He necessarily dies. This, said Warner, is the power of the sacred:

> The power of the black magician and his technique and the power of relics used to harm one's enemies . . . find their source in the *sacredness* of the dead. It is the mana of the dead which gives this power to magic and which *is* this power. To the living, the greatest and most intense dysphoria which finds expression in the life of man is death. The more dead souls that cluster about the evil point of the killing stick, the more power the killing stick possesses.[1]

The dead are the source of the power of the magician. It is fear of the dead that kills. But who are the dead and what is their power? And what does it mean to say that their power is "sacred"? For Durkheim, and others as well, the sacred is set apart. Sacredness among the Murngin and the other peoples indigenous to Australia is bound up particularly with totems. And totemic power is associated with the dead. Murngin souls, after death, go to the totemic well. The dead are thus separated from living society and become fused with the totem. The totem, it is well known, is the symbol of the group and, according to Warner, the source of the power of the sorcerer. By that reasoning, magic is social power. The power of magic comes not from its "agent," as Warner terms the magician, but from the social group as a whole: "It is not the leader who has this power but the ritual of his group. The power and efficacy of the ritual comes from the mana of the entire group" (222).

Voodoo death (this is not a term that Warner himself uses) comes about through a direct expression of the power of society. Those around a man affected by sorcery withdraw. Warner offers a description of how death occurs:

When the supposed theft of a man's soul becomes general knowledge, the sustaining social fabric pulls away from the victim. The familiar attitudes of the kinship personalities change, the collaboration of the victim and his society, of which his social personality has always been an integral part, ceases. The group now acts with all the ramifications of its organization and with countless stimuli positively to suggest death to a suggestible individual. (230)

The group distances itself. The person menaced with sorcery is deprived of society. He no longer has any normal form of communication and he dies. In Warner's view, the person dies because, though deprived of the usual social intercourse, he continues to respond to his fellows, who now consider him dead. But he is still among the living and he still sees himself in the eyes of others. He dies because of an impulse to maintain his sociality. Normal society has withdrawn from him. His only possibility of responding to the social is to accept its withdrawal. To do so means to die, and that is what he tries to do. He tries to act dead in order to become so. The problem for him is not that he must die, but that he does not do so. The solution to the problem is to accept a definition, a social definition. To be "dead" is to have a sociological definition; to be bewitched is to lack one.

Before death takes place the group, then, begin the mourning ritual the object of which is to transmute the social personality into a spiritual being, that is, to make the soul enter the totem well safely. Even before death the soul starts behaving like the sacred totem; the ancestors and the dead relatives come for him and enter his heart; the soul "ceases" reciprocal relations with the profane living, relating itself to the sacred dead; and the living cease acting their everyday roles and become virtually related to the sacred part of the dying person. (231)

The bewitched person "starts behaving like the sacred totem," while "the living," that is to say, those not bewitched, "become virtually related to the sacred part of the dying person." The problem is that the bewitched person can only act, only feign, his new position because he has not yet acquired it, while his fellows, for the same reason, can only be "virtually" but not actually related to the sacred because they are classed with the living. The sacred has not yet possessed the person. For that reason, there is a funeral ceremony, the purpose of which is precisely to turn the deceased into a sacred person.

There is a "sacred part" to this person because, believed to be on his way to dying, he is visited by totemic ancestors and dead relatives, themselves sacred. But one cannot say that his group believes the victim to be dead. More accurately, they hope that he will die, understanding "die" to mean to become part of the realm of the dead. He is, we shall see, termed "half dead." The problem is that he is not dead and it is not sure that he will "die." All funeral rituals are intended to separate the dead from the living. But in this case, the man being still alive, which means he is capable of responding to those around him, it is even less certain that the separation of dead and living can take place.[2]

In Warner's view, in this case to die is to conform to what society expects. But, once again, the source of the problem is that the victim is afflicted in such a way that social expectations are not effective:

The soul ceases reciprocal relations with the profane living. . . . He becomes what his society's attitudes make him, committing a kind of *suicide*. The social configuration in which he finds himself operating at this time is one of anomia for him. His ordinary social personality is removed, his part of the social structure not only having disintegrated but largely disappeared. Such a man is neither in the world of the ordinary nor in that of the sacred. He is, to use the Murngin expression, "half-dead." (230–31; Warner's emphasis)

The dead man is pursued by totemic figures: "Ancestors and the dead relatives come for him." It is in response to these sacred entities that he dies. "The soul 'ceases' reciprocal relations with the profane living, relating itself to the sacred dead." This is what Warner calls "a kind of *suicide*." The power of the sacred to attract causes the man to turn away from the social and hence to die.

Totemic power is called upon to effect the radical separation of the victim from his fellows and thus to enable the continued functioning of Murngin society which, like any other, cannot tolerate those neither alive nor dead among them.

The personality of the victim . . . has the ordinary attitudes of society removed from him. . . . He responds by recognizing his change of states: the wounded feudist killed [i.e., cursed or affected] by magic dances his totem dance to make himself like his totem [thus, he is not dead by our measure] and insure his immediate passage to the totem well; the man dying of an illness moves his hands convulsively like his crab totem or flaps his hands like his black duck totem, listening for the sounds of his ancestors' approach as he follows the suggestive sequence of the mourning song and ritual wailingly sung and danced over his body. His effort is not to live but to die. (231)

The man does not try to save himself from death, but from being pulled away from his totemic definition. To say, then, that sacred power, the power of the totem, is the cause of death by sorcery makes a certain sense. Turning toward his own totemic figures, the man also separates himself from the living. The attraction of doing so is that a proper death, the merging of himself with his totemic figures ("The man dying of an illness moves his hands convulsively like his crab totem or flaps his hands like his black duck totem, listening for the sounds of his ancestors' approach") ensues.

The ordinary daily activity of the victim's social life is removed. The society itself creates a situation which, if unchanged, makes it impossible for the individual to adjust himself to it even though he tried and in addition he usually not only makes no effort to live and to remain part of his group but actually, through the multiple suggestions from it, cooperates in his withdrawal therefrom. (230)

This Warner calls suicide, though one could as well call it murder or perhaps execution. In any case, what we see is how society turns against one of its members, as is always the case in witchcraft. Warner says, in fact, not "suicide," but "a kind of suicide" (231). It is, he says, anomic suicide, in which, according to Durkheim, the individual is isolated from society and dies because social norms no longer apply to him: "His ordinary social personality is removed, his part of the social structure not only having disintegrated but largely disappeared. He is no longer socially integrated and thus he kills himself."[3]

But one could argue that it is not release from norms but belief itself that causes death. And Warner, in a footnote, said just that (230 n. 2). Another, less common suicide, termed by Durkheim "altruistic suicide," also characterizes the Murngin example.[4] In altruistic suicide there is excessive application of norms. As when, Durkheim says, an army officer, protecting his honor, kills himself. If this, too, is the case with the Murngin, there is clearly a contradiction: voodoo death is caused by a lack of application of norms and also by too great application of norms.

If the victim of voodoo death exemplifies anomic suicide, that is, if he is killed as the result of the lifting of all norms and thus having no sanction for his very life, he can be said to be murdered. If we follow Warner, as we have seen, we cannot decide what to call his death. To avoid these contradictions, I propose to speak now not about norms and their effects but about language, using a view of it that does not see it as exhausted by its function as a generator of norms.

Warner collected accounts of sorcerers describing how they killed their victims. A sorcerer named Lainjura begins his story this way: "All of us were camping at Maringa Island. We were looking for oysters. This woman I was about to kill was hunting for lilies that day, for the other women had gone another way to search for oysters (189)." As Lainjura tells his story, the encounter and, for that matter, the killing, is fortuitous. It is a question of running across a woman while both he and she were gathering food, as was their habit. The next sentence continues, "I carried a hatchet with me and watched her." He goes on to describe the killing in detail.

Compare the beginning of that story with this one: "I came to the mission on the Crocodile Islands. They were making a Narra ceremony here. I killed Boniras's wife brother (Marawa), a Burera man, while he was here" (190). Once again, there is a coincidence, not really different from the story of a city. One meets someone on the street and, by accident, something happens. These are stories of lives interrupted. Not only the lives of the victims, but also of the sorcerer/killer. In this story, a reason is given for the killing. Lainjura had fought with Marawa earlier. The next story begins with the reason for the killing: "I killed her because she and Dorng had promised Waryi Waryi a tomahawk, but instead of giving it to him they gave it to Jerrimerrili. This made Waryi Waryi very angry. He told me and asked me to kill this woman" (192). The story of the killing follows, once again commencing with daily activities: "I was at the Mission. That woman went to look for palm nuts. I told everyone I was going to look for kangaroo. Before this Waryi Waryi and I had planned how it would be done" (192). Even when there is a reason for the killing, as in this case, the victim is still surprised. As though they are not on guard, they do not know the circumstances, and they suspect nothing. These are stories of people attacked either for no reason or for no reason that they have in mind, according to the narratives.

Lainjura, having said that he watched her, continues his story:

> The woman gathered her lily bulbs, then left the swamp, went back on the sandy land and lay down in the shade. She covered herself with paper bark to keep warm because she had been in the lily pond and felt cold. Only her head came out from the bark. She could not see me. (189)

It is noteworthy that the sorcerer understands the feelings of his victims. He pictures the woman coming out of the pond and feeling cold. We see him seeing her and understanding her mental and physical state. This is not hard to do since he interprets a common experience, one from everyday life. But she, immersed in the everyday, does not know that she is being watched.

> I sneaked up and hit her between the eyes with the head of a tomahawk. She kicked and tried to raise up but she couldn't. Her eyes turned up like she was dead. I picked her up under the arms and dragged her to a mangrove jungle and laid her down. She was a young girl. (189)

The lurid, sexual character of the account continues:

> I split a mangrove stick from off a tree and sharpened it. . . . I did not have my spear-thrower with me, so I took the handle off my tomahawk and jabbed about the skin on her Mount of Venus which was attached to her vagina and pushed it back. . . . Her large intestine protruded as though it were red calico. I covered my arm with orchid juice. I covered the killing stick with it, too. I put the stick in the palm of my hand so that I could push the point upward with my thumb. When she inhaled I pushed my arm in a little. When she exhaled I stopped. Little by little I got my hand inside her. Finally I touched her heart. . . . I pulled the stick out. I stood in back of her and held her up with her breasts in my hands. (189)

The phallic character of the killing stick is evident from this passage. It will be so again when we see that this stick is used to bring the victim back to life. But though the sorcerer's magical power is phallic, it is not, as we shall see, phallocentric. It does not concentrate power in such a way as to make a group, or even to draw those around the sorcerer to him. "Individually the sorcerer is not different from the ordinary man in the community. He participates in the culture and in the daily round of affairs exactly like other men. The difference from the average man lies in his having a special power" (187).

The Murngin sorcerer, like the curer (p. 200), is like everyone else, except that he has power. The magical practitioner uses his power for good (against those outside the group if he is a sorcerer, to cure members of his own group if he practices white magic). But he gains no special place in society or, to put it differently, no group takes shape around him. The sorcerer's power might be phallocentric if it were associated with the power of the totem. But as we will see, it is located outside that power.

To return to our account, the sorcerer has now reached the victim's heart. The blood of the heart is considered different from the blood of the rest of the body. When the sorcerer has his victim's blood, he has her soul, hence her life. He saves the blood and uses it to reconstruct the victim's body and bring her back to life. He repairs her wounds so that they are no longer visible: "'Her large intestine struck out several feet.'" With the aid of green ants it reenters her body a little at a time until finally "'There was no trace of the wound.'" At this point, the phallic weapon overtly becomes a magical instrument:

I took the tomahawk handle which had her heart's blood on it. I whirled it around her head. Her head moved slowly. I whirled it again. She moved some more. The spirit that belonged to that dead woman went into my heart then. I felt it go in. I whirled the stick again and she gasped for breath. I jumped over her and straightened her toes and fingers. She blew some breath out of her mouth and was all right.

It was noontime. I said to her, "You go eat some lilies." The woman got up and walked away. . . . I said to that woman, "You will live two days. One day you will be happy, the next day you will be sick." . . .

The next day she walked around and played, laughed, talked and made fun and gathered a lot of oysters and lilies. She came back to camp that night. She brought the things she had gathered into camp. She lay down and died that night. (190)

These stories recount the same procedure.[5] The sorcerer enters the body of the victim with the aide of a phallic stick. He arrives at the heart and drains its blood, at which moment he murders her or him. He then reconstructs the body and brings it back to life. The victim is told that s/he will live for a specified period of time, and often that s/he will be happy at first or that s/he will engage in some ordinary activity and then, the next day, s/he will die. The victim does not remember what has happened even though s/he is told by the sorcerer that s/he will die. Moreover, as Warner remarks, s/he "will not be able to tell anyone" (187).

Moreover, the person who has been magically attacked by a sorcerer bears no sign of the attack. The man who has been treated by the magicians still has a wound showing where the spear has hit him. When he gets near the camp so he can hear the murmur of the camp voices, the flies come out, bite upon the wound, and close it up, so that when he gets into the camp there is *no indication* that the flesh has been disturbed. By the time he has reached the camp, the magic has made him *forget* the operation of the medicine men, *although he has some kind of vague memory of it,* about which he tries to tell his relatives. He says to them, "I will tell you one thing." The relative says, "Yes, tell me." The victim replies, "Oh, nothing." He tries to remember, but all he can say is "Oh, nothing" (214).

The narratives specify a certain suspicion. Any Murngin might feel that he or she has something to say but is unable to say it. One might answer our initial question, "What can be shared when it is indefinite?" by saying that any member of a Murngin tribe, hearing a sorcerer tell his deeds, knowing that other sorcerers from outside his group are at work, can feel that he might be a victim and might, therefore, die the next day. But he knows that he does not and cannot know. At most, he might try and recall something he feels he has forgotten. Such an expectation is without any support but the myth. No trace is left either on the body or in the memory of the workings of lethal black magic. Nonetheless, the victim might feel that he wants to talk. He speaks, but he finds out that he has nothing to say. Here is the beginnings of suspicion; the victim suspects he has something to tell and he does not. This is not taken as evidence of sorcery in this account. But the narrator links the desire to speak, the inability to do so, with affliction of sorcery nonetheless. The victim suffers from an inability to find a reference. He does not suspect sorcery, but, according to the sorcerer, he should. A blank should serve as a clue and does not. A person cannot remember that he will die.

According to the Murngin, death comes only as a result of sorcery (183). It is not the natural end of life. It comes from a source that is accidental to human activity, as we have already seen in the examples quoted, and to the life cycle, and is foreign to both. Death is not then a normal expectation, but, given the existence of sorcerers who cause it, it is a constant. The implication of Warner's description of Murngin attitudes toward death is that, thinking of it, a Murngin does not think of drowning while gathering lilies or dying from exposure afterward or from illness. Nor is death something that comes with age and that one can think will be put off. Rather, without making itself felt, the normal trajectory of life might have been bent in its direction. To think of death is to think of something arriving at right angles, as it were, to one's thoughts and activities. Death is a surprise. One can well be in line for death without expecting it. One never knows and one knows that one does not know. Death comes, unsuspected, as an accident, but this accident is built into Murngin culture in such a way that one is not on the lookout for it. Even if one were, it would do no good. Only *après coup* does one recognize it

One cannot say "death" without having an idea of it. Such an idea is, of course, necessarily conjectural. Even where death is considered merely a question of biology, there is still dispute over when, exactly, it occurs. For that reason, one cannot say that the Murngin either "deny death" or give it its proper place, as though we know what it is that they deny. This would be unacceptably ethnocentric. One has, instead, to follow the Murngin narrative of murder. I speak of murder at this point, as that is the aim of the sorcerer. But the victim dies at least twice and is brought back to life once and, if the rituals work, given a proper shape among the totems eventually (though it is not evident that this is necessarily thought to be the case, as we will see). The sorcerer mutilates the body of the victim and drains it of its heart's blood. But he also reconstructs it, revitalizes it, and then predicts its inevitable death.

This death, however, is not death, only "half death," by Murngin thinking. It is only when there are not only funeral rituals but when these are believed to be effective, that one can say that death has been accomplished. But the sorcerer aims not at this cultural death but at the death that occurs before it, the half death. That is the source of his power. The more souls cling to the end of his killing stick, souls not in the totemic well, the more powerful he is. These souls are said to be stolen, pulled away from their totemic definitions and not returned there. It is these unsuccessfully ritualized, not to say "unmourned," souls that he controls and that are the source of Murngin fears. The repetitive shock of Murngin culture takes the form of their sudden presence.

If, then, the stories establish "shock," enabling one to recognize, at a certain moment, what is happening to one, confirming one's necessarily inchoate suspicion, one is not by that given any certainty. The narratives give shape to an uncertain fear (how they do this remains to be seen) and enable it therefore to be installed in the center of the community. They picture a force which, affecting as it does not merely the victim but the persons around him, causes the community to disintegrate as it becomes paralyzed by fear of pollution by a death that is outside definition and in that form is invulnerable to mourning.

Let us turn to the sorcerer. "Individually the sorcerer is not different from the ordinary man in the community. He participates in the culture and in the daily round of affairs exactly like other men. The difference from the average man lies in his having a special power" (187). He is neither a hero nor a villain to his own group. He gains his power from his father or his uncle, usually his maternal uncle but sometimes his uncle through his father, who teach him "'how to kill a man and make him alive to die'" (187). How, in other words, to install death in a society. The power to kill comes through an apprenticeship. In the stories told to Warner, first one aides his father or uncle to murder someone. As it was explained to Warner, the instructor says, "'You do this way and that way, and by and by, after I die, you can do this too'" (188). Warner says there is "almost a right" for someone to be taught by his uncle or father. But one does not become a sorcerer simply as a result of being taught.

The novice must associate with the older sorcerer in a killing or two before he can secure sufficient mana in his group to be considered a sorcerer. First, the power is transmitted from a man who is a killer and master of the souls of several dead men; and second, the beginner must have been associated with the killing of a man and therefore with the dead before he is given the social personality of a sorcerer by his community." (188)

The power to kill is not natural but, in part, cultural and transmissible. It is part of a body of learning. But this learning is insufficient. Presumably, Warner, for instance, who obviously learned the techniques of sorcery, was not for that reason a sorcerer. He would have had to taken part in killings first. The body of learning is not appropriable as such. It comes only with association with death. Thus, the new sorcerer can himself only kill when his teacher has died: "'After I die, you can do this too.'" Warner uses the word "association" twice in the last quotation. The man who becomes a sorcerer "must associate" with another sorcerer first. And he "must have been associated with the killing of a man and therefore with the dead." Only then does he have a sorcerer's power himself.

What does "association" mean here? The use of this word stands in place of a precise description (which would be impossible) of how the power of the dead comes to a man. It is clear that it is not the "sacred dead" themselves who are its source, but the "half dead." One must have something to do with them. And that can only be by killing. One has to kill, then one has the power to kill. The paradoxical sequence tells us not only that killing, under the instruction of the teacher, is the means to appropriate power. It also says that the power to kill comes from the dead. What one learns without experience of death—imagined experience of course—is useless technique.

If the sorcerer has a "sacred power," this sacredness is different from that of the dead. The sacredness of the dead comes from their association with totems which are set apart, the object of taboos. The power of the sorcerer is sacred, if the term is properly used here, simply because it is power set apart, not available to everyone. The sorcerer gains power because he is close to the half dead. It is, again, a question of "association" with half death.

The killing by the sorcerer is, of course, entirely fantastic. It might be called fiction, since it has an author. But if it were fiction, one could say that the author allowed himself to imagine something that he would not allow to be attributed to "himself," the person addressed in everyday life; or at least he has the privilege of having it not be attributed to him. The author looks at everyday life, sees a woman gathering food, and says, "What if . . . ". The sorcerer fantasizes differently, not in the mode of the "What if . . . ," but, rather, of confession. The confession is made up, but it is not, strictly speaking, false for that. It attests to an association which is real, even if it is imaginary. The sorcerers' stories are the inventions of people who imagine facing the nearness and the inevitability of death. And who do this in face of the normality of everyday life which precludes such thinking. If one can imagine in this way, one can be a sorcerer.

The opposed terms "imaginary" and "real" are inapplicable where there are no genres of fiction. The sorcerer attaches himself to his imaginary ventures, as does the author. He attributes them to himself, which means that they are his. Obliged to choose a genre to describe his productions, we choose confession because the sorcerer does not give up his everyday persona. He remains the person of everyday life when he speaks of what he did and when he does what he does as a sorcerer.

The sorcerer confesses, which means that he speaks of an event after the fact, the fact being someone's death for which he claims to be responsible. Imagined death is the source of his story, if not its actual beginning. The sorcerer imagines the person in life before death, and then in life after death. "After death" since the death occurs before his story, and "after death" since his victim is pictured living after he has been killed. Imagining he has killed someone, inventing the details of this act, picturing the person alive, then dead, then alive again, then half dead, the sorcerer asserts that he has come close to experiencing what others might know but cannot keep in mind: their own death as this might occur at any instant and as it removes them from their fellows. Only a sorcerer can find death in life and thus find death where it is otherwise unknowable. Or, once again, to be able to find death in life is to become a sorcerer. It is to remember what everyone has forgotten and to be able to relate it. His otherwise unspeakable truth is so powerful that anyone other than a sorcerer affected by it will do his best to die a Murngin death.

At the same time, the Murngin sorcerer is an ordinary neighbor. Speaking of a particular sorcerer, one known to have killed many people, Warner says, "There was nothing sinister, peculiar, or psychopathic about him; he was perfectly normal in all of his behavior. Among his own people the attitudes were no different toward him than toward any other man in the clan" (188). His power does not threaten his neighbors, and for that reason, perhaps, he is not sinister. But that his power does not entitle him to a special position within his community indicates the degree to which its basis is put out of mind.

The killing stick, dripping with dead souls, is the emblem of this power. It is the killing stick that reaches the point where death, or, rather, "half-death," occurs. The killing stick reaches a point of indefinition which, finally, is the impediment to memory and knowledge. It arrives at the point where memory fails. By holding onto it, which means holding on to association with the half dead, a man achieves the power to "kill," which means to further associate and to articulate what he imagines. What we, the possibly half dead, cannot do, the sorcerer, through this power of association, can.

The power of the killing stick is attributed to the souls dripping off of it, souls of those killed by the sorcerer. It sums up the sorcerer's association with the dead in the past. Its power is to stimulate yet another story. It is the sum of everything told before, the archive, as it were, of the sorcerer's literary productions (if that is what they are). Without it, one has no associations with death that come to mind. With it, one must want to kill, which means to tell some more. The impossible associations of the past press on whomever bears this horrible weapon. It is the stimulus to the production of associations which for everyone else are unthinkable. The killing stick reminds all within its ken that what one cannot remember presses toward expression but arrives there only exceptionally and only by virtue of a special power.

The potent ingredient of the killing stick is thus words. Mauss tells us that each element of magic is composed of words. Here we see them pictured or phantasized. They are, of course, available only through an impossibility. They belong to the sorcerer, with his special capacities. They are attained only through association with the "half dead." They bring these creatures, these others, into the world of the living. The sorcerers' words do not originate with himself. They were taken by him when he was close to the dead. No doubt for that reason he feels compelled to pass them on. Which is once again to say, to relate, to become a sorcerer.

This might be the truth of sorcery. Something only suspected because it cannot be expressed is nonetheless said. Its expression is worth more than justice. But there is also the victim. The Murngin victim cannot speak. We know that, not only from the stories of the Murngin sorcerer, but from other descriptions of those afflicted by voodoo death. He lacks the power of the sorcerer, who not only makes associations but claims them for his own person. The sorcerer speaks in the first person in a culture where there is no convention of fiction, thus no taking on of another persona except that of "sorcerer," neither that of the author nor that of the narrator who might appear within the text. The person who has seen the killing stick directed against him cannot say what he wants to say. And he cannot evade the moment when he wants to say to his relatives, "I have something to relate. . . . " He cannot continue. Were he able to tell us why someone, not himself, could not speak, he might be able to do so. But it is not possible. The closest one comes to that is the association with death by stories of oneself as the murderer.

The victim is a person overcome by the inability to speak. If the community breaks all communication with him, it is because such communication is already impossible. If he were to speak nonetheless, to say what he wants to say, he would say, "I am (half) dead." This sentence, avoided even by the sorcerer who relies only on association with the half dead, is what he wants to say but cannot remember. The sorcerer's ability to speak rests on his capacity to avoid this sentence, which might apply to himself as well as to anyone else, by speaking of himself as the murderer. That is his association with (half) death. He confesses one thing in order to avoid another.

It is not truth that the sorcerer speaks, but evasion. The sorcerer is someone who avoids the consequence of association with the half dead, which is to be like them. He tells his fellows about death. He has experienced it at close hand, he says. By virtue of knowing death, he should say, "I am (half) dead." Were he to do so, there would be no witchcraft. Instead, the sorcerer would be his own victim. Witchcraft depends on the sorcerer being exchangeable with his victim and on this exchange being dissimulated. It is at the point where the witch does not say "I am dead," and where, in his place, there is someone else who ought to say it but cannot, that witchcraft takes its structure. And it is just here that witchcraft becomes a social phenomenon. A person might have private fears of his own death. When, however, the fears of one become attributed to another, a social scene takes place.

The communication that pertains in this scene is special. The community withdraws from the half dead person. Ordinary communication with him ceases. He withdraws from himself. There is fear and even panic. This fear is not to be dismissed as merely imaginary, nor explained by the sheer indefinition of the half dead. The community is faced, in the person of the victim, with something that the sorcerer alludes to or hides. It is that in the process of speaking, in the desire to speak, something is evaded. This something is nothing, but not in a nihilistic sense. It is the point where reference is necessarily indefinite but where it is also necessary and even compelled. We give the word "death" to this point since we know that death is unknowable and that it is put out of mind but that, somehow, it "is."

And because at that point between language and its speaker there is a gap; the victim cannot speak but he has something to say. Demonstrating his inability to speak, he communicates what he cannot say: "I am (half) dead." The embodiment of what is contrary not merely to wishes but to logic, and what is left out of words, is demonstrated to exist. It becomes a possibility for anyone who, having listened to the sorcerer's tales, finds that in them there is truth, even if he has evaded it himself up till that point.

The sorcerer cannot exist without his victims. First he imagines them; then they come into being. Witchcraft is often said to be the persecution of those considered different. In Murngin witchcraft this is only tenuously true. The sorcerer who is feared is from another group, yes. But sorcerers' stories begin not with the recognition of difference but with the everyday, common to both groups. The victim is not originally different. He is originally the same. It is through the narratives of sorcery that he becomes different. The difference that he comes to embody is embedded in language that brushes the surface of half-death. It is neither the force of norms nor their absence that accounts for Murngin death by sorcery. It is, rather, a power of narration that we, readers, find only in literature and then only rarely.

Sorcery is installed in Murngin society at the moment that an impossibility of speech, the conveying of an absolute negativity, is made to seem possible. At that moment, Murngin society is riven in two unequal parts as it turns against one of its own and claims his life which he is eager to give up. His death eventually banishes half death for a time. Those who kill him by turning away from him avoid the contamination of half death. Were they not to turn away and were they to survive, they too could become sorcerers, contaminated by half death but avoiding the consequences by telling their stories, thus reminding people of what they cannot suffer to remember, installing the awareness of immanent half death in them. Those who turn aside from the victim commit murder in fact; the sorcerer does so only in stories and thus only indirectly.

There is something like a sublime moment in Murngin sorcery. It occurs at the moment when the sorcerers tell their stories. They have faced death and survived. They speak not out of fear, which, Kant said, would prevent a feeling of sublimity. They appear rational, and by the standards of Murngin society, they are so. If they cannot overcome death themselves, they seem to demonstrate the effects of having separated themselves from it, at least momentarily. But their stories offer no reassurance. Quite the contrary. Without their stories there would be no sorcery-induced death.

The sorcerers do not claim that there is an absolute line between life and death. They may be present to tell the stories, but their words are permeated with death. The conviction they carry is so predicated. Sorcerers, in place of the admission of the inability to comprehend an overwhelming power, the basis of sublimity, claim to possess it. They do not separate themselves from death; rather they bear the traces of their association with it.

As a result, Murngin society has an uncanny cast. At any moment anyone alive may also be dead. Anyone who believes their words, and we are given no evidence that there are Murngin who do not, is vulnerable to them. Words kill in Murngin society because they mark a place where death might always already dominate. The words of the sorcerer are saturated in this negativity. To take them at their worth is to become deprived of the power to stay alive. One cannot speak. Words which, spoken, should prove one's existence, remain unsaid because they assert that one is dead. Feeling the urge to say "I am dead," one is afflicted by paradox. One is and one is not, alternately and at the same time. It is not only that were one able to speak one might live. It is also that some words bear the force of their origin and so are unsayable.

3

Institutionalizing Accident

> "A moment earlier the regularity had been broken by a sudden oblique move-
> ment: something had spun round, skidding sideways—the abrupt braking, as it
> appeared, of a heavy truck, which was now stranded with one wheel on the edge of
> the pavement. In an instant, like bees round the entrance to their hive, people had
> collected round a little island of space in their midst. The driver, who had climbed
> down from his seat, stood there, grey as packing-paper, gesticulating crudely,
> explaining how the accident had happened."
>
> —ROBERT MUSIL, ´THE MAN WITHOUT QUALITIES´

I. Evans-Pritchard and His Followers

The anthropological study of witchcraft as we know it today began
with the books of the American Clyde Kluckhohn and the Englishman
E. E. Evans-Pritchard, but particularly the latter. Kluckhohn's work on the
Navajo was important in showing the logic of witchcraft beliefs and their
social place, but it did not set off an increasingly coherent line of interpretation and further study. The contrary was the case in Britain and the academic world centered on it. Reading Evans-Pritchard's *Witchcraft Oracles
and Magic among the Azande* in 1937 when it was published, however, one
might not have predicted what followed. The section of Evans-Pritchard's
book that is anthologized in America and that is taught in introductory anthropology classes concerns the explanation of misfortune. Witchcraft explains what otherwise would be accident and as such would be inexplicable. Evans-Pritchard's followers were more concerned to show the
place of witchcraft accusations in social life than to demonstrate the logic
of witchcraft beliefs. As John Middleton and E. H. Winter noted, Kluckhohn and Evans-Pritchard elucidated "the logic of wizardry," but left un-

developed "the problem of explaining particular forms taken by beliefs in wizardry, and the problem of the relationship of these ideas to the social structure."[1] Evans-Pritchard, they said, made a cultural study. What was needed and which, by the time they wrote, had already developed, was "a sociological explanation," which they believed had the advantage of making comparison and verification of results possible.[2] This was seen as a natural step forward suggested by certain sections of *Witchcraft Oracles and Magic among the Azande.* Mary Douglas, at least, read Evans-Pritchard as describing "how a metaphysical system could compel belief by a variety of self-validating procedures."[3] Douglas, like other British social anthropologists, thought this would be better posed as a problem in the sociology of knowledge. Finding the social functions of the beliefs, one could account for their persistence and, to a degree, their form. She gives as an example work done by the anthropologists Clyde Mitchell and Max Marwick: a village reaches a size larger than its resources will permit, and witchcraft accusations become the "idiom in which the painful process of fission could be set going."[4] In this Durkheimian thinking, there is an underlying reality, "society," and in particular, social tension, which is reflected in a particular idiom. Witchcraft is an idiom of conflict, reproducing, or perhaps representing, conflicts which exist in the structure of society.

The British school produced sophisticated studies showing in admirable detail how social processes worked. Its very success, however, led to a difficulty. Mary Douglas: "Wherever belief in witchcraft was found to flourish, the hypothesis that accusations would tend to cluster in niches where social relations were ill defined and competitive could not fail to work, because competitiveness and ambiguity were identified by means of witch accusations."[5] One could always find social tensions, perhaps because they always exist. Witchcraft, in this view, was a way of making them visible. Marwick, for instance, notes that "the divining situation [in which the witch is identified] is important sociologically since it is during the divination that vague feelings of tension are organized and formulated into a belief that a particular person is responsible for a particular misfortune."[6] This brings him close to Lévi-Strauss's notion that vague suspicions, otherwise inexpressible, are consolidated and brought to expression in witchcraft accusations, giving the community a coherence that, till that point, it lacked. The difference remained, however, that the first were "vague feelings of [social] tension," the social being at the base, whereas little about social tension appears in Lévi-Strauss.

Mary Douglas's criticism suggested that if these suspicions pointed to underlying social tensions, it could never be verified by the methods anthropologists followed. Nonetheless, she remained convinced that a better method would reveal the relation between witchcraft belief and social conflict. For her, the formulation of Lévi-Strauss could be at best a starting point. Indeed, in her telling survey of witchcraft studies, published in 1970 in honor of Evans-Pritchard and in particular of *Witchcraft Oracles and Magic among the Azande*, she does not mention Lévi-Strauss's essay, published in English in 1963 and in French in 1949.[7] Witchcraft pointed to social tension; the problem was to establish the relation between the two in a verifiable way.

For his part, Lévi-Strauss was not interested in a correlation between social tensions and witchcraft accusations. He had moved a step beyond, or at least away, from Durkheim, looking at the linguistic character of accusations. His point was that, regardless of the social and political situation surrounding them, charges of sorcery had to be seen as first of all linguistic in character, or, at least, as a mode of thinking modeled on language. In their basic functioning, witchcraft accusations were not motivated by a situation whose reality could be independently expressed by the anthropologist.

Lévi-Strauss's essay had the strange effect of making witchcraft functional in a way quite different from function understood by British social anthropologists. For Lévi-Strauss, witchcraft confirmed and even established a community. Where there were only vague sentiments shared between people, their articulation promoted not merely shared understandings but shared investment in objects and words beyond their conventional meanings. However, from the point of view of anthropologists who worked for long periods in societies, Lévi-Strauss's approach had the disadvantage that it said nothing about the workings of society outside the moment of witchcraft accusations. From Lévi-Strauss's perspective, to show the motivation of symbols of witchcraft would be to take a false trail. He wanted to explain the power of signification when no particular signification ensues and yet a symbol, necessarily incomprehensible, is formed. It is around such odd symbols that articulation takes place as such and that, beginning with structural (Sausssurian-Jakobsonian) linguistics, one sees a power deriving from the very capacity to form signs rather than to refer to already constituted meanings. As such, Lévi-Strauss said little that was of help to social anthropologists who were interested in the daily workings of the societies they studied. One had to wait for his ideas to pass through those of Jacques Lacan for them to come back to social anthropology in the work of people such as Janet Favret-Saada and Vincent Crapanzano, to name only two.

In Lévi-Strauss, witchcraft accusations center on signs which must remain incomprehensible. The incongruity of such signs to the cultures in which they are found produces the witch. The power of the witch is an anti-social power. But the revelation of this power, instead of upsetting social life, becomes its basis. The Zuni witch seen by Lévi-Strauss is an ordinary Zuni who is revealed to be someone entirely different from his fellows by virtue of his relation to the power that inheres in these signs. And yet this otherness, though initially thought harmful, turns out to be valuable, at least as Lévi-Strauss understood it. The "truth" of sorcery, à la Lévi-Strauss, was more important than justice, which meant that the person of the witch was left unharmed as, around an initial incoherent suspicion, a communal voice formed itself. The difference between the witch and the community is forgotten as the "truth" of sorcery becomes the focal point of social formation and renewal and a "truth," initially foreign to the community, is incorporated into it.

In the analyses of British social anthropologists, accusations of sorcery revealed points where social life was upset already. But, as in the example given by Max Marwick, the result is social integration. Fission is necessary for demographic reasons. It must take place. Witchcraft accusations allow it to do so and thus allow East African societies to work once more. The social system needs conflict and thus needs witchcraft to change latent conflict into action. Witchcraft is thus integrated into society not as harmfully disruptive aggression (on the part of either the witch or the witch hunters) but as disruptive aggression which is useful, perhaps necessary, and which should not be thought foreign to the constitution of the societies involved. As in the Lévi-Straussian explanation, it is not a question of suppressing a force thought disruptive and harmful but rather of looking at the system as such and thus understanding that a force, either the need to articulate what one only feels one knows or unconsolidated feelings of enmity, needs expression. Disruptive secret power, contrary to ethics, contrary to the social, is in fact needed. Witchcraft, by definition a foreign power, not belonging to the approved sources of social power, contrary to the good, nonetheless functions for the good. Its foreignness is thus domesticated. It is a short step to the thoughts of Steve Biko on the subject.

In the wake of World War II, historians, notably H. R. Trevor-Roper and Norman Cohn, studied European witchcraft in order to find the devastating sources of conflict in Europe.[8] On the other hand, anthropologists posited the exchange of truth for justice outside of Europe. Only in these ways could witchcraft escape its reputation as harmful and even lethal. The cost was that the sources of fear and violence that historians found in Europe were largely neglected.[9] Looking in retrospect at studies which served their times very well and which also advanced our understanding of social processes, nevertheless one wants to ask if there could not have been another path, one that opened onto the sources of disruption without denial of their consequences.[10] And one wants to know also how it was that witchcraft could function without violence and accommodate, if not integrate, impulses antithetical to social life. An answer is contained in Evans-Pritchard's study. I want to look back at his book and ask about paths of explanation left aside as functionalism took its course and as the structuralist approach was little advanced. Accident, we have already seen in the Introduction, is at the beginning of Evans-Pritchard's explanation. Much of Azande life functioned around the attempt to incorporate accident into the daily. To expect the unexpected, to know that one cannot anticipate it, to have conventional ways of reacting to it when it occurs; these are themes one finds in Evans-Pritchard's description of the Azande.

II. Magic Versus Trauma

leprosy and there is a history of incest in his use of leprosy and not witchcraft."[11] But when rse to the breaking of conventions or laws, then s witchcraft. Witchcraft, as all anthropologists st quoted section of Evans-Pritchard's study, ex- means that while what we term natural causes

Institutionalizing Witchcraft   75

for events are not denied, the reason that something happened to a certain person at a particular time is accounted for in a way that naturalistic explanations could not. Thus, says Evans-Pritchard, his old friend Ongasi was injured by an elephant while out hunting. The reason is witchcraft, in part because the question posed is not how the elephant hurt the man, but "Why he and not someone else? Why on this occasion and not on other occasions? Why by this elephant and not by other elephants?" (69). And in his most famous example, a granary collapses while people are sitting beneath it. "There is nothing remarkable about this," he tells us. There are termites at work all the time and eventually granaries, no matter how well made, collapse. But the question is, Why should there have been people underneath it at that moment? It is not unusual for people to sit under granaries to escape the heat. But this does not explain the conjuncture of two trajectories: the ants eating away until the supports are weakened and certain people at a certain moment choosing to sit under just this structure to avoid the heat. "To our minds, the only relationship between these two independently caused facts is their coincidence in time and space. We have no explanation of why the two chains of causation intersected at a certain time and in a certain place, for there is no interdependence between them" (69–70). Azande seek an explanation, whereas we do not, presumably because we cannot.

Witchcraft, it is often said, stops with Descartes. Once there is a notion of a mechanical universe, one ceases to ask unanswerable questions. Or, one might say, the questions that prompt accusations of witchcraft are left unanswered. But it is not true that we simply let the matter go. We understand that we cannot answer the question posed by Azande. But we pose it also, all the same. When, for instance, we are involved in a bad accident, the sign of our being traumatized is precisely that we feel compelled to repeatedly recall the scene of the accident. A similar accident happening to someone unknown to us is less likely to stimulate such memories. If it does, we believe we identify with the person in the scene with ourselves. We might be shocked at seeing an accident that happens to someone else, but if the shock does not produce the same effect it is because we can think of the accident without reliving it. What happened to the person we speak about did not happen to us. We do not worry about why it is the accident occurred. But when we relive the scene as it recurs to us, it is as though the normal forces that produce an accident—a slippery street, a speeding car, neglecting the red light—are insufficient to explain how it is that "I," in particular, suffered the effect of those forces. There is a singularity about the event when "I" am involved in it. At that point, I say to myself, "If only I had crossed the street one minute sooner," and "Why did I step off the curb just before the light turned red," and so on. I construct another scene, one that did not happen, because while I know that the accident happened to me, I cannot believe it. It is not simply the harmful consequences of the accident that make me feel that way. There may have been none. It might have been only the feeling of a chance event that stimulates in me dread of what might have happened. In reaction to that, I say to myself, "If only . . . ," and in doing so I construct a slight narrative in which nothing happened. I crossed the street. I arrived on the other side without event. There was only the normal course of events in which I made my way through traffic, obeying the laws that regulate circulation as did everyone else. I understand very well that the law is often broken; consequently I look left and right before stepping off the curb. It is not the breaking of the traffic laws that makes the accident abnormal. It is that they were broken in such a way that I became a victim. A victim not merely of negligence and perhaps criminality but a victim of circumstances. In response, in my mind I reconstruct "normality" by contrast to what actually happened to me, or I repeat what occurred. I do so because what I cannot grasp I think of as abnormal. I was in the grip of forces which applied to no one else. Out of this presumed abnormality comes witchcraft.

We have no idiom for expressing such forces. Which is a weak way of saying, in Kantian terms, following Mauss, that no judgment is possible. We cannot judge the nature of the coincidence that occurred. At this point, a term heterogeneous to all judgment appears, according to Mauss. This is "mana," or "power," or, in our case, "witchcraft." As Evans-Pritchard puts it, "What [the Azande] explained by witchcraft were the particular conditions in a chain of causation which related an individual to natural happenings in such a way that they sustained injury" (67). Evans-Pritchard speaks of Zande "philosophy." What he means, I believe, is that witchcraft, as he puts it, "explains *why* events are harmful to man." The sentence continues, " . . . and not *how* they happen" (72).

Witchcraft is not a mistaken science. Perhaps it can be called speculative, as philosophy is also speculative. Not all misfortune is caused by witchcraft, but there seems to be no debate about whether witchcraft is involved in a particular event. The question is put to an oracle and the oracle's message is decisive. Witchcraft, Evans-Pritchard tells us, supplements empirical determination of causes. "The Zande accepts a mystical explanation of the causes of misfortune, sickness, and death, but he does not allow this explanation if it conflicts with social exigencies expressed in law and morals" (75). Other causes are adduced if they are socially relevant. One cannot claim that one lied or committed adultery, for instance, because one was bewitched: "Since Azande recognize plurality of causes, and it is the social situation that indicates the relevant one, we can understand why the doctrine of witchcraft is not used to explain every failure and misfortune. It sometimes happens that the social situation demands commonsense, and not a mystical, judgment of cause" (74). This means that misfortune cannot be accidental. The Azande universe and its "philosophy" rules out interpretations of events that occur for no decipherable reason.

Zande speculation starts from seeing a peculiarity that makes an event not explicable in ordinary terms. Thus, Evans-Pritchard says that "it is the particular and variable conditions of an event and not the general and universal conditions that witchcraft explains. Fire is hot, but it is not hot owing to witchcraft, for that is its nature. It is a universal quality of fire to burn, but it is not a universal quality of fire to burn *you*. This may never happen; or once in a lifetime and then only if you have been bewitched" (69). It is the singular quality of an event that prompts explanations of witchcraft. But Azande [the plural of Zande, the later being both a noun and an adjective] witchcraft is not itself singular. That is, there is not a different power for every event. There is one power, that of witchcraft, though we have seen that among the Zuni, for instance, there are particular objects that are the instruments of that power and that "witchcraft" seems to arise from different places each time. Azande witchcraft explains the particular, the singular even, by reference to a general power. It thus annihilates its singularity; which is to say, it rules out accident. We could at this point say that witchcraft among the Azande institutionalizes accident by making of it a category.

This might be thought to be a simple denial: "there is no accident," no singularity, in which case witchcraft would be merely an ideological prop. It would be the tool, the belief, the deception necessary to support a denial. But to say this raises certain questions. First, one asks why it is necessary to deny accident. It is not an absolute necessity, as we know. And next one asks why the denial is made with reference to occult power. Is there not more to this notion of occult power than the means of making a denial?

This question about myself as I am found in an inexplicable conjunction of circumstances—termites at work, passing by the granary at a certain time, deciding to stop—divides "me" in two. Compare it, for instance, with a man who comes across someone who bears him a grudge and who decides at that moment to take his revenge. I might curse myself for having taken a walk at that moment and in that place and thus having met my enemy. But I might also simply think about the injustice of the man's view of me or the inappropriateness of him striking me. Questions of "Why?" might not arise, in that case. But if they do arise, "I" find myself in a scene which is larger than one of the encounter of two subjectivities. What I have encountered is something that I do not imagine was controlled by anyone. I see myself, at that moment, from outside myself, shaken out of my own world. At that point, a question of articulation arises. There is something to say, but I do not know what. I cannot account for the event. Saying what happened to me does not account for the event. There is something else to say, but I cannot say it because I cannot grasp it.

This, once again, would be the point of trauma. The point where "I," in particular, cannot say what happened. Where even if "I" can say that in the afternoon, as I was sitting under the granary, it suddenly collapsed, my words feel inadequate. This inadequacy has a strange quality. Traumatized, it means that I relive the experience. In that sense, my words are, in a certain way, more than adequate to describe the event. They even pull it into the present. But they are inadequate because they are not "my" words. If I could describe the accident "in my own words," as we say in English, the "mineness" of the words would locate them at the time of speaking. What they described would be before that. But they are not exactly my words. "I" seem to have no choice. The words I use are as if given to me.

Ordinarily when I relate my experience, I feel that my words reflect what happened to me and that I choose them in order that they might do so. The traumatized person speaks with urgency; his words seem not to be chosen but to be forced on him. He has to say what happened to him. The words come to him, it seems, automatically, practically indistinguishable in their effect from the event itself. It thus feels as if a power is at work. This force comes into existence just at the point where words fail me because they are not my words. They say what happened, they even bring back the event, but a dimension is missing. The effect is paradoxical. The words issue from my mouth; they describe the event; they embody it. But these words have no authority because they lack a voice. One cannot tell where they came from. It is not merely that they are not "my" words, but they are no one's at all. They are an effect of accident, of the "force," one says, for lack of another term, that is responsible for accident, though, of course, "responsible" is inexact and that is the problem. Between the urgency, which indicates a force, and the naming of that force, there is a gap. My voice is "filled with urgency," one says in English, and yet it is hollow. It is a question of articulation. The articulations lay outside my control. Or, one might say, following our introductory remarks, an unknown third person speaks through me.

The hollowness of my voice is the sound of a power located outside myself. In magic, this power is named; in trauma, it is not. What is at stake is recognizing a power that cannot be recognized in the limited sense of this term. In the crucial moments of magic, one recognizes that one cannot recognize, that events are linked to each other in ways that seem to reveal something one cannot grasp. When magic is culturally sanctioned, the articulation of events comes to be accounted for by it and voice is restored. Exactly what makes words sound hollow without magic, that they are not "my" words, that they are determined from elsewhere, makes them convincing once magic is invoked. Magic, said Mauss, depends on a heterogeneous term, impervious to all logic, and which, for this reason, accounts for linkages where otherwise there is no accountability. And, he stressed, it depends on belief. Here, "belief," however, can not be understood as the credence given in common by members of a society to something they know. Rather, as Derrida points out, it depends on something one does not and cannot know. When this can nonetheless be given a name, there is magic and magic words at work.

III. The Oracle

The person who believes himself bewitched is likely also to think that there are many who hate him. He knows who they are. He consults his oracle. It is at this point that the narrative of accident changes registers. From a story of daily life it becomes a story of magic. Which is to say that it becomes a story, the events of daily life ordinarily remaining outside extended narration. There is then a shift from the first person to the third. The "I" that speaks when I tell you a story becomes "he" when one can speak of a "narrative voice" which is not that of the author and only problematically that of one of the characters. The voice that speaks in fiction seems somehow to bring us language from an indefinite point. When Maurice Blanchot says that the narrative voice is impersonal, he means that the third person is not really a person, as are "I" and "you." As Benveniste pointed out, the third person is defined as not being the other two.[12] "He" or "she" or "they" are not present in discourse. They occur outside it. The narrative voice of fiction is behind the scenes, somewhere else. The origin of speech has shifted to a place whose locus is uncertain. The "he" rather than the "I" narrates. There is no notion of fiction among the Azande to my knowledge. But there is a shift of narrative center. The Zande man consults his oracle. Someone else, present only through signs, speaks. The estrangement of the voice that makes it recognizably not the speaker's own voice takes place. The man's own voice would not be acceptable. He knows who hates him, but this is not enough to establish that any particular one of them is a witch. Just where his own voice would not be acceptable, a foreign and therefore acceptable voice takes shape in the consultation of the oracle.

The Azande have well-defined procedures for identifying witches. The most important is their oracle. When a man feels he might be bewitched, he takes a bundle of chickens and a special poison (*benge*, from the vine of that name) into the bush. He feeds the poison to the chickens, asking it questions to which the fowl replies by dying or by surviving. With the care and patience that marked his work, Evans-Pritchard gave his readers examples of the working of the oracle. For instance:

Is Namarusu's health all right? (Does good fortune await her in the near future?) The fowl DIES, giving the answer "No" (her condition is bad).

Is Kisanga's illness due to any one living on the opposite side of the new part of the government settlement? The fowl SURVIVES giving the answer "No."

Will either of Kamanga's wives die in the near future? The fowl SURVIVES giving the answer "No."

Is Namarusu's health threatened by any of those living near her? The fowl SURVIVES giving the answer "Yes."

Will Kamanga one day beget a child? The fowl DIES, giving the answer "Yes."

Will Kisanga be all right in the future? Is the bad magic which caused his sickness finished? The fowl SURVIVES, giving the answer "Yes." (303–4)

There are no special formulas for asking the questions. Though there are stereotyped phrases that recur, these are not ritualized. The oracle does not work because of what the man says or repeats. The questioner merely administers a certain poison, one that comes from far away and has gone through a ritual process, and this enables an answer to appear through the survival or death of the animal. The chicken, of course, cannot speak itself. It yields an answer nonetheless. We might also apply to the oracle; or at least Evans-Pritchard did, but probably without the eagerness and pleasure of the Zande who asked these questions.[13] The opposition Life/Death conveys a message to the Zande but not to others. The answer comes from knowledge of a special code which, even if we could speak the language of the Azande, we would be unlikely to credit. And this might be the case even if we posed the questions ourselves.

The difference, once again, arises at the point where neither the questioner nor anyone else knows the answer, where the reaction we would impose on ourselves would be either silence or speculation. Neither is the case here. The bird, dead or alive, speaks, or, rather, conveys a voice from elsewhere. This answer is not simply given by the code, or even by the code believed in. Rather, what belief consists in here is allowing a conjunction to be made between question and answer which evades recourse to experience. "If Adiyambio, who is suffering from a deep-seated ulcer, remains in our government settlement, will he die?" (302). The possibility of linking the survival of Adiyambio with staying in the settlement for us would have to involve intervening factors. The presence of medical care, the existence of water to wash his wound, etc. Here, however, two states are linked only because the oracle allows the possibility of such linkage.

The oracle here furnishes the magic word, the copula that allows anything to be linked to anything else. It not merely allows it, it stimulates such connections. It allows it to be authoritatively said that "X is a witch." The operations of magic in that sense are the opposite of those of hysteria. The hysterical symptom is a compromise formation. The compromise is between the censoring agency, which does not want a wishful impulse to emerge into consciousness, and that wish. As a result, an odd and indecipherable sign comes into existence which contains that impulse without allowing it to reach its full expression. The oracle, however, as the source of knowledge of unthinkable possibilities, stimulates the expression of impulse. It finds an object for a feeling of hatred that before that was unclear. It is this, I believe, that accounts in part for the pleasure in consulting the oracle.

The impulse issues in the speech of the oracle. It is, of course, the voice of the interlocutor estranged from himself. The bird speaks only when the interlocutor "performs" it. It responds to the interlocutor's question, but, unlike addressing a person who has the freedom not merely to say various things in response but not to respond at all, the bird must "speak" when the interlocutor feeds it poison and must say only "Yes" or "No," and only that.

The "speech" of the person who consults the oracle as it passes through the bird is analogous to traumatized speech. Analogous because the person hears his own voice without being able to feel himself to be the origin of its words (or signs). But it differs because instead of feeling that his words are inadequate, as does the traumatized person, the interlocutor feels them to be significant. What makes the difference is the appearance of a narrative voice that cannot be equated with that of the author but that seems to issue from the text. It is the transformation of "I" into "he" of which Maurice Blanchot speaks.[14]

This is not mere slight of hand, any more than it is when, in a culture where the genre "fiction" exists, a writer transforms his voice into one that seems to emerge from the paper on which he deposes his words. Azande themselves noted the similarity when they compared the poison oracle to paper as used by Europeans:

Azande often say: "the poison oracle does not err, it is our paper. What your paper is to you the poison oracle is to us," for they see in the art of writing the source of a European's knowledge, accuracy, memory of events, and predictions of the future. (263)

The Zande comparison with paper invokes memory and predictions, among other things. The comparison with writing comes when, achieving an impersonal voice which speaks from the page, the person writing is relieved of the strictures he puts on himself when he speaks as "I." There is also authority ("knowledge, accuracy") which comes when an impersonal voice speaks, as with writing and with the oracle. It is in the change of person of the speaker that the Zande oracle becomes influential as well as pleasurable.

The oracle is a form of writing, but the difference in genre is important. When we see a written page, we automatically ask ourselves what sort of thing is written on it. Is it a shopping list, a story, a journalistic account, and so on. Without knowing that, we do not know how to read it. But the Zande oracle gives only one form of language. The quotation above is preceded by these words of Evans-Pritchard:

For how can a Zande do without his poison oracle? His life would be of little worth. Witches would make his wife and children sick and would destroy his crops and render his hunting useless. Every endeavour would be frustrated, every labour and pain would be to no purpose. At any moment a witch might kill him and he could do nothing to protect himself and his family. Men would violate his wife and steal his goods, and how would he be able to identify and avenge himself on adulterer and thief? Without the aid of his poison oracle he knows that he is helpless and at the mercy of every evil person. It is his guide and his counsellor. (262–63)

The only thing comparable in authority in Zande thinking to their oracle is paper for Europeans. Paper understood by people who, in 1926, when Evans-Pritchard was in Zandeland, could not read or write but who remarked the place of literacy in the lives of Europeans. The (to them) indecipherable signs of writing answered all questions, including important matters about themselves. The only difference between poisoned chickens and letters on paper in their understanding is that only the first are legible to them.

This is, of course, a form of literacy. It is magical, however, because its signs, and there are only two, authorize or forbid connections. "If Adiyambio, who is suffering from a deep-seated ulcer, remains in our government settlement, will he die? The fowl SURVIVES, giving the answer 'No'" (302). The chicken's death, meaning "Yes," would say that the connection between Adiyambio's survival and remaining in the government settlement is authorized, as we put it. It is a magic sign, as we have understood magic from Mauss: it allows connections where otherwise none could be made. The oracle furnishes the magical copula.

But when everything that comes to mind is acceptable, some of it produces fright nonetheless. The oracle does not forbid such thoughts. When it says "No," it means, in the example given, that the witch has not been identified. But there is a witch. Another name is placed before the oracle. This time it dies, and so says "Yes." The witch has appeared. The witch kills; the threat of death has materialized. The possibly worst thought that one might have, "I am dying," is valorized. A small sign, stomach trouble perhaps, means that, indeed, someone is trying to kill me. The oracle justifies my fear. Denial of fear is not one of its modes any more than is repression. In place of both there is the exteriorization of anxieties. They no longer belong to me, to my psyche. Instead, they have been given a place in a story about the world. I might have barely escaped death when the granary collapsed; my near relative was perhaps killed. The witch is still at work; my stomach pain indicates that that is the case. But I did not know it to be. I only suspected the worst. Now I know it.

I know it through my own words estranged from myself; which is to say from my own expression of my fear. It is not merely the recourse available once one can identify the witch that lightens this heavy load of anxiety. It is also the appearance of authority I can trust even when that authority announces a menace to me. If the verification of suspicion ameliorates life, it is because it returns one to the social. Which is to say that it unifies me. When I merely suspected, I was speaking to myself, giving myself various opinions (A is the witch; no, B is) and, by definition, since it is suspicion that is involved, finding my words unreliable. I do not know how to act toward A and B, or, for that matter, others, any of whom could well be the witch. When my words return to me through the oracle, I am unified again. I present a single face to everyone. I am now in a state to approach the witch. Precisely what "witch" means in its most virulent form, that he is anything or anybody, preventing any consolidation of myself in front of him, has been avoided.

Magic, seen in this perspective, was an intermediary between impulse and authority, converting the first into the second. It did so, how-

ever, only at a cost. The singularity of accident, its inexplicability, was reduced to the generality of "the witch." Accident itself is obscured. The
witch, one is tempted to say, is "revealed" by the oracle. But it is more accurate to say that "witch" is a word which conceals accident. The naming
of the witch, whether through the oracle or simply through assertion, as is
the case in most places in the world, is therefore unstable and comes only
through an unverifiable procedure.

The wishfulness that sustains this procedure nonetheless can be seen
in conjunction with another form of Zande magic, namely, special plants
which are thought to have magical potency. These grow in caverns hollowed out along streams. They are difficult to reach. Evans-Pritchard describes these places:

These streams arise in springs which have eaten out of the earth dark chasms,
shaded by tall trees and obscured with dense brushwood. Sometimes the erosion
has burrowed short tunnels into the earth, which lead off from the main cav-
ern, buttressed with roots of gigantic trees and roofed with thick foliage of shrub
and creeper. Azande fear these caverns, which house snakes and are the homes of
ghosts and of the Supreme Being. (215)

In these dark places, where one is frightened and imagines ghostly figures,
in fact one welcomes them also because they show the way. "The ghosts
merely show them where plants are growing in the darkness" (216). Ghosts,
instead of leading one astray, show one where to go. So that exactly where
one might think that imagination misleads, ghosts of the dead lead one
straight. To restate this, ghosts, instead of being terrifying figures, validate
one's meanderings, or at least they did so in this instance. Azande, wander-
ing in dark caves, cannot be led astray by illusions produced by an evil genius. Whatever comes to mind is not merely acceptable, it is for the best.
Here, magic does not lead one to insupportable associations and eventually to unrestrained and unrestrainable anxiety. In place of a superego which
prevents the emergence of old wishes, incompatible thoughts, and impulses, the past in the form of ghosts and ancestors protect and allow one to go
where, under other circumstances, one would be said to go astray.

We ask ourselves if deadly violence against "others" is a structural
feature of society. The Azande, to this point, do not support this supposition. Their obsession with witches might have done so had not witchcraft

also supported sociality. At the same time, when one looks at Zande social life, as we shall in a moment, we will see that witchcraft was a major cause of social fragmentation. Witches, at the time of Evans-Pritchard's study, were seldom killed. At the same time, without the imposition of colonial authority, witches were likely to have been. Before colonization, witches were often put to death.

What is at stake is whether through witchcraft accusations a voice of the community can be formed, as Lévi-Strauss says was the case for the Zuni, and which would be the case if the workings of the oracle and the subsequent process of accusation and acknowledgment worked perfectly and worked without the support of externally applied force. Is the voice of the community in a witch hunt the basis for sociality? Is the formation of an enemy the foundation of a society?

IV. The Ambiguous Return to the Social

Witchcraft, Evans-Pritchard said, was normal in Zande society. "Witchcraft is . . . a common place happening and [a Zande man] seldom passes a day without mentioning it" (64). An accident happens, a misfortune of some sort. Azande understand the natural causes of the event. But they ask, "Why did it happen to me?" and "Why did it happen just then?" At that point, they suspect sorcery or witchcraft. (Evans-Pritchard distinguished the two terms, but the majority of anthropologists did not follow his distinction. Hence, I use them interchangeably.) Evans-Pritchard observes:

Those who speak in a roundabout manner and are not straightforward in their conversation are suspected of witchcraft. Azande are very sensitive and usually on the look-out for unpleasant allusions to themselves in apparently harmless conversation. This is a frequent occasion of quarrels, and there is no means of determining whether the speaker has meant the allusions or whether his hearer has supplied them. For example, a man sits with some of his neighbors and says, "No man remains for ever in the world." One of the old men sitting nearby gives a disapproving grunt at this remark, hearing which the speaker explains that he was talking of an old man who has just died; but others may think that he meant that he wished the death of one of those with whom he was sitting. (111)

There is an "apparently harmless conversation," but Azande are "very sensitive," and listening to it, some find in it "an unpleasant allusion to themselves." But no one can be sure whether the illusion was intended or not. Evans-Pritchard speaks of "apparently harmless" words. Evans-Pritchard himself would not have found the sentence, "No man remains for ever in the world" a threat. What in other places passes without remark, among the Azande leads to quarrels and to accusations of witchcraft. Once something bad happens, the sentence is recalled and interpreted as a menace. No matter that it was not meant that way.

Azande can prove that the sentence was intended as a threat. After a misfortune, they put the name of the speaker to their oracle and ask whether he was responsible. The oracle confirms (possibly) that the speaker caused the accident. It does not say it was merely an accident and that there was no witch. A witch is always found; if it is not the first name put to the oracle, it is the next, or the one after. And the founding of the witch, after the fact, recalls the ambiguous sentence. In this way, the oracle offers "proof" of witchcraft and resolves an ambiguity. But on the other hand, the existence of witchcraft offers the possibility that many sentences might, in retrospect, have had another sense. It is a cause of suspicion as well as its resolution.

In such a society most exchange becomes suspect. Evans-Pritchard experienced this himself when he tried to do favors for his friends:

I found again and again that I had only to be generous to, even very friendly with, one of my neighbours and he would at once be apprehensive of witchcraft, and any ill-luck which befell him would be attributed to the jealousy my friendship had aroused in the breasts of his neighbours. The Zande believes that his fellows cannot bear that you be generous to him or publicly show him any favour, and he who lives in Zandeland must be prepared for malice that he has caused by ill considered benevolence. (111)

One gives and the result is suspicion. Not suspicion of the giver, in this case, but of those who were not party to the gift. One might think of Evans-Pritchard's gift as a sort of accident. A strange white man appears where one is rarely seen. He lives with "us," which must have been unprecedented, and he gives us things. There is unlikely to have been a way to anticipate this event. He is benevolent, and "I" profit from him. But I know at the same time that the result is that I will be the target of witchcraft.

A man's crop is successful, his nets are full of game, his termites swarm, and he is convinced that he has become the butt of his neighbors' jealousy and will be bewitched. His crops fail, his nets are empty, his termites do not swarm, and by these signs he knows that he has been bewitched by a jealous neighbor. How the misfortunes of others please a Zande. Nothing is more pleasing, more assuring, to him, more flattering to his self esteem, than the down fall of another. (102)

One does what one should, one becomes prosperous, and for that reason, one will be bewitched. One suffers, and one is convinced one has already been bewitched. If one's own good efforts attract witchcraft, it means that one cannot find a reflection of oneself, not merely as one knows oneself to be but as one should be, in one's fellows. One is always reflected wrongly. Or it might be that something of oneself unknown to oneself but known to others becomes public. One suffers and one knows that one does not deserve it; one has done as one should. Something is at work and it is the result in the first place of the way one is seen by one's neighbor. Whether he sees correctly is the issue. Since, as will become apparent, no one can be sure he is not a witch, the neighbor may be correct. For that reason, when one sees others fall, one feels gratified and reassured; it is him and not me. What one suspects about oneself and sometimes finds confirmed is true of others.

Exactly the force that is condemned when "I" am the victim is celebrated when someone else is affected by it. At this point, we see how occult, anti-social power is cultivated, apparently by the whole of adult Zande society, or at least by men. It is the way in which something inappropriable, a power which remains always outside the possibility of being made an approved part of Zande society, which never becomes the basis of authority or social position, is nonetheless celebrated. When "self-esteem" is enhanced because the power of sorcery has caused the other's downfall, one sides with this destructive power to one's own psychic advantage. This advantage apparently is never publicly celebrated. One never reads that someone "deserved" what he got, which would make sorcery an auxiliary to social values. It remains contrary to ethics and approved values. But as power it attracts. This attractive power, always disowned, is at the base of the jealousy Evans-Pritchard describes, as it allows Azande to celebrate the misfortune of others. Each wants to be on the side of this power, and yet, socially speaking, this is an impossibility.

The existence of such a power in the heart of Zande society would be unsupportable if there were not some way of dealing with it. The Zande way was not to exclude the witch, nor even to deprive him of his witch-craft. It was to unveil him, at which moment the witch, unaware of his witchcraft, apologized. The acknowledgment of witchcraft was enough, in the circumstances that pertained during the time of Evans-Pritchard's study, to allow an accommodation to a power that could only harm. This form of accommodation, it seems to me, could never have worked if there were not the restraint put on vengeance by colonial authority.

A man who believes himself or his relatives to be bewitched consults his oracles. They confirm the identity of the witch. He now behaves cautiously. "We must remember that they must avoid an open quarrel with the witch, since this will only aggravate him and perhaps cause him to kill his victim outright, and will in any case involve the aggressors in serious social, and possibly legal, difficulties" (92). He is likely to make a public oration. He declares that he knows the name of the witch but that he will not disclose it to spare the witch shame. Evans-Pritchard cites the case of a man whose kinsman fell ill. All death is caused by witchcraft. The man warns the witch that if his kinsman dies, there will be vengeance. He climbs a tree and gives a public oration, for which there is a term in Azande, *de kuba*. From a high branch he shouts:

Hi! Hi! Hi! It not an animal O! It is not an animal O! I went today to consult the rubbing board oracle, and it said to me that those men who are killing my kinsmen are not far off, that they are right here near by, and that it is those neighbours of mine who are killing my kinsman. It is thus I honour you [meaning the witch] by telling you that I will not speak his name[the name of the witch]. I will not choose him out by himself. If he has ears he will hear what I am saying. Were my kinsman to die I would make magic and then someone would die and my name would be tarnished because I have kept silence. This is why I am telling you that, if my kinsman continues to be sick unto death, I will surely reveal that man so that every one will know him. . . . That man that has ears, one speaks but a few words and he can hear them. After what I have spoken to you I will not burden my mouth again, but I will choose out the man himself and expose him before his face. All of you hear well my words. It is finished." (93)

A certain public, those within range of his voice as he shouts from the tree top, hear him. Climbing the tree, he is no longer *en face* of those whom he knows. His shift of perspective changes also the identity of his intended audience. They include his neighbors, but they are now also anyone who hears in the possible capacity of "witch" but from whom no immediate response is called for. He relays news of what has happened to him; the oracle has spoken to him and revealed a secret. He does not transmit what the oracle says, but he says that he is capable of doing so. He declares that he knows a secret, but he does not reveal the identity of the witch. It could be anyone within hearing. Anyone might be the witch at that point. There is thus another audience than the one he addresses on the ground, where whomever he speaks with answers as neighbor or in another sociologically defined capacity. Here, he speaks to everyone as though any one of them was a witch. But he wants the secret to be kept so that he can once again address these people in the way he did before. He does not expect a verbal reply; only an improvement in the health of his kinsman.

If his kinsmen does not get well, he reveals the witch, but he is unlikely to do so directly. He asks a deputy of the king to send a wing of the poisoned chicken oracle to the presumed witch. The deputy does so himself or asks someone else to do so. Again, a public element is invoked. Witchcraft is not a private matter, it is clear. It involves notions of a public, at least of a certain kind, and of the Zande state.

On his arrival the messenger lays the wing on the ground in front of the witch. . . . He treats the witch with respect, for such is the custom, and anyhow it is none of his business. Almost invariably the witch replies courteously that he is unconscious of injuring anyone, that if it is true that he has injured the man in question he is very sorry, and that if it is he alone who is troubling him then he will surely recover, because from the bottom of his heart he wishes him health and happiness. (95)

A man accused of witchcraft, says Evans-Pritchard, is "astonished." "He has not conceived of witchcraft from this angle. To him it has always been a reaction against others in his own misfortunes, so that it is difficult for him to apprehend the notion when he himself is its objective in the misfortunes of other people" (118). One might think that he would repudiate the charge, Evans-Pritchard says, "since witchcraft is imaginary and a man cannot possibly be a witch" (119). But this is not the case. "A man cannot help being a witch; it is not his fault that he is born with witchcraft in his belly. He may be quite ignorant that he is a witch and quite innocent of acts of witchcraft. In this state he might do someone an injury unwittingly, but when he is exposed by the poison oracle he is then conscious of his powers and begins to use them with malice" (121–22). It is rare, however, for a man to refuse the accusation. "A man who behaves in this manner is acting contrary to custom and is insulting the chief's deputy who ordered the wing to be laid before him. He will be laughed at as a provincial who is ignorant of the manners of polite society, and may gain the reputation of a hardened witch who admits his witchcraft by the anger he displays when he is found out. What he ought to do is to blow out water and say: 'If I possess witchcraft in my belly I am unaware of it; may it cool. It is thus that I blow out water'" (122–23). The best defense against an accusation of witchcraft is to admit to it. Not to do so will convince people one is a witch. To do so will confirm the accusation, of course, but it will also show that the man behaves according to the rules of polite society. The acknowledgment is itself the sign that the social and not the anti-social reigns.

Evans-Pritchard tells us that the accused might well feel offended. If so, however, he conceals his feelings. He blows out water as a sign both of acknowledgment of witchcraft and of lack of hostile feelings. A man told Evans-Pritchard it "was not only polite to do so when requested but also showed an absence of ill feeling which ought to characterize all good citizens" (124).[15] Accusations, one should add, are so common that "a man will be very lucky if he escapes occasional accusation, and after the poison oracle has declared on several occasions that a man has bewitched others he may doubt his immunity" (125).

Witchcraft is inherited by men through their fathers and women through their mothers. It is a substance attached to an indefinite organ, but likely to be the intestine or another organ concerned with digestion. A person may not know that he is a witch. He may activate his witchcraft simply by his ill-feelings for another. Even when it is established by autopsy that witchcraft substance is in the father, the son may not be considered a witch until the oracle reveals him to be so. This, according to Evans-Pritchard, is because witchcraft is thought about practically and not theoretically. Theoretically, a Zande could know that so-and-so is a witch; but practically, he is not interested until misfortune leads him to search for its agent. Even then, it is the oracle and not previous knowledge that determines who is responsible for a particular misfortune.

From the point of view of the accused, witchcraft is treated here as a lapsus, a bêtise, as the last quotation illustrates. One does something, it is by error, one did not know it, and one makes one's excuses. Partly this is mere convention, but it is also believed in. Because witchcraft is beyond the control of the witch, someone accused has no trouble admitting his witchcraft; before the accusation it was unknown to him. The admission is enough to end the matter. The witch says "he is not causing the sick man injury with intent. He says that he addresses the witchcraft in his belly, beseeching it to be cool (inactive) and that he makes this appeal from his heart and not merely with his lips" (96).

Everything is done to make admission of witchcraft easy. The accused blows on the chicken wing as a sign that one has only good wishes toward the bewitched—a tacit or perhaps ambiguous admission of witchcraft. Evans-Pritchard calls it an enactment of guilt: "The fact that a man has publicly to enact a confession of guilt by blowing on the fowl's wing [and this enactment becomes believed] must render him at least doubtful about the existence of witchcraft in his belly" (125). If it can be admitted to, it is not simply because the nature of witches means anyone might be a witch, but also because, according to Evans-Pritchard, witches are not uncanny. By which he means that witchcraft is a daily occurence, at least in speech, and in that sense normal rather than strange. But, of course, if witchcraft were normal, not only in the statistical sense but in the sense of conforming to a standard by which it could be known, it would not require the extraordinary measures Azande take to confirm their suspicions. Moreover, Azande witchcraft involves a mood, a state of mind or feeling, as attested to by the suspicion that surrounds it and that therefore merits the term "uncanny." It is precisely to alleviate this mood that there is accusation and acknowledgment. Such relief can only be temporary, at least so far as the accused is concerned. His public admission is also an admission to himself, if not of guilt, then of the frequently realized possibility of being a witch.

Social recognition of witchcraft, as exemplified in the accusation and the assertion that the accused bears no ill-will toward his accuser, is ambiguous. On the one hand, the accusation is made because harm, even lethal damage, is being done. On the other hand, the acceptance of the admission as the end of the matter seems to turn witchcraft into something acceptable and even benign. The juncture between the good neighbor and the bad witch is obscured by the ease with which one is transformed into the other and back again, and by the acceptance of this fact. The witch is tolerated, not in his capacity as witch but because "witch" can quickly become "neighbor." And, of course, "neighbor" easily changes into "witch." The solution to the problem of witchcraft is thus also the making of further difficulties.

Contrary to our association of witches and violence, there was, in Zande Land of the 1920s, little violence associated with witchcraft. I believe this was for legal reasons. "If you suffer some misfortune you may not retaliate by assaulting the witch who has caused it, for, with the possible exception of loss of an entire elusine crop, the only act of witchcraft that is legally recognized by punishment meted out to a witch is the crime of murder. This must be proved by a verdict of a prince's poison oracle and he alone can authorize vengeance or indemnity" (86–87). Moreover, witchcraft accusations do not lead to vengeance, except at death. A man whose relative has died consults the oracle to find the witch who killed him. A public announcement is made that the witch has been found. But the name is not revealed and nothing more happens. If, later, the man not publicly named or one of his relatives suffers, it might be said that this was vengeance. But vengeance remains imaginary. However, once again, one must keep in mind that colonial authority forbade witch killings, which earlier had taken place.

To believe that one has taken vengeance without making any public act means that one targets not the social person but the witch, and that the two do not coincide for long. The witch and the social person are easily pried apart and pasted together again. Accusations of witchcraft are based on the oracle, which "never errs." The names placed before it are, however, those whom the Zande believes hate him. Hatred is certainly an emotion that belongs to the social. Witchcraft is tied to social identity, but not for long and not consequentially.

It is . . . to the interest of both parties that they should not become estranged through the incident. They have to live together as neighbours afterwards and to cooperate in the life of the community. It is also to their mutual advantage to avoid all appearance of anger or resentment for a more direct and immediate reason. The whole point of the procedure is to put the witch in a good temper by being polite to him. The witch on his part ought to feel grateful to the people who have warned him so politely of the danger in which he stands. We must remember that since witchcraft has no real existence a man does not know that he has bewitched another, even if he is aware that he bears him ill will. But, at the same time, he believes firmly in the existence of witchcraft and in the accuracy of the poison oracle, so that when the oracle says that he is killing a man by witchcraft he is probably thankful for having been warned in time, for if he had been allowed to murder the man, all the while ignorant of his action, he would inevitably have fallen a victim to vengeance. By the polite indication of an oracular verdict from the relatives of a sick man to the witch who has made him sick both the life of the sick man and the life of the witch are saved. (97)

I may feel that my neighbor hates me and that he is a witch. It does not mean that we should not try to get along. Hatred and suspicion permeated Zande society. But they were accommodated to. One can even argue that witchcraft made hatred acceptable. Rather than long-held, pent-up emotions whose only outlet was violence, one blamed the witch and excused the neighbor. But if witchcraft and hatred were integrated into Zande society, it was true as well that belief in witchcraft fostered hatred because it fostered suspicion, as we have already seen.

"We must remember that since witchcraft has no real existence a man does not know that he has bewitched another, even if he is aware that he bears him ill will." No one can know for sure that he is innocent, the power of witchcraft having the capacity to act without the knowledge of its agents. The public admission of witchcraft is not merely for the sake of social harmony. It is also the admission of the accused of the possibility that he has witchcraft substance in him. On the one hand, the admission of guilt allows the return of the social personality of the accused. On the other, it is the admission to himself that he is a witch. If Azande witchcraft appears abstract, in view of the ease with which it is detached from the social personality, a person's realization of his own witchcraft, meaning the presence of death within him, must have given it added reality.

This makes it all the more striking that there can have been no dialectical movement of Zande society in so far as it centered on witchcraft. Just at the point where recognition of witchcraft might be thought to mean a change in the status and the identity of the accused, the opposite is the case. There was rather a restoration to a normality that, for its part, had been disrupted only in the mind of the accuser. Each time politics and identity seemed to coincide, they broke apart. And each time they broke apart, they came together again, but in a way that never changed social arrangements. Or, to put it in other terms, each reflection of myself by an other was admitted to without being reflected in established social relations.

Everyone was affected. Evans-Pritchard said that no Zande he met would admit to being a witch. But he added that the answer was not always believable:

> I sometimes asked a man, if I knew him very well, "Are your a witch?" I expected a prompt unqualified denial couched in offended tone, but received often a humble reply, "Ai, master, if there is witchcraft in my belly I know nothing of it. I am no witch because people have not seen witchcraft in the bellies of our kin." However, it was less the replies I received than the tone and manner in which they were given that gave me an impression of doubt. Had I asked them whether they were thieves the tone and manner of their reply would have been decided and angry. (125–26)

> But though many men declare in private that they are not witches and that there must have been a mistake, my experience of Azande when presented with hens' wings has convinced me that some think, for a short time at any rate, that perhaps after all they are witches. (124)

In the Zande view, everyone, including in a vague but nonetheless real way the speaker himself, was potentially a witch. Zande society thus reflected the situation Jacques Derrida described when he spoke of "tout autre est tout autre," which means both that every other is an other and that every other is wholly other.[16] In Zande society, I accept my reflection of myself in the eyes of my accuser. I, too, am other than I knew myself to be. I am a stranger to myself. And everyone else whom I know is also, at least potentially, entirely different from their social appearance. Zande identities slipped between the social and asocial, between the known and the revealed, though in the largest sense, witchcraft itself was never revealed. It is this constant sliding that makes Zande witchcraft irreducible to whatever social conflict might have preceded it. In that case, witchcraft would be another name for "rival," while a successful accusation would resolve a conflict of interest.

In place of conflict, the admission of witchcraft led to a disinvolvement. Just at the point where the other is recognized as totally other and totally inimical, there is a restoration of identity.

[Witchcraft] is a planned assault by one man on another whom he hates. A witch acts with malice aforethought. Azande say that hatred, jealousy, envy, backbiting, slander, and so forth go ahead and witchcraft follows after. A man must first hate his enemy and will then bewitch him. . . . Witchcraft tends to become synonymous with the sentiments which are supposed to cause it, so that Azande think of hatred and envy and greed in terms of witchcraft and likewise think of witchcraft in terms of the sentiments it discloses. (107)

One seems to have here a complete socialization of witchcraft. Hatred comes first, witchcraft follows. One therefore expects war, but there is peace. Zande society seemed to consist of terrible accusations and peaceful reconciliations, or, one can say, of constant change between the socially defined and the appearance of the asocial and anti-social. Zande witchcraft is hatred, but hatred does not result in conflict but reconciliation.

The assumption which makes this possible is that witchcraft is self-enclosure. The person closed upon himself, unaware of what he is or does, is a witch. Hatred might be embedded in conflicts of interest, but these have no chance to play themselves out in the idiom of Zande witchcraft. If the witch could be indissolubly wedded to his social person, things would be different. As it is,

in their representation of witchcraft hatred is one thing and witchcraft another thing. All men are liable to develop sentiments against their neighbors, but unless they are actually born with witchcraft in their bellies they cannot do their enemies an injury by merely disliking them. (108)

In this passage, witchcraft might still be trigged by hatred. But as Evans-Pritchard described it, it operates with a certain autonomy, in part because witchcraft is linked to accident independently of hatred.

Notions of witchcraft are evoked primarily by misfortune and are not entirely dependent on enmities. Thus a man who suffers a misfortune knows that he has been bewitched, and only then does he seek in his mind to find out who wishes him ill and might have bewitched him. If he cannot recall any incidents that might have caused a man to hate him, and if he has no particular enemies, he must still consult the oracles to discover a witch. Hence, even a prince will sometimes accuse commoners of witchcraft, for his misfortunes must be accounted for and checked, even though those whom he accuses of witchcraft are not his enemies. (105)

Witchcraft, hidden even from oneself if one is a witch, reveals itself through accident or through lapsus. Evans-Pritchard speaks of "belief" in witchcraft. Which is to say that Azande know that someone can do harm without necessarily knowing what they are doing. It is a Freudian error. An "error" because it is contrary to the social; "Freudian" because it is done without the consciousness of the actor. The situation is ambiguous and some may think that the witch acted knowingly. But the act is treated socially as though the person acted without awareness, as though it precedes from accident. In this way, Azande acknowledge something similar to our idea of the unconscious. Their acknowledgment is in the interest not of suppressing or eradicating what emerges from there, but of neutralizing it. Consider this description of Azande behavior:

Europeans do not always understand why Azande are so restless; why each man likes to live far from his nearest neighbors; why a man sometimes leaves one homestead and builds another one; why he chooses to live in one place rather than in another place which to our eyes looks better suited for a home; and why he sometimes leaves his homestead for weeks and lives uncomfortably beneath a grass shelter in the bush. But Azande go away to live in the bush because they are sick and the poison oracle has told them that if they hide in a certain place the witch who is devouring them will not be able to find them and so they will recover. (263)

Evans-Pritchard describes something more than the usual bewilderment attendant on unfamiliarity with a culture. Usually, one comes to a strange place and what one learns about it helps one to find a place there. This was not the case in Zande Land. Even after one knows that Azande live for periods in the bush because they believe they are attacked by witches, it does little to help one understand the person whom one is looking for who, it turns out, is somewhere in the wilderness. His reasons for being there remain inaccessible.

The same is true on a larger scale. One cannot say, for instance, that Azande do not live in clusters but apart from each other for reasons that have to do with the structure of their lineages or for ecological reasons. One has to look at individual motivations. The oracle has told someone he will be bewitched if he builds next to someone else. The person there-

fore decides to build his homestead away from others. The distribution of
the population depends not on traditions or on environmental exigencies
but on impulse. The Azande thus give the appearance of being directed by
something incomprehensible. Impulse is acted upon, made part of "normal" life, even instituting its own patterns on Zande life.

This "pattern-despite-itself," as it were, is the result of the strange
relation between witchcraft and accident. Accident, the singular, as it is
seen as Zande become involved in misfortune, is submitted to the oracle
to know who the bewitcher is. The singular event, classed with all other
singular events as the effect of witchcraft, then acted upon, yields a pattern
which is at once social because most Azande seem to have led their lives according to their oracles, and yet is also asocial since it is the result of a mere
agglomeration of singular accidents and their effects.

A society marked in so many places by the valorization, or at least the
interest and perhaps the obsession with the accidental, raises many questions. Accident in the first place is made acceptable by being neutralized.
The revelation of the witch means also the evaporation of his menace. In
place of the superego which censors impulse, the Azande seem to have had
an agency to welcome or at least tolerate it. But the permeation of Zande
society by accident is also the generation of suspicion and the setting of
Azande against each other.

V. The Oracle Again

The oracle says only "Yes" or "No." It thus simplifies suspicion. One
might have suspected X of envy, for instance, after mentally reconstruct-
ing incidents which pointed to that. The oracle, however, does not speak
of intentions or of suspicions. Its voice is similar to the voice of a person
in trance. It is a voice divorced from subjectivity. The obscurity of its provenance alone guarantees its lack of interestedness.

The Zande oracle does not say what cannot be said but only suspected, à la the Zuni witch as seen by Lévi-Strauss. Rather, it says what
can be said and is said ordinarily, but when said ordinarily is without certainty. It is fiction that gives this certainty, if we can use "fiction" as a universal category. This is not, of course, because it is seen as contrary to fact.
Rather, it draws on what fiction draws upon. It commences from a condi-

tion for linguistic expression that precedes subject matter. This is not the innate capacity of certain social types who, according to Lévi-Strauss, have more words than referents and become socially useful for that reason.[17] It is, rather, in the estrangement of someone from his own concerns that he discovers (another) voice.

The oracle speaks from afar. The magical poison fed to the fowl to make it talk has to be sought on a journey that takes six or seven days and passes through lands foreign to the Azande.[18] And it must be treated ritually before it is effective. Only in this way does the chicken's survival or lack thereof matter. An interlocutor is constructed as the speech of the person who interrogates it is separated from himself, just as Blanchot said about writing. What returns to the interrogator is not his intentions. These are confused; he only suspects. Rather, the "it" that speaks is purged of intentions, hence of suspicions, as this "it" speaks through a code similar to mathematics. (The code consists of only binary oppositions. For that reason, one does not need to know the Azande language to understand the Azande oracle, though, of course, one needs to know the language of the man who asks the question.) An answer is given, in a voice no longer that of the interrogator, which is precise and purified of doubt, just as it is purified of language, speaking now only in a single binary opposition which, like numbers, have the same graphic sign despite the particularity of the language spoken.

This purification of voice of language and doubt at the same time is accomplished through distance. The distance from which the *benge* poison comes and its ritual separation from ordinary substances indicate the length which the voice of the operator of the oracle travels. One might think that addressing the oracle is comparable to speaking to a stranger from a distant part of the earth. One does not know his language. Nonetheless, for some reason, one is confident that, if he raises his left hand and not his right when one finishes speaking, it means "Yes." How he arrives at his answer is of no concern whatsoever. One only knows that one cannot know. And one is in no way concerned that the person is wholly unacquainted with the circumstances one recounts to him. But one believes, nonetheless, that he always answers accurately. It might be better to say, here, that "accuracy" is defined by the supposition of an answer rather than by its content.

"Distance," in this case, means distance from present circumstances. The oracle in that sense is truly a third person, one not present in discourse. The oracle, when it speaks, never says "I," never indicates itself as the bearer of language. If it is somehow there nonetheless, its absence from discourse is taken as the presence of a code particular to itself, even if not belonging to a particular language. It poses simply as a rudimentary form of language itself.

If the oracle is stripped of subjectivity, the person whom it answers becomes the same for the moment that a discourse pertains between the two. The oracle returns questions with suspicions, miscellaneous thoughts or waverings all gone, replaced by one of two indicators. The interrogator of the oracle is no more responded to as a person than is the driver of a car at a stop-and-go light. Who he is socially, even his name, does not matter. He is not reflected back to himself as a social persona, nor even as a subject of the law, as is the person who stops for a red light. He is subject to accident, either in the past or the future, but this cannot render him a "subject," one capable of holding contraries together, in Hegel's definition. When the oracle confirms some of his suspicions and puts others at rest, and allows him, armed with the certainty furnished by the oracle, to speak, he is again a normal subject of Azande society.

Before consulting the oracle, speaking to someone else, suspecting witchcraft, the speaker might hesitate to make an accusation for fear that it would not be accepted or would be subject to doubts and modifications. He might be afraid that his words would not be well received and find, as a result, that he is tongue-tied or at least unpersuasive. Facing the oracle, however, he is not before a censor; quite the opposite. The oracle will give him words which are not subject to the difficulties of assessing the justice of his accusation. The truth (as opposed to justice) of his claim to being bewitched does not rest on facts; it rests on avoiding them. It depends on the avoidance of reference to the world in favor of an application to a source of language. That is why the oracle can be compared to fiction or to a source of speech.

The conditions of Azande life make authoritative language difficult to come by. One is almost constantly obsessed by suspicion. One therefore cannot find one's own voice, to use the common phrase. The oracle is the wish for the recuperation of voice, realized through the commonality of conditions that pertained in Azande Land. It is a collective illusion, which is not to condemn it, since every culture probably needs and has such an institution. To speak of "illusion," here, is to say that the oracle carries its own justification with it. It is its own law, generated in the moments of its address, rather than being subject to the sources of authority rooted, for instance, in genealogy or rank.[19]

The man who receives the signs of the oracle may then shout from the treetops, warning the witch of possible retaliation if he does not cease his nefarious activities. Or he may confront the accused, at least indirectly, sending him a wing of the chicken. Whatever the case, "witch" is then a word that can be spoken authoritatively. This is the effect of the sacrifice of subjectivity and of reference to the world; it establishes a voice.

The accused person admits that he may be a witch. But that does not end the matter. He proves not that witches exist, that there is "really" a referent for the word, but that there is a source of language and that the accuser can speak and that the word produced can be put into circulation. Once set off, the word "witch" passes throughout Azande society, re-embedded in social concerns, triggered by revived suspicion and triggering suspicion in turn. Exchange is then found to be imbalanced. One gets something one has worked for, hence deserves, but one is the target of witchcraft. One knows it. Something else, the word "witch" has inserted itself into the evaluation of what one has received. In addition to the two parties who exchange, there is a third and this third is sinister.

The witch is established in Azande society in order to banish him, or at least to end his effects. But he is never definitely limited. When one is found and exorcised, there is soon another at large. Why? It is not necessarily because the witch is a fiction since this fiction is so strongly established in Azande society. Nor is it because there is much doubt about the way the fiction is created. It is rather that establishing the witch resulted in an imbalance in exchange. Whatever one got was thought not to match what one gave. Something unpredictable was likely to act from outside the terms of exchange. Accident, the embodiment of extraneous logic, in that sense was endemic to Azande society. "Witch" summed up these accidents and this unbalance. To establish the witch meant to disrupt social life. Thus, witchcraft is a "strange institution," in that it led one to expect the contrary of normality.

On the other hand, to expect disruption is to make a place for it. There is no equivalent institution among the Murngin to which those who suspect themselves of being ensorcelled can apply. There is nothing among them that establishes a single source of language through the estranging of the voice of the bewitched or through any other means. Without this stabilizing element, Murngin hear uncanny voices and have no identity through which to speak except that of "sorcerer." They cannot speak; the unspoken word ravages them; they die.

If Azande society was relatively peaceful, however, it is not, in my opinion, because Azande in a certain manner institutionalized witchcraft. "Success" here can only mean disruption. The ability to speak accusations of sorcery does not mean the acquiescence of sorcery as a force but rather the contrary. It means the installation of fear, the disequilibrium of exchange, and the circulation of accusations. We should not forget the putative beginnings of recourse to the oracle. It is accident, but it is, in particular, death. All death is the result of sorcery. "Witch," then, means "death." This word, produced by the oracle, detached from all circumstances, referring only to an incomprehensible event, produced fear. We are only a step away from the stammering of the bewitched Murngin.

The oracle authorizes speech. But the speech so authorized is not controlled by the speaker. Evans-Pritchard reports no consultation of the oracle about witches without ensuing accusations. The accusation of witchcraft starts in authority, but it continues through the *on dit*, the "they say." Precisely because an Azande charge of witchcraft is not the opinion of an individual it remains outside the control of the person. No one can revise it. And, being unable to do so, one can only repeat it. Precisely because the prejudices of the accuser have been put aside, along with all other aspects of his subjectivity, there is no possibility of integrating the accusation into the thoughts of the speaker. His only recourse is to diffuse the charge for himself by disseminating it. The truth of sorcery remains unacceptable.

Colonial law imposed peace. But there was also the politesse of Azande society which worked in favor of settlement and amicability. Without it, the acknowledgment of witchcraft would have been more difficult. The strength of the social thus aided the suppression of violence. Evans-Pritchard describes this without, however, indicating its source or the nature of its strength. In any case, politesse did nothing to limit suspicion or the circulation of accusations. I have no evidence that Azande are among those Africans who complain that colonial society did not protect them from witchcraft. But they might well be since during an imposed peace fear circulated in their world. The oracle of course was a vehicle for the circulation of this fear. But it also has to be counted among the strengths of Azande sociality, establishing as it did an object in the world for the word "witch" and thus obscuring a deeper fear of something nameless and therefore less subject to control. Without the oracle, no doubt there still would have been suspicion and no doubt witchcraft as well, but without the integration we have seen into procedures of accusation and acceptance.

The authority of the oracle came not merely through the general acceptance of this institution, widespread in Africa. It derived primarily from the ability to establish a connection between a word, "witch," and an agreed on limit beyond which one knew nothing but which was believed to be the source of something that inflected that word. It consolidated a place where Azande could not themselves penetrate, where they agreed they could not penetrate further, and which was a source of truth. Through it a word was redefined with practically every important usage. It is the wedding of a word to a source of knowledge that enabled there to be a certain institution of witchcraft in their society.

We might think of the finding and bypassing of that limit in this way. The victim of accident wants to know "Why me?" He cannot answer the question. It would be better to say he becomes aware that he cannot answer this question. But he rehearses the accident to himself and goes on to formulate the causes ("witch"). It is this very attempt at formulation that generates the possibility of a response. By saying to himself what he suspects, he hears himself. He hears that he cannot know; that he can only suspect. It is not his confusion that is important at this point. It is that he finds a limit to his powers of thought and speech. He knows he cannot know or that he cannot speak with certainty. The movements of the ritualized chicken reflect his knowledge of this point back to himself. He is in face of something he cannot know, and yet the questions he poses press in a consolidated fashion. It is just at that moment that the motions of the poisoned chicken are taken as response.

The oracle thus converts suspicion into certainty. But, as an effect, witches multiply and suspicion is further stimulated. The certainty of the

oracle is spurious. It is agreed upon, but this agreement is on a name—
"witch"—whose connection to the cause of accident can only be tenuous.
The name, appearing at the limit of knowledge, in fact only names that
limit. The agreement to accept the accusation as accurate means that it becomes part of discourse but this cannot, finally, solve the matter. Suspicion
continues and a search for another name is set underway.

Accident fragments the subject, producing multiple voices. One
might expect that the wish to unify the subject would produce trauma,
as the person feels himself alienated from his experience, unable to put it
into words convincingly. The Azande had another solution to accident.
The victim of accident has been displaced from his ordinary social identity. "He" does not understand why the accident should have happened
to "him." At the point where a debilitating dissociation between experience and speech would allow us to recognize trauma, he consults the oracle. Instead of trying to say what happened to him and not finding an adequate way to do so, the man who consults the oracle listens to it to find
the witch. As with narrative as Blanchot describes it, a limit of language is
established. One comes to the point where one can say nothing further;
a point is reached beyond understanding. To try to speak further would
make one inarticulate. But nonetheless one can hear something, as we have
said. This limit makes itself felt through the *benge* poison. Killing a chick-
en with this poison seems to authorizes one to speak to it. But it would be
more accurate to say that the person who consults the oracle now has an
audience or an interlocutor for what up till then has been inexpressible, or
at least unacceptable to others and to the person himself. The person says
what is on his mind, what presses him to speak but about which he has no
certainty himself and for which he can find no certain reception in ordinary circumstances.

In a normal situation, his speech might merely produce an echo of
himself. This not merely because of the unfathomable nature of accident,
but also because as a victim of accident, even at the second degree, he has
been affected in ways that have nothing to do with his experience. Nothing
that he is by virtue of his life in society or the status he has by birth explains
why the accident happened to him. To ask about it from that point of view
produces only bewilderment. But when he consults the oracle he draws on
his experience only in order to reach a point where it does not count. The

response is in no way tailored to who he is. It is not the person in his ordinary capacity who consults the oracle; it is the victim of accident who as such knows only bewilderment. Nothing he says in his ordinary capacity matters. It is not that ordinary language is now restored to him and he can therefore speak about the accident drawing on what he knows. It is rather that the accident victim himself, the person who is, if we are allowed to say it, "beside himself," can speak as such. To the greatest possible degree, he is deprived of his subjectivity and this is an asset. It would only get in the way. Once the chicken is fed *benge* poison, the victim speaks only in his capacity of someone subject to accident. His own speech, once again, is not restored. Rather, now he speaks as someone who cannot speak in an ordinary way on the topic of accident, but who in an extraordinary way can expect a response to a sentence that arises out of bewilderment. Someone, something is listening. His bewilderment is the very basis of his speech.

He is not a free subject; he has been drained of his subjectivity, of his experience, for the moment. But he puts himself aside, as it were. In this way, he avoids trauma, the relation between the speaking subject and his memories felt to be inadequate. With the consultation of the oracle, there is no previously defined speaker. The "speaker" here is an effect of the oracle. Only because the oracle is present can he speak as he does. The man who announces the identity of the witch after consulting an oracle does not tell of his experience. He merely repeats what the oracle has said. He is bound by it. The lack of a sublime moment, of a separation from a power that overwhelms, which was his infliction up till that moment, becomes his triumph. He is still subjected to an obscure power, but now it grants him the right to speak, or, more accurately, it speaks through him.

Not by working through his suffering, which would be his acceptance of it and the reunification of himself, but through the use of the very fragmentation of his identity which made him think of witchcraft, the victim regains himself. As one of those fragments, he finds a place for himself in the social and thus aides in making witchcraft an institution. There was thus created a class of people in Azande society, "victims of witchcraft." This was not an exclusive identity; it did not replace ordinary social identity, but stood beside it, making these victims like those curers who, in trance, assume the names of spirits but who, outside of trance, are normal people. The making of witchcraft into an institution depended on giving it a place while at the same time keeping it apart from normality.

This solution, if that is the correct word, could only work intermittently. "Institutionalizing witchcraft," accident in its worked-out form, meant locking it up, as one might do to someone disturbed. Not at all to cure it, but to be make it capable of being released in order to roam society once more. Thus, witchcraft replaced another fear which lacked a name and hence a means of response.

Consulting the oracle, someone or some thing speaks in my place, and as a result, I can speak. In my place, where I am not, someone else appears. This "not me" substitutes for me and hides the multiple subjects caused by accident and expressed through suspicion.

Witches can mean nothing unless they are inflected by whatever it is that the oracle can bring from a distance that cannot be measured in human terms and that can be reached by humans only through ritual means. But this distance only comes into being with the production of a third person out of the substance of the disabled speaker. In my place, where I was, are the hidden remnants of uncertainties which prevent me from speaking authoritatively. These multiple uncertainties remain hidden only by the insistence that I am in face of an alterity completely different than me. This entity speaks to me and, being univocal, speaks authoritatively. It marks the place where there is something I must know. Such an alterity overpowers me, and I am grateful to it for doing so. *En face* of it, the phantasm of the witch, richer than any stereotype, emerges.

For Blanchot, the narrator's voice issues against a negativity which it cannot recapture. Such, too, is the case with the Azande oracle which, speaking of witches, speaks of death. The certainty of knowing a particular menace of death adjoins the impossibility of saying definitively what death is, where it comes from. Thus, witches reappear within a "strange institution." For Evans-Pritchard, Azande witches were not uncanny, but we have disputed his assessment. Evans-Pritchard, in making this judgment, made Azande witches a form of the sublime. Azande, overwhelmed by a force they could not comprehend, nonetheless gave a name to the phenomenon and thus separated themselves from it. Once again, the reappearance of suspicion and witchcraft shows that this separation was never completed. With the oracle, however, it seems as though certainty was achieved. The oracle asserts that there is a capacity to know whose provenance is not within me, but in someone or something from a distant place. The oracle established an other. And in doing so also claimed that this other could name, hence dissolve, the uncanny. It is this, finally, that institutionalized the witch.

PART TWO

WITCHES RESURRECTED

Suharto, Witches

" . . . no one is around for anyone any longer, and that this is indeed death, this dying of which Blanchot has complained not that it is fatal but that it remains impossible."

—JACQUES DERRIDA, *Politics of Friendship*

In Banyuwangi, on the eastern tip of Java, at the time that President Suharto left office in 1998, in a space of three months, about 120 people were killed after being accused of being sorcerers.[1] Later, in December 1999, ten people were killed after being so accused in the nearby area of Malang Selatan. There were similar incidents in other parts of Java. Let us start with one instance.

On the night of December 9, 1999, in the village of Hardjokuncaran, south of the city of Malang, four members of the same family, all accused of being sorcerers, were attacked. Three were killed and one escaped. One of the men arrested for the murders said, "My father was killed by sorcery." He knew this because his father could not stop urinating until the moment he died. His was one of a number of strange deaths. Some people swelled up, their abdomens or an arm doubled in size, until several died. About Muki, the father of the family of sorcerers, one man said, "If he wanted to borrow money from you and you didn't give him any, he got angry"—the implication being that one then fell ill. Another man, in his early twenties perhaps, was indignant. His brother was being held for trial. He was outraged, not because his brother was innocent but because his court-appointed attorney was asking for expense money; his brother was quite justified in killing a sorcerer since the man was a murderer. This youth was upset as well because the night of the killings he was not present and so was unable to participate in slaying these hated witches. His own house was a few kilometers away and his mother was ill, the result of sorcery. The very distance between his house and the sorcerers' proved how powerful the latter were. They could make his mother fall ill even when she was far away.

A man who had been an itinerant seller of noodle soup said that Bukhori, Muki's son, entered his house while he was out working.[2] Bukhori was a relative of his wife but ran off with her. Then the husband himself was bewitched. His arm swelled and he was in bed for months. He went to the doctor, who told him he had an infection. But, the man said, "There was no wound," thus clear "proof" (*bukti*) of sorcery. Bukhori was known for his predilection for other men's wives, and each time, after the wife was stolen, the husband was bewitched. A woman said that at first she was grateful to Pak ["Pak," a shortened from of "Father," is used as we use "Mister"] Muki. When she fell ill, he would give her large pills and she got well. But as time went on, she did not recover. And, she said, "many others got sick and they stayed ill and were killed." The pills Pak Muki gave her had pieces of rice inside. When she was ill, she felt there were strange things in her stomach. She was sick for two and a half years. The doctor told her her illness "came from outside" and "was not the kind of illness he could cure," so she was sure she had been ensorcelled. When Pak Muki was killed, she got well. All those who died, she went on, had swollen abdomens. They were all bewitched "for almost no reason at all." For instance, people would not lend Muki money, or, if they did, they could not get it back, and either way, they would fall ill. At this point in the conversation, a young man broke in to say that if sorcerers did not use their knowledge it would attack them. This was meant as an explanation for why it was that Muki was so violent. It was not simply his character; it was a part of the structure of sorcery itself. One could not understand how much harm Muki and his family had done if one did not see that they were compelled to deflect the lethal force of sorcery away from themselves and onto their neighbors.

Another seller of noodle soup said that Muki owed him Rp70,000, the price of twenty-some bowls of soup, and that he could not collect the money. If he asked for it, Muki would say, "'No problem. I'll pay later.'" I asked him why he continued to give Muki his wares; why not stop after, say, the fifteenth bowl? He replied that he was afraid he would die if he did so.

Another man added that, "If you did what he said, he helped you. But if not, you died." Muki made no explicit threats. In the minds of his fellow villagers, he did not need to do so. Villagers were terrified of him. It was not at all clear to most of them that if one did as he said, one would not be affected. Muki's own brother, who had helped him on many occasions, was also bewitched. And the parents of his daughter-in-law, who gave him land, were bewitched, too.

The mother of Muki's daughter-in-law, a woman who appeared to be in her seventies, said Muki sent an emissary to ask for her daughter's hand. "We were forced [to agree]. If not, I would get sick. So my daughter said yes." Muki said nothing menacing, but they understood that if they did not do what he wanted, they would suffer. In any case, the woman fell ill, and her husband also. Muki said, "A whole water buffalo won't cure him." That is, they could spend the price of a water buffalo on cures and he would not get well. "Proof," she said. Her abdomen swelled to the point where she could no longer lie flat, and her thighs swelled so much she could not urinate. But as soon as Muki was killed, she got well, and her husband got well too. Time after time, the swift recovery of ill people after Muki, his wife, and his son were killed was taken as "proof"; theirs was a family of sorcerers.

The entire village population, according to the testimony of the people we met, felt themselves enthralled by sorcerers. The result was the end of social reciprocity. A man asks for a family's daughter. There are none of the usual negotiations around marriage. There is only a tacit understanding on the side of the girl's family: if the daughter does not marry the sorcerer's son, himself a sorcerer, the mother will fall ill and die. A man gives Muki a month's supply of soup. He is convinced that if he does not, he will die. Muki never pays. Someone is so sick, the result, it is certain, of Muki's efforts, that no matter how much he might pay, he could never get well. "Whoever had anything to do with Matrawi [Muki's formal name] would have a mysterious [misterius] illness soon after," the local paper reports.[3]

Muki, his wife, and Bukhori, his son, were beaten and hacked to death, then strung up on display. Nineteen people were arrested for their participation, most of them later released. It is likely that many more were present. All those we met in the village, present at the killings or not, rejoiced at these murders.

The people of this village are convinced that death has visited them in unnatural ways. The father of one of those arrested whom we have already mentioned had to urinate so badly that he did so the whole day. "My father died dried out," his son told me. Death is no longer natural. And its unnaturalness makes it unbearable. If someone dies of comprehensible causes, his survivors usually do not remain preoccupied with his death. On the other hand, the bizarre quality of death by sorcery makes the passage to death and the deceased unforgettable, at least when sorcery is reinvented rather than being part of ordinary expectations, as we shall see it is in this case. Ordinary or natural death is followed by a series of funeral practices. Biological death is followed by the washing of the body, the interment, a series of rituals at punctual intervals. This has the intended effect of funerals everywhere: the separation of the living and the dead, though in Java the terms are quite different from our Western understanding of life and death.

Javanese practices at death are marked by certain qualities. The memorialization of the dead is minimized. It is not the purpose of the funeral to ensure that the living remember the dead as he or she "should" be remembered. Separation of living and dead does not mean that the memories of the deceased are put into a past from which the deceased person can never return. It is expected that the dead might reappear autonomously, as it were, without being consciously called into memory. They come back in dreams, or even in waking life. The spirit population itself, and Java is densely populated with ghosts, spirits, and supernatural effects, is vaguely thought to be the living transformed into the dead. Their supernatural effects are always startling and usually unwelcome. But they are expectable nonetheless. "Did you die, father?" the son of a murdered man accused of sorcery asked the ghost of his father. "I only moved away" was the reply. The mother of another murdered witch was visited by her slain son one afternoon. He was dressed in blue clothes. She asked him if he was healthy, but he disappeared without answering. She was startled. But she must have been reassured as well; I was told that his dress indicated that he was fine.

Javanese accept such phenomena as the usual intrusions of spirits into the world rather than as the impossible reappearance of someone who is dead and therefore incapable of returning. But the place made for involuntary memory and hallucination, to put their experiences in our terms

of understanding, still does not allow for "unnatural" death. Death is unnatural not only when it takes strange forms and when it seems to be in
the power of the sorcerer. It is unnatural when it is contagious. By that I
mean that everyone seems menaced with death and, since it is the human
condition to be so menaced, unable to put the threat out of mind; such
people look for a source of death in order to put an end to its contagion.
Even when they find that sorcery is the cause and the sorcerer is dealt with,
they are not at ease because the nature of sorcery is unclear to them. Soon
the sorcerers' power will reach me is their ineffaceable assumption. Hence
the obsessive quality of sorcery. And with that, the hunt for witches.

The idea that the sorcerer must use his power on pain of its otherwise
being turned against himself is important. The sorcerer is accused of focusing his malevolence against certain people. But everyone is a likely eventual victim. The sorcerer is only a vehicle for something that originates beyond him. He must continually find new targets. He is, in that sense, like
the curer, or *dukun*. The supernatural curer in Indonesia, as in most places,
himself falls ill. To be cured he must allow his or her body to be visited by
the spirits which have caused the illness. Often there are two sets of spirits,
good and bad. The curer becomes their receptacle and allows them to be
used for the good. He or she thus gains a double identity. S/he is who s/he
is in everyday life. And s/he is someone or something completely different
when s/he cures. The sorcerer, in this view, is the curer inverted. Both offer their bodies for the use of supernatural powers which possess them as
much as they possess the spirits.

Magical curing is, in effect, the making reasonable and useful of supernatural power. When the curer becomes the sorcerer—and, in a few
cases this is what people thought happened, though most people accused
of witchcraft were not curers (*dukun*)—this power loses its reasonableness, its capacity to be made part of ordinary thinking. The curer produces health, but the sorcerer causes death. The difference, perhaps, is in the
verbs "produce" or "make" versus "cause." The sorcerer is not productive
but destructive. No doubt this opposition is a useful element in explaining the workings of the world. But the sorcery that followed the leaving of
office of President Suharto surpassed it. Few of those murdered were curers (*dukun*). The possibility of using Javanese mysticism to explain fortune
and misfortune or to alleviate anxiety was unavailable when sorcery was

dislocated from the *dukun*. The identity of the sorcerer and the source of his power then became unclear. The very thought of sorcery then became a way to imagine that unnatural death has appeared or will do so.

The sorcerer in the period after the fall of Suharto was and, at the moment I write this, continues to be, one's ordinary neighbor. Some accused of sorcery, such as Muki, were curers. But most were not. The post-Suharto witch is just like everyone else. But he has a second identity as well. One that, according to the Javanese theory of witchcraft that still applied, he did not choose. The lack of choice is often obscured by the enmity people bear the person of the sorcerer. But it remains an important element of sorcery. The sorcerer is a repository of lethal power. This lethal power affects—one can say "infects"—people, making them fall ill. The cure, if there was one, was, indeed, sometimes the removal of strange objects from their stomachs or other parts of their body—objects which contain or communicate the sorcerer's power. But usually there was no cure. The sorcerer's victims are inhabited, as he is. The difference is that they, for some reason, are not offered the sorcerer's possibility of deflection of that power. There was an uncontrolled emergence of forces that could not be identified with the known spirit world; they invaded practically the entire community. With only the slightest reason, or none at all, one was ensorcelled. Explanations of envy or conflict of interest that accompany accusations of sorcery in other times were often left aside.

The motivations of the witch were thus often obscure. Muki, for instance, was not rich. But, according to villagers, he could have been. "If only Muki had sold his services he would have been very rich," we were told, as, indeed, some curers have become in Indonesia. As it is, Muki, the sorcerer rather than the curer, acted for reasons that were indecipherable. When someone fell sick, it became a sign of Muki's powers, particularly when the person had had something to do with Muki. As we have said, whether one did what Muki wanted or not, one suffered from him. Interests could not explain his actions. If one dealt with Muki, giving him what he wanted was no help at all. Being in touch with him meant being brought to his attention and therefore becoming his victim. And this, simply out of his need to be malevolent.

As an intermediary between the spirit and human worlds the sorcerer should be a figure. But, unlike the case in the West, there is no image of the witch, at least the witch of this period of mass accusations. The curer who does evil is a figure. One can see him on television. But the sorcerer of today's East Java is just like anyone else. These witches were not set apart by appearance or even by status, since rich as well as poor, prominent as well as humble people were accused. Of course, elements of thinking about traditional sorcerers remain. Thus, there were experts who could tell if someone has supernatural power. But as we shall see, such expertise could not be relied on.

A sorcerer could be a man or a woman, and he or she could be old or young. Sometimes children are killed along with their parents because sorcery is said to descend in families. But I do not know of young children accused of practicing the art. Even the name, *tukang santet* or, in Banyuwangi, *tukang sihir*, gives no clue. *Tukang* denominates someone who practices a trade and has a particular skill. But one cannot assimilate this skill to a merely technological one, for one reason because the older sense of *tukang* retains the implication of esoteric knowledge. The word can also refer by metonymy to someone who works with something, thus a *tukang botol* is someone who collects bottles to sell. A sorcerer is associated with magic—*sihir*—the way a *tukang botol* is associated with bottles. The name, in other words, while it seems to link the sorcerer to a class, when pushed ends with mere metonymy. The witch is defined by association with witchcraft. But in many cases that seems not to have been known in advance. No one reported seeing the accused practicing his craft, for instance, so far as we know.

Hence, a name without an image. The contemporary witch is located behind the normal appearance of one's neighbor. Nothing about him or her yields definitive proof of sorcery. "I told them to look wherever they want," the son of a slain sorcerer said to the masked men who invaded the house and killed his father. "You won't find anything but holy books here. There is no witchcraft anywhere." In fact, they did not look. Muki, it was said, was often seen returning home at two or three in the morning. Doubtless he had been sitting in the river or visiting a site of magical power. Sitting in the river at night is a common Javanese mystical practice. Many people do it who have no intention of becoming witches. Some of the accused sorcerers were curers for whom such practices are quite normal. In any case, anyone might try out these techniques without being a professional mystic, as it were. Muki, by his appearance and even by his esoteric actions did not differ from those who live in the same village. He lived there for at least thirty years, according to his neighbors. It was only in the last five years or so that, they said, he became feared. And then he came to embody an absolute, unbridgeable, and unbearable difference.

The frequent recurrence of the word "proof" (*bukti*) in the mouths of the killers (and also of the survivors, preceded, naturally, by "There is no . . .") leads us to speculate on what this word means. It does not mean "evidence" (of the criminal). The reader will note that the usage of the word seldom bears on the identification of the witch. That is self-evident to the accusers. "Proof" means, first of all, "There is something strange." Someone swells up; it is "proof." After Muki was killed and such swellings disappeared, it was also "proof," as much for the strangeness of the disappearance as for the coincidence with his murder. "Proof" means that what the speaker expected was born out. One might expect the opposite. In the face of bizarre happenings, there is no explanation. In effect, to say "proof" is not to say "He did it, here is the evidence" but "I knew it." After the fact, the uncanny event is claimed to have been anticipated.

Only the survivors protest that the murder victim was not a sorcerer. Everyone else is sure. They are certain that sorcery is at work, and there was no dispute about who was the witch, except, of course, from the accused. The sorcerer is not recognizable by anything in his appearance. But he is known all the same once there is "proof"; once, that is, the uncanny has manifested itself. The witch becomes "known" as the source of malevolence precisely when all one can think of is malevolence and one is bewildered as to the cause. Just when one cannot know the reason for so many bizarre and frightening occurrences, one is certain: "It is Muki." Presto. The insistence on "proof," as well as the strange context of its usage, lets us see that it is a denial. "I do not know what is happening or who or what is causing it" is the real meaning of this word.

The East Javanese witch is not like the Communist in America during the McCarthy period, or Jews during the pogroms, or gypsies at periods when they are attacked. These are recognizable types. Contemporary Javanese witches are not. The fact that the witch's appearance reveals nothing but the ordinary in part accounts for the brutality of the killings. Muki was bashed in, slashed, and stabbed, and then, when he was dead, strung up in the doorway of his house. His wife and son, similarly slain, were hung, the first in another doorway, the other from a tree in the grove to which he had fled. When the witch lacks a figure, it seems necessary to disembody him to get at the essence of witchcraft. Simply killing the person does not do. To be rid of the witch, particularly given the lack of ritual means to do so, means killing something that one cannot find. It means killing more than the body, and therefore it requires the witch to be slain multiple times, as it were.

The *Malang Post* reports two killings of *santet* on the same day, both of which illustrate the difficulty in killing a witch. One, a woman, Mbok Siamah, forty-five, did not resist her killers.

> Her body trembling and her voice shaking, she begged not to be killed. But the woman's supplication was ignored by the savage mob [*massa yang sangat beringas*].[4] The woman gave in to her fate as they beat her body with various clubs and sharp weapons.
>
> Without significant resistance, the woman . . . collapsed onto the ground. The moment was critical and there was no way out but the woman still was able to show her supernatural powers [*kesaktian*]. Even though they struck her dozens of times with sharp weapons and objects she did not die. This widow was even able to find blankets to cover her face.
>
> Seeing that the victim was not yet dead, the mob even tried to choke her to death with twine but this did not do her in. In fact, the twine broke several times.
>
> Finally, the mob went back to beating her with various clubs. Finally, Mbok Siamah could not hold out against the blows and she died straight away. The brutal mob needed a half hour to finish off this opponent not at all equal to them.

The newspaper report goes on to describe seventy-year-old Pak Gito, who

> . . . swung a staff. Pak Gito drove back the mob; those who approached him crumbled. Pak Gito made the mob in front of him retreat several steps out of fear. But, because their number was so large, they fearlessly kept on trying to kill him by swarming around him with sharp weapons.
>
> Pak Gito finally was overwhelmed in the face of this opponent, so much greater than himself. Finally, this former village government official fell.
>
> Seeing their enemy fall, the masses straight away clubbed him. In fact, one person who had brought a sword with him slit Pak Gito's throat. Besides that, several others who had brought sharp weapons stabbed his right leg with a sword. Pak Gito finally died a horrifying death.

During this time the mob also ransacked the victim's house. A Politron 14 inch television set was beaten till it was smashed to pieces. The household furnishings were also smashed.

The next day, Pak Gito's corpse was found lying in front of the house, curled up. Next to him were rocks as big as his head used to beat him. This was proven by the splattering of fresh blood on the rocks.[5]

This case, which I know only from the newspaper, involves two witches who were lovers. Pak Gito, married and seventy years old, had bewitched the widow, Mbok Samiah, so that she fell in love with him. Mbok Siamah became a witch as a result of her relation with Pak Gito. Villagers warned the pair about their immoral behavior, but they continued to see each other. Pak Gito was only recently discovered to be a witch. It is said that he caused the deaths of many, something presumably known only in retrospect. The proof in this case was the finding of the tools of witchcraft—scissors, hair, and nails—hidden in the kitchen hearth.

Traditionally, people with mystical power in Java are difficult to kill. Usually, to kill them one has to find a certain weak point or use ritual means. In stories before this time, the victim, in pain, finally tells his accusers how to bring about his death or he himself removes his magic invulnerability. This report comes closest to such stories, but it lacks mention of magic invulnerability and ritual means of murder.

This narrative about the killing of a witch has, however, another element. In other cases, too, the house of the witch was ransacked and the contents burned. This, indeed, is also sometimes the practice in urban riots against Indonesians of Chinese descent. Here, the television set is given special notice. We will see later that this is not necessarily by chance and that it has something to do with the nature of the new witch. In riots against Indonesian Chinese their goods were also often burned. In the incidents I witnessed in Central Java in the early 1980s this was meant to repudiate the attraction that wealth, associated with Chinese, had for the rioters. In that way, Javanese rioters asserted their difference from Chinese.[6] Here, too, rioters tried to eliminate all trace of the witch and consequently any contamination by him and certainly any identification with him.

But the television set, so prominently marked by its details ("a Politron 14 inch television set") is an extra element. This set is not just destroyed; the household belongings (unspecified) are beaten in the same way as the witch ("beaten till it was smashed to pieces"). In one village we visited, an extremely poor man was watching television at the house of a neighbor, there being no set in his hovel, when masked men, called Ninja, arrived at the door, summoned him out, and killed him. His mutilated body was found at the corner of the village road the next day. His wife and children were watching a soap opera with him. I asked them if they still watched it. "Of course," was the answer.

These family members, who suffered materially from the father's death, and who were already poor, had no hesitation in resuming their television habits without him. They did not fear feeling his absence. There are reasons for this, having to do with Javanese death practices. But one sees also that television fascinates. Whatever one sees on it, watching it one is removed from daily concerns. We might reluctantly guess that the family does not miss the father because the attractive power of television is so great. *Dukuns*, or magical practitioners, who can also practice black magic are represented on television. But these are not the witches involved in our account; the new witch could be anyone. The habitual programs of this family and most other peasants I know are the soap operas, which deal with the lives of rich people in the capital and in which sorcerers rarely appear. The source of television's fascination may be the power that brings foreign elements into the village. The destruction of the television set in order to disengage from the force of the witch suggests a power vaguely associated with the new witchcraft whose source includes not only the traditional world of Javanese spirits but something beyond it.

The sorcerers' corpses were mutilated. But what is a corpse if not a mutilated body? One can say that corpses are the living deprived of life and thus deformed. The decay of the body that comes with death is evidence that the person is deceased. In Java, the ghost is the restoration of the corpse. Not only is the person again present, if in an ambiguous manner, it is also whole again; it has a complete form. Some types of Javanese ghosts, such as the woman with a hole in her back, are monstrosities. But the ghosts of murdered sorcerers reappeared whole, at least to their families. These ghosts are not the opposite of living persons, but their continuation. They are not anomalies, but, in a certain way, entities wished for. These Javanese ghosts ameliorate the shock of death. They obscure the moment of decease and hide the "deadness" or absence of the person turned into a corpse.

In order to mourn, the instant of death and the corpse as corpse, as the body mutilated by death, has to be forgotten. Or perhaps the process of mourning, when it works and if it works, is this forgetting. We replace our knowledge of the corpse with the memory of the person when he was alive, using the past tense when we effectively separate the living from the dead. The deceased then are elsewhere, not part of the living world, relegated to a past that prevents their return. Javanese return as ghosts. But despite this return there is still the separation of life and death to the degree that the ghost conceals or denies the moment of death, the time of transformation of the body, a moment immune to cultural integration.

By contrast, the trajectory of events after the death of the sorcerers was in the opposite direction. Instead of the restoration of wholeness, frequently enough there was the cutting of the body into pieces and the bashing in of the skull and other cruelties I do not have the courage to repeat. Often the bodies were dragged through the streets. In place of the ghost, there was the display of deformation. One can say that there was a procedure since, unless the sorcerer escaped, there was always murder and mutilation and usually the corpse was put on display. Rather than the production of ghosts, there was the display of a death which resisted amelioration and which was in opposition not only to the usual Javanese cultural practices but, I think one can say, to all cultural practice. The production of figures, the work of imagination, was set aside in order to search for something else.

This search could only be done through destruction. Revelation of "death" could not be accomplished through constructing a figure of death through writing, telling, or painting, for instance. Whatever was to be seen could only be shown through displaying the essence of the corpse, and that could be done only by opening the body, by smashing it and by severing its members. The displays had the usual effect of the representations of death the media furnish us with. They said, "It is not me." The murderers hoped if not for the end of death, then for the ability to put it aside. They searched for its essence, sorcery, inside the body of the sorcerer. Once the sorcerer was dead, and it is clear that they were never confident of killing him definitively, the corpse was intended to give death a certain visibility. Death being in the dead body, it was not, or was no longer, in them. The revelation was supposedly also the cure. And yet death was never defeated.

One knows because the reputed sorcerers were killed multiple times, as it were, not merely because traditionally witches are difficult to kill but because the killers were not sure that the witch was definitively dead and because the witch hunt continued in other villages.

Murdering their neighbor, they tried to avoid the possibility implicit within the logic of witchcraft that, because they too had death within them, they too were sorcerers. This possibility starts in the feeling of invasion by a lethal element heterogeneous to themselves. This element disables them; it makes them incapable of becoming what they should already be: living beings and also social beings. They are already inhabited by death. If they have death within them, but somehow are still alive, they are, at least potentially, witches. One sees the strong similarity to the Murngin "half-dead." They need, after that, only to become the switching point, the diverter of death, to fully be witches. Under that condition, one kills the witch because one is the witch oneself.

Some who were accused of sorcery were not sure that the accusation was false. A man in Banyuwangi was warned by the village headman that he was suspected of being a sorcerer. He refused to flee, telling the village headman that he was innocent and therefore he would stay. But when his house was stoned, he ran off. He traveled widely, going to Bali and other places, to escape possible death. It is believed that certain people, sometimes thought to be witches themselves, have the capacity to see if someone is a witch. He went to a religious school in the countryside and asked the teacher (*kijaji*), "Am I a witch?" "No" was the answer. The man went back home. On the way, he met the officer in charge of the local military post and repeated his question. This man looked carefully at him, the radiance of his face indicating to those with the power to see it whether someone is a sorcerer. He said, "Yes, you are a witch." As a result, the man postponed his return.

This man could not tell from his own interrogation of himself whether he was a sorcerer. He asks how he is seen by others, and he thinks that they may know something about him that he does not know himself. He got two answers to his question. Neither was definitive. Neither he nor Udi, another man whose story we shall soon hear, could find in their surroundings a reflection of themselves as they thought they were up to the moment of the outbreak of witchcraft. To ask, "Am I a witch?" when the "proofs" of witchcraft are signs of an identity concealed from oneself is to rely on other's appraisal of oneself. But these others are not convincing. They may know something or they may not, but whatever it is does not match what the accused knows about himself. There is no verification possible, at least for anyone who did not admit before the accusation to being so. (There were two cases of people who admitted to being witches, but in these cases it was impossible to tell whether the persons thought that only after the accusation. Confessions to suit the wishes of the community are, of course, quite common in cases of witchcraft.) The witch's identity is apparent to no one except those with special powers, and even then, as we have seen, not authoritatively. This, of course, did not stop villagers from finding "proof."

The feeling of being possessed—if not the posing of the question "Am I a witch?"—seems to me a condition for the unprecedented outbreaks of witchcraft in Java at the end of the New Order. It indicates that at a certain moment there was not merely uncertainty about identity, which means that one doubts who one is, as though one had a range of known possible identities. To be a witch, at least in Java, is to be invested with a power heterogeneous to all social identity. Thus, there is also the possibility that one could be someone completely different from anything or anyone one knows. The impossibility of relying on social opinion opens up infinite possibilities within the person. These possibilities are beyond the ones imagination presents.

To ask if one is a witch is to say that I cannot put myself in the place that others once placed me. I can no longer see myself as they saw me at an earlier time in my everyday identity. Earlier, I would be able to say "I am not a witch," because I would be unable find in myself the confirmation of my accusers. But under the conditions that prevailed during the witch hunt, self-image disappeared, as multiple possibilities of identity thrust themselves forward. "Witch," under that condition, is a name for the incapacity to figure oneself.

Muki is the "proof" of his fellow villagers' collective disability. He took no account of their persons; he gave them no credit for who they were. However you behaved toward him, you died. In their descriptions of their dealings with Muki, they picture themselves not merely as powerless but as denuded of social attributes. They got no reflection of themselves as they thought themselves to be from Muki. Rather, acting in every case against their will, their feelings, their habits, and their customs, they had no life in themselves with which to resist him. Their only recourse was murder. They picture themselves as, in a certain sense, already dead, but terrorized by a death that will arrive again, as it were. What happened, then, was a cultural failure. It was an inability to put death aside, and with it the incapacity to manufacture either ghosts or social persons.

The heirs of these sorcerers, all of whom claimed that the victims were not sorcerers and that they themselves are not, produced ghosts often enough. That they were able to do so shows a difference between culture on the one side versus a certain deculturation. But why and how they could do so, and why, at a certain time, cultural processes failed remain to be explained.

Let us look at the case of another murdered witch (I mean, when I use this word, "accused witch"). Munakip was slain in his bed on the night of December 21, 1999. He was, according to the *Malang Post* "dieksekusi massa" (executed by the mob because he was suspected of having black magic).[7] Here is what his son, Udi, told us:

Dad chanted the Koran in the prayer house [in front of their own house]. After he finished praying, he read a magazine, talked with the kids [his students] and went to bed. The kids went home. I locked the door but left the window open. I heard someone at the prayer house and thought they might be thieves. Maybe they were after our cucumbers. I said, "Who's there?" Then about ten o'clock they started to throw rocks and broke the windows. There are no nearby neighbors.

Someone came in the back of the house by the window. I shouted for help. "Don't do that. If you scream, you'll be cut up," someone said. I went out another window to find a neighbor with a telephone. I didn't pay any attention at all to being cut up, I just kept right on screaming. But I [had to] telephone the police. [Later, Udi would say that the police had come within fifteen or twenty minutes, there being a police post not too far away.]

Mom was in the kitchen, getting the meal ready [the meal eaten just before dawn during the fasting month]. They locked the door and wouldn't let her out. There were many people at the mosque, but they were afraid to help.

Dad was asleep when they came. He was kidnapped, is the word. [In fact, he was murdered in his bed.] Then he was cut to pieces.

They could have come one by one, but they came lots at a time.

Later I saw pictures of the corpse. It was *sadis* [a word derived from "sadistic"]. The police didn't want to show me them, they are afraid of raising the urge for vengeance. But I am not after revenge; I want the law.

There is someone here who envies (*iri*) us. So far as the *santet* issue goes, there is no truth in it. Just envy. He wants to smash this family.

I asked Udi if the family had had problems with the neighbors.

There have never been any problems. But if you mean envy, sure, there's a problem. The problem is, Dad and I don't work but we live as well as those who do. [He goes on to explain that he is a producer of weddings; he dresses and makes up the couple and rents them clothes and decorates the house, for which, the newspaper reports, he gets about three million rupiah a month, many times more than the neighboring farmers. His father, he repeated, is a teacher of the Koran.] The one who envies us, he sees that we don't work [by which he meant "work in the fields, work manually"] and yet we live as well as they do.

Udi went on to explain that Mariano, a *préman*, or hood or street criminal, who had lived in the village but then went to Jakarta and had returned two or three years earlier (the newspaper reported he had returned two or three months before the incident), has been blamed for organizing the killing. He is said to be behind three other murders. But, said Udi, "the *provakator* is someone else. Someone very envious of this family. This man has not been arrested. He worked from behind the scenes; he was the real instigator."

Mariano escaped a few weeks after I spoke with the victim's son and was later arrested in Jakarta. The newspaper reported that Mariano had named a *provakator*, implying that it was someone involved in national politics from Jakarta. But later a local man, one matching Udi's description, was arrested. Thus, the designated *provakator* was not at all someone who was part of a national conspiracy (*konspirasi*).

The house in which we spoke with Udi was built with his money. He had earned enough in the three years since his return from Jakarta to build a larger-than-usual house, which was not yet finished. He had also bought a truck, which someone drives for him and which he uses in his wedding productions, and a motorcycle. My Javanese friends agreed with him; this display of wealth, in the context of the village, was very likely to arouse envy. What is more, the rapidity by which he, and hence his family, had become wealthy, was likely to be attributed to magic. And, we learned later, other *kijaji*, religious teachers, said that Udi's father had been a very powerful *tukang santet*. This reputation, preceding the acquisition of wealth, was used to account for the family's fortune. All of this fits the description of witchcraft as it has operated traditionally. Earlier, jealousy or envy seem to have always been mentioned as the elements that would spark accusations of witchcraft.

We can ask what it means when Udi says that villagers are *iri* (jealous, envious) of his family. He speaks of how he is seen by others. He "knows" what they think of him. He sees the difference between himself, his father (he does not speak of his brother or his mother), and them. This difference, as he puts it, does not consist merely in having wealth while they are poor. It is also that "they see that we do not work and yet we live as well as they do." He minimizes his relative wealth in favor of a difference which, he implies, they do not understand. He pictures himself and his father as a mystery to their neighbors. They have an enigmatic characteristic which is unacceptable. *Iri*, says the dictionary, is "to feel or to have the feeling of discontent seeing someone else's good fortune." Udi, judging from the newspaper reports that say that a neighbor was responsible for plotting the murder, seems to be correct in his supposition. It was a neighbor and not a plot concocted in Jakarta, and it was someone who saw how Udi waxed rich rapidly. The "discontent" here was obviously unbearable. It was, of course, his father who was killed, while Udi himself was left untouched. This, it seems to me from talking with people in the neighborhood, is because the father was long involved in the affairs of the village, whereas his soon was much less so. Udi's neighbors, in his account, never perceived him at work when he produced weddings. They only saw prosperity where there was none before. In Udi's understanding, his father, who had been a Koran teacher for decades, who others, possibly unknown to Udi, suspected of practicing sorcery for some time, was innocent and was nonetheless hated. It was their envy and their lack of comprehension, Udi feels, that was behind the events.

Udi knows the perception of himself is occulted and transformed. He stresses the aspects of himself mysterious to villagers in order to explain how his father was accused of being a witch. He, of course, thinks he has been misperceived. He explained how he lived in Jakarta for ten years and learned his trade, and how eventually he plans to return there. For him, the making of money is nothing. He sees that "they," his murderous neighbors, cannot understand him. At the same time, they accuse him of nothing. His capacity to become different is, if not explained, at least left without need for explanation because it took place in Jakarta, outside the village. Whatever he is—hairdresser, earner of money—it belongs to the city and not to the village. Villagers, it is implied and frequently said by others, are *bodoh*, "ignorant." They do not think of interpreting what is outside their world. They merely find a local cause for what they do not understand.

Elaborate weddings with expensive preparations were a feature of the New Order which penetrated the village. They were a ritualized sanction for the wealth that was gained during that period. Precisely because weddings were an occasion when wealth was redistributed, differences in wealth were made tolerable, though only uneasily. What was found intolerable was differences of wealth which seemed to have no provenance. This, at least, is Udi's understanding of how he is seen. In his view, it means that, to them, his father, an extension of himself, could be anything at all. Of course, Udi knows that "they" are mistaken. He does not accept their view of himself or of his father, perhaps because he retains his confirmation of himself from his time in Jakarta.

In Udi's explanation his neighbor's murderous impulses are not directed toward social differences. Indeed, they stem from an inability to perceive difference in the first place. The envious want what someone else has. But while the word "envy" (*iri*) is used, it seems to me to fill in for the lack of a word. In Udi's understanding, it is not that neighbors wanted his riches. And, in fact, when they broke in, they took nothing from the house, nor did they do what we have seen anti-Chinese and some attackers of accused witches do: destroy their victims' goods as a sign that they, the rioters, renounce them. *Iri*, or "envious," here is directed not against a consolidated social distinction but against its provenance. Our wealth, says Udi, is in their minds a sign of not laboring and still living well. For them, this has mysterious origins that indicate sorcery. It is not that "we" have what "they" want. It is rather that we seem to be vaguely or indistinctly different.

"Envy" here indicates that "our" mystery is insupportable to "them." And that can only be because they might become like us. There is a desire to live without work, and therefore envy. But there is the fear that if one did so, if one became like us, then one would also be a sorcerer. "Envy," as used here, indicates an identification that is both desired and feared. Finally, it implies that one is, indeed, already in the place of the envied, unable to break an identification with him. The attempt to do so was murder. In Udi's analysis, the inability to generate a reflection of himself in the minds of his fellow villagers was the result of this identification. Murderers and victims were, he thought, the same in the minds of the former. Both were witches in the sense that a menacing force had them in their grip.

In the instance above, there is nothing that contradicts ideas about witchcraft from an earlier time. The witch here is also a curer, as was the case before. But there is a new witch in East Java today, even if sometimes he appears also as a curer or *dukun*. New, because this witch has sources of power which, remaining inchoate, surpass those of the witch of the past. Most witches were not also *dukun*, or magical curers of the traditional sort. But even when it was a *dukun* who was involved, the recourse against him was different. This difference was an implicit acknowledgment of the new powers of the witch. We were repeatedly told that there have long been witches in East Java and that sometimes they were killed. The main difference, people told us, was that, then, only individual witches were attacked. The ethnographic evidence is slim, there being no extended ethnographic studies of Javanese witchcraft to my knowledge. What we have, however, does not support the idea that there were many killings earlier. In any case, Clifford Geertz, whose extensive ethnographic studies were conducted in the 1950s, said this:

Accusations of sorcery are common enough, but they are never made openly and directly against anyone; they are only whispered to others as malicious gossip or discussed rather abstractly as hypotheses to account for peculiar behaviors. . . .

In many instances the immediate suffering from sorcery is psychologically real and the accusations fervent. . . . Even in cases of this sort where the hurt is real and immediate, accusations are never expressed directly to the assumed culprit, nor is a public charge made; gossip to all one's neighbors is the typical pattern.[8]

Of course, in our cases, accusations were made collectively and there was action rather than mere gossip. Traditional sorcery is discussed by both Geertz and Koentjaraningrat in terms of particular types of *dukuns*, each of whom specializes in such things as love magic or thieves' magic. The only accusations were against *tukang sihir* or *tukang santet*—generalized practitioners of magic. This reflects the difference between then and now. Then, in the 1950s, "sorcery [was] always practiced for a particular reason, never for sheer malevolence" (110). Furthermore, Geertz notes:

> Although one may gossip about it and make secret accusations to one's heart's content . . . any open attempt to organize public opinion against an accused sorcerer would be almost certain to fail. Similarly, one finds no private individuals in Modjokuto [the pseudonym for the place in East Java where Geertz worked] with a wide reputation for instigating sorcery. Although some dukuns are suspected as all-too-willing agents, even these are in no way socially ostracized. (110)

Koentjaraningrat mentions that sorcerers might be accused of causing death but he mentions nothing at all about the killing of sorcerers themselves. The recourse against sorcery was first of all gossip. And after that it was the hiring of another sorcerer.[9] Geertz again:

> In all the cases of sorcery of which I heard, I never discovered a case in which direct confrontation by the victim of the accused took place or where any general open accusation was made or any claim for punishment or damages instituted even informally—there being no formal procedures in any case. *Sorcery is a mystical act to be mystically combated.* (110; my italics)

Geertz then tells of one man who, having been robbed twice, went to a *dukun* who practiced evil magic to get retribution.

Today the accusations of sorcery are often divorced from particular injuries. And even when this is not the case, the threat of the sorcerer is general. Somehow the malevolence that issues from him will harm everyone even if only one person in a village feels himself to have been injured. Thus the need felt for collective action. This is the case with Udi and his father. Udi was convinced that one man was behind the murder, a man envious of his family. But this man, if he existed, was able to convince many in the village that they too were in danger. No doubt the *provakator*, as Udi termed him, had been jealous for some while. But at a certain moment his perception made many sufficiently afraid for them to take collective action. This, following after Geertz, was new.

The remedy against sorcery is no longer sorcery. Gossip no longer satisfies. The power of the *dukun* will now not prevail against sorcerers. When sorcery was the answer to sorcery, the spirit world was in equilibrium. This is presently not the case. The menace is general and catastrophe threatens. Thus the attempt to banish witches, if not witchcraft, forever. The defenses against sorcery have disappeared. The implication is that witches today have another source of power, one proceeding from outside the world of Javanese spirits. Even where the elements are seemingly traditional, the generalized panic indicates a fear that has no known origin.

It is tempting to think that it was a question of the inability to understand the penetration of the market. But this cannot be so since, as I have said, the poor and the desperately poor were also attacked, and those who had no connection with the world outside the village except through television were as well. I do not want to discount the market entirely. But we cannot find the exact source of this power. Witchcraft here was not a metaphor for something that we as analysts could name but they, the witch hunters, could not. Something amorphous and unnameable was at work. Up to this point, one can only say this: at a certain moment there was a menace felt whose origin was unknown and which was general. It surpassed the usual understandings of sorcery. With this, a new social type came into being: the village mob. People, using the idiom of sorcery as it had been known, invented a new witch; only the name and a few associated beliefs were the same.

How did such a change come about? We can look for a first answer to the history of the Suharto regime. The New Order, as it was called, narrowed and rationalized national identity. It was a time when the emergence into adulthood which, in the Sukarno period, was a time full of undefined opportunity, became restricted. It is only apparently paradoxical that though the development of the market allowed new careers the imaginative opportunities of the Old Order evaporated. Only certain social types were allowed. Walking into the regional parliament, for instance, one had to have proper attire, especially shoes and not sandals, and the right identification. Dressed in the form that indicates the greatest wealth of possibilities, as a revolutionary, one would certainly be refused admission. Getting a national identity card was a recurrent problem. This card specified, among other things, which of the five authorized religions one belonged to. The need for letters of identification, identity badges, and permits multiplied. Since the fall of Suharto there has been an abrupt decline in the insistence that identity be continuously officially confirmed. Government surveillance has decreased considerably, as the operation of a free press, for instance, indicates.

One should not exaggerate the degree of the new freedom, but once again, though without the euphoria that pertained at the time of independence, there is the possibility of becoming nearly anyone. This time, however, it is not that the government or the nation approves of such development but that it is simply not doing the work of surveillance to the same degree. The assumption that one is seen in the eyes of national authority is greatly weakened. The youth in the revolution knew they dressed in the same way as their compatriots. They could find their double next to themselves. Youth who marched against Suharto merely imitated this look from the past. The model vanished quickly, as though it were only one more fashion. By contrast to the early days of independence, when eccentric attire of various sorts was accepted, perhaps as the possible look of the future, there is today a certain indifference, the general effect of the lack of confidence in a generalized other.

It seems as though there is the substitution of the surveillance of the market for the surveillance of the nation: on the one hand, the new indifference of the state; on the other, the rapid change of fashion. Even village youth, for instance, dress in T-shirts, imitation Nikes, and so on. But there was no substitution, at least for villagers, as we shall see exemplified below. During the Suharto regime the market was allowed a place without the relaxation of governmental surveillance. A space was made for fashion and for consumption, but on the condition that they would be ultimately subordinated to national identity, with all that implied in terms of recognition by the state. We must add to this the untransformed nature of the village, in which the pressures for consumption were felt without a place being made for them. An example, of course, is the case of Udi. The effects were felt not so much in Udi himself, who forged ahead, building his house and buying a truck and a motor bike, but in the reaction toward him by those who were mystified by his sudden production of wealth. Had the circulation of money and, with it, consumption, been a normal part of village existence, perhaps villagers would not have thought that sudden wealth implied sorcery. They themselves, even the poorest, by their dress showed that they nonetheless depended on the market to a greater extent than ever, without, however, any thorough transformation of their mentality. The New Order introduced "development" (*pembangunan*) even for villagers. But it contributed nothing to the cultural development necessary for making a place for new social types. On the contrary, the surveillance practiced by the government had the effect of suppressing the assertion of wealth as a form of social status in the village, at least for those who held no government position.

It was not only the pressure of new wealth that was felt at the time of the witch murders, however, as evidenced by the killing of the poor as well as the new rich. The effect of the New Order was to make it seem as though only certain forms of social expression, principally those that were traditionally found in the village, were available. Retrograde as it was, this conferred security on those who appreciated authority. For them, safety continued to depend on governmental surveillance. They may not all have been supporters of the New Order, but its ending meant the end of that security. The lifting of surveillance meant that much, if not everything, seemed possible. That included, in particular, asocial and anti-social drives.

Hate in Java is often spontaneous. Muki had been accused of practicing witchcraft for as long as people could remember and of having had ancestors before him from whom he inherited his sorcery. I do not know the facts, but the debts of the soup seller, who spoke as though these were the debts of a lifetime of sorcery, extended back only about a month. The second soup seller, who lost his wife to Muki's son, had suffered this loss, it turned out, several years earlier. However, he had been bewitched only recently. The intensity of the feelings against Muki may have made it seem to villagers that he had always been a witch. In other places, the witch was said to be recent. In all instances, the intensity of animosity cannot be doubted, and in that sense, "hate" is the correct word. But Javanese hate as evidenced in most of the cases of witchcraft was unpredictable and uncontrolled rather than savored and slow-growing. It suggests the resurgence of unconscious drives hitherto repressed rather than a long-standing resentment cultivated in memory and cultural representations.

Perhaps it is possible, however, to characterize the violence against witches historically. In Pramoedya Ananta Toer's vignette of the revolution, called "Revenge" ("Dendam"), young men waiting for a train become convinced that a haji is a traitor.[10] He has magical powers, and until he gives them up they are unable to kill him. The possession of these powers convinces the youth the haji is guilty. Benedict R. O'G. Anderson used this story in his earliest written formulation of his idea of nationalism. He made the point that murder and the impulse for revenge were a part of the revolution, something forgotten by Western scholars.[11] One sees these traits here attached to suspicion and magic, as with sorcery. And, as in the cases discussed, suspicion arises suddenly and for no reason we are told about. (We know only that someone is a traitor, but there is no evidence that it was the haji.) Since the revolution, violence has also been put out of mind by Indonesians as part of their past. The revolution is often discussed in Indonesia, for instance, without mention of the word "Dutch," unless "negotiation" also appears in the sentence. The massacre of 1965–66 has remained unspeakable, aside from the initial murder of the generals. Iconographically, Indonesian soldiers are shown in heroic poses, but seldom, in my experience, with a visible enemy. Violence remains, in my opinion, in the cultural memory of Indonesians, but largely in their repressed memory.

In the Indonesian view, the revolution was a push toward national expression, one which took modernization as its goal along with independence, and for which violence supposedly was a means. However, revolutionary violence was seen by the educated as threatening the achievement of these aims rather than accomplishing them. Its targets uncontrolled, it could mean social as well as national revolution.[12] Only in a few locales was there a successful social revolution, but it may be that in many places violence surpassed even revolutionary goals. It may have been inevitable that such violence was repressed, feared, and built into the national memory under the form of fears of Communist resurgence, sadistic criminals, and social disrupters.

The Suharto regime, which committed several massacres on a scale well worth world cognizance, at the same time contributed to this repression by attributing violence to the unformed *massa*, or "mob," or perhaps "masses."[13] Whatever its real origins, as, for instance, in ordinary criminality, or with the army itself, violence during the Suharto regime was usually associated with the *massa*, a term increasingly used in opposition to "the people," or *rakyat*, though the actual persons who fall under the term are the same. The revolution in official retrospective view, one widely shared, was the work of "the people" under the leadership of the educated. Its violence, put out of memory, reappeared in the fear of the *massa*. With the discontinuation of the populism of Sukarno and the increasing distance of the regime from the people it governed, "the people" receded from view. The *massa* became prominent as the Suharto regime justified itself through the security it claimed to afford in preventing violence. Such a claim required a national menace. The *massa*, as transfigured revolutionaries, spectral communists, and criminals were this menace. Though I say that the *massa* are transfigured revolutionaries, it would be equally accurate to say that they are the decomposed people, by which I mean "the people," deprived of their moral sense, without goals and without form, revolutionaries without the goals of independence or any other aims, which leaves collective violence as their only property.

As we will see, the responsibility for the murders of sorcerers was taken not in the name of the people of certain villages, and not by individuals who had quarreled with the murder victims, but by *massa,* or the "mob." That they accepted a pejorative term for themselves indicates how desperate they were for a form of identification of any sort. To murder in the name of "the people" would be an assertion that this violence was justified within a moral framework. To claim to be the *massa* means claiming an incoherent violence, one resorted to desperately, as we have seen was the case, and without reflection. *Massa,* in that use, as a mere negative term, that is, "not the *rakyat,*" is the analogue to *tukang sihir* or *tukang santet,* the Javanese "witch," in this respect. It indicates not an instrumental violence but possession by violence of those who become murderers, just as witches are said to be possessed by lethal spirits.

One would not expect the word *massa* to be used, not only because it is pejorative but also because until recently it most commonly designated an element belonging to the city rather than the countryside. That villagers applied it to themselves, given the historical evolution of that word, shows how violence during the Suharto regime took on a hidden attraction which we can only in part attribute to its subterranean transformations.

The word *massa* is ambiguous in the first place because of its honorable connotations in the past. In the Suharto period it came to indicate people whose violence is without goals, and at the same time those whose violence is captured by nefarious members of the political elite for the latter's own purposes through deception. (The *massa* are easily deceived, being, like the *rakyat*, without the capacity of formulating their own goals.) Thus, any group calling themselves "the *massa*" indicates that it is violent and that its violence is pure of any aim, and at the same time, its members enter themselves into the vocabulary of Indonesian political discourse in such a way that they can be used for certain aims, though these do not originate in themselves. As we will see, the witch hunters were thought by some to have been manipulated from outside. From their own point of view, however, they acted without goals, insofar as they acted with an urgency so great that it precluded any formulation or consideration of their actions. To say that they acted against witches and thus had a goal is to overlook that to say "witch" is merely to expel an unbearable hatred, violence, and the feeling of being possessed. Any object, simply because it is exterior, might do. But afterward, as we will see, these groups justified their acts. If they did so without leaders to speak for them, it indicates that they had a source of political action outside constituted discourse. They are the *massa*, but they are then close to being revolutionaries.

During the revolution, there were examples of such pure violence and they came at moments when the other was obscured. In the accounts of revolutionary fighters, violence sometimes appears blind, occurring at times when there is no cognizance of the identities of those surrounding one. What was left was killing, which, in its disregard of the surrender of the eventual victims, can be called murder. Here is the account of one revolutionary youth:

No more enemies were taken prisoner; they all died, they had to die. The corpses of the enemy were left sprawled out; the destruction continued. Forward, destroy, kill, and kill only.

The writer left his post in the kitchen in order to join the killing:

No matter that the enemy was running away in complete disarray and with hands in the air. We were all mad; mad to shoot the enemy.[14]

When he calls himself "mad" (and after the revolution he was hospitalized for his violent tendencies), he means that the desire to kill made his victims' identities secondary. It was as "enemies" that they surrendered, but their signals were of no consequence. There was something else about them, beyond their status as "enemies," that made it urgent that they be killed. Seen in overall perspective, the violence toward neighbors was similar in its disregard of social identity. This similarity between East Javanese witch hunts and revolutionary actions could indicate the return of a historical situation, but it could equally well show the autonomy of a destructive impulse whose origins are distinct from any particular social situation. Such an impulse is held back under ordinary situations, but it can emerge when, for a variety of reasons, the capacity to see the other and to be seen by him is blunted. But we have more to understand about the relation between murder, the creation of corpses, and the inability to see oneself in the eyes of others or to see others in their social identities before we can draw conclusions.

This account of a revolutionary recalls a Javanese practice called *keroyokan*, which is a form of *main hukum sendiri*, or "taking the law into one's own hands," at least seen from the outside.[15] It consists of a spontaneously formed mob chasing, catching, and usually beating to death a thief or other culprit. It occurs usually in markets or in villages or city neighborhoods. To my knowledge, the victim is always an outsider, which makes recent cases of witchcraft anomalous, except when one pauses to think that the new witch is, underneath his appearance as neighbor, the embodiment of a foreign force. In the case of a traffic accident, for instance, involving a villager struck by a passing motorist, a group of men often quickly forms to hunt down the outsider. In the market, petty thieves, or those suspected of being such, are often the victims.

Middle-class Indonesians often take *keroyokan* to be a primitive form of justice and they disapprove of it. I have heard it explained by scholars as a continuation of village justice after law codes from the state were imposed. Some see it as a desperate recourse to justice in the face of the notorious failure of the Indonesian courts, in which, it is commonly known, decisions are for sale. Lacking justice, the *rakyat*, the people, take it upon themselves to see that it is done. There is a reflection of this in the statement that the *massa* took vengeance (*dendam*) against witches. But one cannot see *keroyokan* as a form of class conflict since, judging from newspaper accounts, the victims and the murderers are overwhelmingly from the same class.

The problem with these lines of explanation is the difficult word "justice." One might better reserve the word for occasions that are reflected upon and allow the hearing of various voices. In *keroyokan* there is a single sentiment (to avoid the word "opinion") and it is formed (to avoid the phrase "decided upon") nearly instantly. Thieves are often killed for stealing the most trivial items, and this in the moments after they are caught, usually after a chase. In a neighborhood in which I lived in Surakarta, a man was killed for stealing a towel, for instance, and this is common.

My concern here is not moral. It is to understand how it is that a group with murder in mind can form so rapidly. Indeed, the root of the word *keroyokan* means "to spread," as in "an opinion spreads." Something triggers a response and it is practically instantaneous. Justice, as I say, is considered. This reaction is automatic. But what is it that triggers it? It is always an instance of aggression. Not all crimes are aggressive, of course. And those which are not do not figure in *keroyokan*.

Aggression triggers *keroyokan* but not in the first place as a matter of justice if that means certain norms have been violated. In that case, there could be a discussion of the merits and an interpretation of the facts. This is, as I have said, precluded, giving an unbalanced result: small losses lead to murder. Aggression in these cases is unbearable. It produces, as with witchcraft, murder as the solution. Reflection is not merely avoided, it is impossible. Aggression here is the equivalent of "death" in the cases of witchcraft. One is already invaded by it. One wants, in fact, insists, on banishing aggression and one is the aggressor oneself.

There is a common reaction which means that the inability to tolerate aggression is common. One would like to say that such a reaction is part of Javanese culture. But it seems to me, rather, that it is a failure of culture. In Java there are functioning modes of discussion and recognized ways to formulate community opinion. These are disabled when certain forms of aggression appear in certain places.

The aggression of *keroyokan* is material. There is injury or loss. This marks it off from witchcraft, which deals always with phantoms. But these phantoms are, of course, aggressors. They too are violent. The case of the revolutionary suggests that first there is aggression, whether material or phantasmatic, and then there is the obscuring of social identity.

Alternatively, one might see the outbreak of witchcraft not as the breakdown of identity or as triggered by phantasmatic violence but as a form of social conflict. This, indeed, was the supposition I had in mind before going to East Java. Since these witchcraft accusations arise within the village, in examining this supposition we have to look first at the local situation.

The Javanese village remained culturally untransformed all the while that class differences, for instance, became accentuated within it as, during the New Order, developments in the growing of rice increased the differences between owners of land and the landless.[16] It is clear, however, that culturally the village changed but little. One turns to what Clifford Geertz, in his classic description in *The Religion of Java*, called "the core ritual." This is the *selamatan*, or communal feast. The peculiarities of this ritual, described by Geertz, have been interestingly reinflected in the study of Andrew Beatty. East Java is a region of multiple historical influences and has experienced immigration from Madura, Bali, and elsewhere. The *selamatan*, as Beatty sees it, accounts for these differences while suppressing their importance. The ritual symbols, for instance, have "variant readings," allowing participants to silently hold their own, quite divergent beliefs:

Each symbol has a range of meanings which variously contradict, complement, or nest inside each other. The variant readings which comprise this symbolic ambiguity are not the quibbles of specialists over the finer points of tradition; they reflect fundamental differences of a kind we are not accustomed (nor prepared) to expect in ritual. A few of the participants believe that a transcendent and unknowable God created man and sent down the Koran to Muhammad as his sole guide, and that man's preordained actions lead inexorably to heaven or hell. A few others disbelieve in any kind of afterlife, and question the idea of a personal God, the absolute truth of the Koran, and the divine mission of Muhammad. The remainder—perhaps a small majority, though proportions vary—believe in the continued existence of ancestors and perhaps in some form of karma, but not in a Muslim afterlife. But they all pronounce the same words.

What is not said is at least as significant as what is said. And what is said, though it varies little among speakers, varies greatly in meaning. The formulaic explication of the selamatan address, in its generalities, ambiguities, and wordplay, encompasses diversity and seems, superficially, to deny it.[17]

There is an agreement, one might say, not to bring up differences unless it is in order to minimize them, but this does not mean that differences are denied. On the contrary: "There is still a sense that something important has been said and shared. If this is ritual as consensus, it is a peculiar form of consensus which under the surface preserves contradictions and divisions" (51). Differences are, Beatty adds, buried "in common ground," which is "common only in form, not sense." The result is that "instead of consensus . . . we find compromise and provisional synthesis" [provisional because it lasts only as long as the ritual]: a temporary truce among people of radically different orientation" (25). The ritual consists of the insistence, not to say belief, that locally people have ritual form in common. But, as Beatty points out, knowledge of difference persists; a "truce" implies the continued differences of the parties who have agreed to it. If what sets people apart is put aside during the ritual, it seems not to be ever out of mind. Individual interpretation of common symbols is well known to Javanese, who, in my experience, outside the ritual, comment on the ignorance of others. Beatty's use of the word "truce" seems to me apt.

Selamatan are found throughout Java, but they are local in the first place because the spirits that are referred to in the rites are local in their habitats. They are sometimes Muslim spirits just as they are sometimes "Javanese." Even without the form of ghosts, the spirits of the past haunt Java, if one can use that verb in a general sense, by residing in the persons who participate in the *selamatan*, giving them their identities as Muslims or whatever else. One might think of the *selamatan* from this point of view as a ritual which localizes the major historical forces, largely originating outside Java, which have swept through the island. Through the *selamatan*, these historical effects, taking the shape of participants, humans, and spirits of various origin, are given a place. The assertion of these differences is a significant part of the rite, which in effect says that all of these forces have a place.

The *selamatan* thus acknowledges the multiple historical and cultural currents that have passed through Java, perhaps most densely and with the most variety in East Java. It gives them a place in the local community all the while that it arranges that such differences should remain as discrete as possible. Community beliefs in the *selamatan* comprise both those which originated locally and those which came from elsewhere and were localized. Rather than giving precedence to either, the ritual dampens differences between them. But the ritual makes gestures to authorities outside the boundaries of the village, whether Islamic or Hindu, for instance, or national, since the different beliefs of the *selamatan* are associated today as they were in the 1950s with various national political organizations.

During most of the New Order, there was tight government control of religious activities. Moreover, given the danger of standing out, there was, says Beatty, a reluctance to join Muslim mass organizations, with the exception of the Nahdatul Ulama, which had excluded itself from politics to become a cultural and religious organization. This reluctance "reflects a desire not to upset the political status quo rather than a lack of interest among [those with a strong Muslim orientation] in the promotion of Islam" (131). On the other hand, during the final years of the New Order there was also a push beyond the usual boundaries of self-restraint. During the latter part of the New Order, Islam was given an important part in Indonesian politics and culture. With government acquiescence, there was, among the young, "a true missionary spirit" (140), which though kept within the boundaries set by the government certainly upset the "truce" mentioned above. Beatty describes the efforts in one village to bring practices in accord with Islamic belief (cf. chap. 5, especially 134–57). Furthermore, the newly wealthy had, again according to Beatty, little means for enjoying their wealth. One man told Beatty that were he to do so he would offend his neighbors. He thus lived on a scale far below what he might have enjoyed (149).

Given the push made by certain Muslims and the pressure of increased wealth, one would think that the witchcraft accusations might follow the fissures papered over in the *selamatan*. Udi, for instance, might be taken as an example of how someone made himself a target. But our other example is different. Muki was said to have had "only enough to get by on." Nor did violence follow the lines of social division; it was rather a case of the village, or a preponderant element of it, against a single family. Generally speaking, the targets were usually members of the Nahdatul Ulama (N.U.), but the murderers were also. Nor did we find any preponderance of either wealthy or poor accused witches.

This area of Java was the scene of massive killings of Communists by Nahdatul Ulama members in 1965. The remnants of the Left are now distributed among other organizations allowed by the government. One might expect charges of revenge by the descendents of Communists and, in fact, these emerged from the military. But the N.U. itself denied this possibility, reasoning that such a charge would divert guilt from those they assumed to be their political rivals, the army, and would alienate their allies in other parties where descendents of leftists were members. In the N.U. view as expressed to me by its leaders in the city of Banyuwangi, the only divisions at play were between the military and their organization.

The N.U. claimed that there was a hidden identification underneath the charge of witch. They asserted that many Koranic teachers, members of N.U., were targeted. Such people were vulnerable to being called *tukang sihir*, or "witches," not because they actually were so but because they often practiced white magic, helping their neighbors and fellow villagers. They thus left themselves open to confusion. If they were "good witches," as it were, they could also be "bad witches." And, they added, witches had been known for centuries in the area and, they believed, there was such a thing as black magic and it is difficult to know who practices it. Their political opponents used this obscurity to eliminate village N.U. leaders. As I have said, however, it was not only N.U. leaders who were targeted. Nor did we find evidence of outside forces.

What happened in East Java was not communal politics following the weakening of national authority and pressure on the fragile village religious mechanisms for the keeping of order. It was not a case of Muslims against Javanists, or one sort of Muslim against another, or Muslims against Christians. There was rather a collapse of the structures that generate identities and the subsequent surge of untamed impulses.

To take a contrary case, that of Ambon, where there was conflict between Christians and Muslims, preliminary reports suggest that the conflict began with an individual dispute. A bus conductor argues with a passenger who does not want to pay. They turn out to be from neighboring villages. Later, the conductor leads a group of his friends to the other's village to continue the conflict that started on the bus. One village is Christian and the other Muslim. It seems that at this point the conflict becomes one of Muslims versus Christians, though it could have remained one of a dispute of gangs of youths or simply of particular villages. But each side at a certain moment acted in the name of their respective religion.

By contrast, in East Java, with only the apparent exception of acting in the name of the *massa*, no one acted "in the name of." In a village some took action against a witch. Each group who did so acted separately and one by one; there were none of the large-scale actions such as those against mosques and churches in Ambon, where the local origins of the actors was indistinct, or at least unimportant, compared to the religions they espoused. In one instance, in Banyuwangi, one group sought three witches in different neighborhoods. But these were adjacent neighborhoods on the edge of the city and the murderous youths hung out with each other. The witch hunts were the actions of clusters of unself-conscious young men who not only did not but, in my opinion, could not act "in the name of." They lacked the ability to see themselves in assumed identities such as "Christian" or "Muslim" at the moment of the attacks.

Precisely what did not work were the projections and identifications that underlie coherent politics, violent or peaceful. When these identifications are in place, the actors become "the people," or *rakyat*, who are, in Indonesia, always spoken for by their leaders. The *rakyat* sees itself in its leader. The lack of the ability to do so is one condition for these witch hunts, as I understand them. The decomposition of "the people" or the failure to form "a people" left the actors as the mob, as an incoherent group, without any particular identity. *Massa* is a word which indicates this lack and perhaps tries to compensate for it.

The settlement of cases of *tukang santet* in the thirty-six cases we found originated outside the village. The police investigated and, as usual in Indonesia, arrests were assumed to mean guilt. While not everyone was satisfied that all those guilty were arrested, no one, to our knowledge, protested that those arrested had not participated in the murders. Usually, the arrests meant that the village settled down. Families who had been attacked resumed amicable relations with people whom they suspected or even knew were among the killers of their fathers or mothers or spouses. It was not only the police who participated in making peace. The local authorities, meaning the village headman, the camat or government administrator above the headman, the police, the army, and often officials of the Nahdatul Ulama and other organizations convened meetings of the village and explained the need for national law to take its course and for villagers not to take the law into their own hands.

It was astonishing to me that feuds or vendettas did not ensue. But that they did not testifies to the restoration of authority. We can begin to see why there were no vendettas when we see how it is that the survivors of murdered "witches" asked for justice. In every case, the family protested that the murdered person was not a witch. ("If he were," said one, "I would have killed him myself.") Usually, peace was made, as I have said, and the families of the village got along as well as they had before the incident. In some cases, better, as one person closely related to a murder victim told me, since "they [the killers] know now that what they did was wrong and they are sorry." Whether this was true or the sort of denial that character-izes the *selamatan* is not clear. But that these Javanese, after the slaying of their fathers, mothers, and brothers can expect to be on good terms with their murderers is revealing. It means, in the first place, that what prompts the desire for revenge, the inescapable memory of the murdered father or mother, does not press urgently. The funeral rituals had the effect they are supposed to have everywhere of separating the living and the dead. The reason for their effectiveness is both that authorities intervened, thus reas-suring villagers, and that the expected result of Javanese funeral rituals is not the sort of transformation of memory that we usually associate with mourning, as we have already explained. Furthermore, the murderers usu-ally attended the funeral, though this was not so in the case of Muki and in at least one other instance. Once the active memory of the dead was given a place, the urge for vengeance lessened. Though, as we have seen, it de-pends also on the quality of the memory.

Let me give an example. Fathidullah, sixty-five, who lived on the outskirts of the city of Banyuwangi and was a retired employee of the pro-vincial government, was murdered when, as usual, a group of men came to the house, saying, simply, "tukang sihir," broke in, dragged the man out of his bedroom, killed him, and dragged his body to the main road. The man's wife and teenage son were in the next room. They could do noth-ing and were left untouched. Eventually, seven men were arrested, includ-ing one, Dul, who, according to the widow "hated" her husband and was, in addition, "arrogant." The mob had worn masks and its members were therefore referred to as "Ninja";; they spoke Indonesian rather than Java-nese. But, Fathidullah's son told me, they were all local; they had used Indonesian as part of their disguise. I asked how they knew. Did they recognize the voices? The adolescent son broke in:

> It wasn't that. They were my friends.
>
> JS: How did you know that?
>
> They asked me to pardon them.
>
> JS: And did you?
>
> Yes.
>
> JS: And how are things now?
>
> Just fine.

He added that he hangs out with them just as before. This young man's mother still has a great deal of animosity toward Dul and his family, even though she meets Dul's wife on the street and things are as usual. Her son, on the other hand, found it easy to forgive his friends. They, he said, just went along because they were asked. They were not the real killers. If the memory of his father pressed on him, he could not have forgiven his friends so easily. Even his mother, more affected than her son, is satisfied that the killers have been arrested and has asked that nothing more to be done.

In many cases, the dead individual returned to his family in the form of a hallucination or a dream. Sometimes the spirit advised that nothing further be done. "I am reconciled [*pasrah*]" said one. Another said, "Don't answer defamation [*fitnah*] with defamation." Sometimes the spirit was silent. Each time a phantom appeared, the body was again whole, the person nicely dressed. These are what we might call productive spirits, restoring the harmony of social life. They ask nothing. If, by contrast, the body were to be seen again in the mutilated form left by the murderers, it would be almost a demand for vengeance. In place of the memory of the mutilated corpse, there instead appeared the image of the dead person restored to his appearance when alive but in the form of a spirit. Such spirits made it easier, no doubt, to put murder in the past. Even if such spirits reappeared without being summoned and even if they demanded something, the effect would be similar. The unrelenting and uncontrollable memory of the dead could be assuaged by answering their demands. Indonesian curing rituals work by establishing a response to what otherwise cannot be answered and has gone un-understood until revealed by the curer. When, however, the spirit requirements are met and illness still persists, sorcery is often suspected. Sorcery, that is, is often a result of the failure of exchange with the spirit world. The result of which is, once again, an urge for vengeance as the only possible alleviation of pressing psychic demand.

The capacity to form spirits is thus a dampening of the call for revenge, though I would not dare to say that the results are final. One can think of Javanese spirits as the form given to repeated urgent inner insistence. Javanese spirits, if this hypothesis is correct, are manufactured out of involuntary memories given the forms of ghosts. But when images do not take shape, sorcery comes to mind. Sorcery, whose locus always remains obscure, is taken as the place from which psychic demands issue, albeit incoherently. The ghosts which appear soon after death articulate memories, even as they conceal the immediacy of death. The "sorcerer," by contrast, marks the point where the failure to manufacture images becomes evident.

The question remains why disputes were often brought up when there were charges of sorcery. In order to answer, it is better to disentangle the elements. Disputes, which always exist and which were extant before the sorcery outbreak, are usually manageable without violence. The unbearable menace that is sorcery comes and goes. The survivors of these attacks clearly had difficulty believing that they could be objects of hatred. We will see that it came as a revelation to them and that they were sure it was unjustified. But extreme violence left without an origin would be all the more menacing. It is not surprising that it finds its purported source in those with whom one quarrels.

But if one eliminates dispute as the cause of the accusations, one has to explain the hatred of the murderers. One can point to the conditions for its arousal in Indonesian political conditions, though these conditions do not completely account for the menace and the murder and the urge for display that are at the core of sorcery. We will return to the question later. For now, we can see that citing disputes and conditions in the village localizes forces which are national and perhaps even global in their origins and gives a precise location for psychic forces, perhaps panhuman, which are nowhere to be mapped. Citing disputes thus normalizes the uncanny.

The impulse to normalize explains why the witch hunts were set within the village rather than the area as a whole. Mobs acted against their neighbors. A mob, at least under the name *massa*, is new to the village, as we have said.[18] It, of course, denies the validity of "neighbor." What is at work is the transformation of village categories, quite against the will of everyone, murderers and victims alike. That fellow villagers were the targets is better understood when one starts the other way around: mobs formed within villages. The word *massa*, "mob," is at once evidence of the breakdown of identities for causes that arose outside the village and the attempt to restore identity by the use of a word recognized from descriptions of national events. It is the attempt to give the uncanny a face, even if that face is one's own, and to give it a place within the village. After that, it can be dealt with. The witch is sought out as the hoped for counterpart of the possessed mob.

The *selamatan*, I have said, localizes differences. In 1998, social differences had dissolved and the bearers of menace had not been identified. The threat had to be dealt with differently. "Witch" is the name given to a nationally derived menace to make it part of the local scene. "Witch," I have pointed out, means "diverter of death." In that sense, the murderers were also themselves witches. But they appeared on the scene in the form of the mob, in the impossible but understandable attempt to give death—now no longer natural, originating elsewhere, outside the village, and thought now to be present—not a permanent place in the local community, of course, but a temporary identity. As the mob, they indicate that they are moved by forces outside the village. But as an entity limited by the boundaries of the village, they say that a new force has a local form. The mob takes shape in the village at the point where the usual explanations of the uncanny no longer avail. Blaming the witch further localizes this force otherwise foreign to the beliefs hitherto surrounding witchcraft.

The sentiment that sorcery not only exists but is imminent and that perhaps "I" am a sorcerer can arise, it seems, out of nothing. N.A., a man we visited in Malang Selatan, heard that there was a list of sorcerers, that the name "N.A." was on it. Fearing that he was going to be attacked, he fled and spent time away from home before returning. His younger brother said that another N.A. was the real sorcerer. Everyone knew the other

N.A. was a sorcerer, he said. Which meant also that everyone knew his brother was not the person designated. But despite this, our N.A. felt that the name could well refer to him. No one made any threats to this man; no one stoned his house or said anything to him except that the name "N.A." was on a list. The existence of the list itself has not been verified. This man obviously felt that, nevertheless, there might be something to the accusation, though he denied he ever had anything to do with sorcery. He remained terrified at the time of our visit. A man's name can suddenly designate his possession by sorcery. Anyone at all can become accused of witchcraft; by himself, by others.

In Banyuwangi, in a neighborhood on the edge of the city, Asari was summoned by the head of the neighborhood (R.T.) after someone fell ill and said Asari bewitched him. Asari, according to one of his daughters, said, "No, it is not true. Its simply that there are bad feelings by someone toward me as the result of an inheritance dispute." Then another person fell ill, and Asari was summoned by the local military official (the *kora-mil*, or military subdistrict commander) and told to move because his life was in danger. He went to a religious school in the countryside for two years and then returned. Again there was trouble, and again he was told to move. He said, "So far as whether I am killed or not, it doesn't matter. I am not guilty." A week later, his house was stoned and the windows broken. That night, the *massa* (said to be all local young men) came. They took his daughter, cut off her hair, and held her. They told her that if her father did not return, she herself would be killed and his house and the six houses of his relatives which surrounded it would be burned down. They made her sign a blank sheet of paper so that later they could write whatever they wanted on it, but it did not become clear to me what it was they thought they might write. Asari returned from the military post and he was killed.

Asari's daughter insists that there was never a problem with the neighbors. The inheritance dispute, over a piece of land, was years ago. The brother-in-law of her mother used the land to put up a house, then fell ill and said that it was the fault of her father, Asari, but it was all in the past. Asari and his relatives wanted to make the violence of their neighbors understandable: there was a dispute, someone was wrong and nonetheless tried to blame Asari. Asari himself had forgotten the whole thing. This explanation risks leaving the animosity of the village as a whole baseless.

Why the entire village set itself against them is left unclear. But the concern of Asari's relatives was to say that Asari was not a witch and that they are not witches. They are completely without guilt of any sort, and this overrides their concern to explain why Asari was singled out as a sorcerer.

We spoke with ten or so of Asari's children and other relatives. I asked them if they were still afraid. One person answered, "No, we are innocent and Dad didn't do anything wrong." His daughter said,

> They [meaning his killers] are afraid because the leader has not yet been arrested. Now that those who were arrested are about to be released from jail, he might well be identified. But Dad didn't do anything bad, he was never a witch, he never did anything. I should know. I am not guilty. I did nothing wrong. They want to kill me, let them go ahead.

Her answer, which is typical of others as well, implies that "they" might well kill again.

As she reports her father's words, she repeats his sentiments about him on her own behalf. The import of her words is not that death is unimportant. If it were a light matter, there would be no accusations of witchcraft in the first place. It is rather that the face she presents to the world represents her exactly as she is; the same is true of her father. They are not different than they appear; they are not witches. On the other hand, the killers refuse to face her. When she meets them on the street, "They look ahead but I bend forward and stare at them. They are afraid."

Fear, here, is based on the emergence of a hidden quality. She is not guilty, she does not fear that she will appear to be a witch. If she does, it is their misperception. Death, in her discourse, is merely a side effect of misunderstanding. Or rather, being killed through a misunderstanding is nothing compared to fearing that the quality of witchcraft, if one can so speak, will emerge. She is innocent of witchcraft; her father was innocent of witchcraft. They therefore are, and were, without fear.

But she was not always fearless. When her father was first killed, she was afraid to talk about it. But then she thought, "Dad is already dead, what can I lose?" She was afraid at first of "the people who count" (*orang besar*). But she gave herself the same reassurance, "I have nothing to lose. I am not guilty." She is upset with the police and "the people who count" for not arresting the instigator of her father's murder.[19] I asked her why, then, not do to them what they did to you? She said, "We can't. The people who count, they can do it, but we, who don't count [*orang kecil*], we can't." In reality, her neighbors do not have a social position different from hers. But in her mind, they have connections. "They know the police, they know the army," and they are protected. On the other hand, she feels she is without recourse to the official world. For instance, according to her, the complaint they filed with the military when threats were first made was lost; at least the military claim they have no record of it. For her, it is an indication of how connections work and what it means not to have them.

Justice, for her, depends on those above. She is convinced that in the world as it is properly constituted, "the people who count" will recognize her lack of guilt. In her thinking, an ideal government would, and in a certain way already does, see her for what she is. It is not only that "We can't" make our own justice, though that is what the people who count can do, according to her, and perhaps that is exactly what the witch killers did. It is also that this ideal authority exists already for her. Somewhere—probably at a level above that of the local authorities—and somehow, they know the truth. Therefore, she is not afraid to show her face. The problem is that she has no access to that structure and the killers do.

An idealized structure exists for her and reflects her innocence back to her. She has no doubt that in showing her face to the world she shows her true face and not a mask that hides witchcraft. She recounts how she stares them down and how they, too, know what she knows about herself. Her confidence comes from believing that true authority knows her and, for that reason, her knowledge of her own experience is right: "I am not a witch."

She has confidence and pride in her ability to formulate her case. She told me, "I only went to school through the third grade, and I can't even sign my name. But my mouth, its not bad, eh?" The assumptions behind her thinking are evident also in the next example.

Atmoyo, a Madurese living in the mountains off a road which even motorbikes cannot take if there are heavy rains, was killed. His daughter, who seemed to me to be in her thirties or forties and who was a widow, said this:

Dad was accused of being a witch by the neighbors. He was a farmer and went to the fields everyday. He wasn't a witch. He was just ordinary [*biasa-biasa saja*]. Every day he would take part in a neighborhood gathering [*arisan*], he would be with his friends [*silaturahmin*, a word popular in the New Order which means something like "forging the bonds of friendship"], and so on.

Then the house was stoned. My brother was in Bali working. I waited till midnight for Dad to come home. Next morning I went to where they were having the meeting for the neighborhood gathering. I saw blood. I followed the traces. I just followed them. Then I looked for him in the gardens and in the fields. Then, at five in the morning, on the edge of the road, covered with banana leaves, there he was. His leg was cut off. He was crushed in all over. His neck had a rope around it and his trunk was cut almost all the way through. (She weeps).

I waited till 9 o'clock to report to the village headman, to tell the police, the doctor, and so on. Then he was brought home. He was bathed like an ordinary corpse. Why not? He was already a corpse.

On top of the leaves, the killers had left a page torn off a calendar from the year before. On the reverse they had written:

Atmoyo
Witch
Beaten by the mases [sic]

She went on:

He was tortured. If you saw him, Mister, if you saw him, you would be afraid to look. There was no proof. What was the proof? The real proof. Where was it?

Everyone has to die, Mister. But not tortured like that, Mister.

They arrested four people. In fact, there were lots and lots of people who came to the house. I couldn't see them all. I was afraid, I couldn't look at them one by one. In fact, they threatened to whip me. They wouldn't believe Dad wasn't here. Really. They came into the house, armed with whips, looking for Dad. They took lots. On top of everything else, they were thieves too.

Please, have something to drink.

They cut him up. Just cut him up.

She went on to say, in answer to our questions, that there had never been a problem with the neighbors. Later, we learned from her and her brother that in fact her father's brother who lived next door had had a dispute with him. He was being sought for the murder, but had fled.

I asked her if she were still afraid.

I was afraid at first. When they were making an issue of it, I was terrorized [*diteror*] before, afraid. Now, I'm not afraid any more.

I only became aware when the neighbors were called [by the "aparat" to a public meeting). "Oh, the neighbors hate my dad." Then it became clear, and so I was not afraid.

She then added that she, too, had been accused of helping her father in his witchcraft.

After four of them were sent to jail and there were no more accusations, sure, I thought, if the accusations start again, I will just report them [to the aparat]. Since here the people are ignorant [bodoh].

At the time, Mom, if she had to leave the house for so much as to go to the well, she shook and trembled. (She imitates her).

If my father had not died, I wouldn't be brave enough to speak this way. I became a skillful talker.

She then imitated how she was before, stuttering and moving her mouth without issuing words.

And if I thought about Dad, I [and she imitates her inability to speak again, this time with noises and without opening her mouth) . . . [20]

Her father's death and the threats against her left her speechless. But, like Asari's daughter, what gave her the courage and the skill to speak was the realization of the situation: "Oh, the neighbors hate my dad." It is their fault, they are wrong. He is not a tukang santet. And she is not, either. She knows, "I am not a witch," and she can speak again and, like Asari's daughter above, it seems, for the first time ever.

Both of these women learn how to speak, how to articulate their place and, one can say, their identities when the necessity arises to deny that they and their fathers are or were witches. Their capacity to do so comes not simply from the realization of conflict in which, to defend themselves, they must take a position contrary to the majority of their neighbors. It is not sheer need that makes them skillful speakers, it is the courage they gain once they realize that, in the eyes of political authority, real or ideal, they are innocent. Once the meeting is held at which, no doubt, the neighbors proclaim that her father was a witch and the political authorities tell her she cannot take the law into her own hands, Atmoyo's daughter speaks. Both women reflect in their voices the situation that has been verified for them by political authority. They do not only speak their convictions; they say truths that for them originate outside themselves and whose content is the denial not merely of acts of sorcery but of having a sorcerer's being.

One could put it this way. When these women realize "They hate my Dad" [and me], they also realize "I am not a witch." Witchcraft, here, is lethal hatred which emerges autonomously. Anyone who bears that hatred, who is a witch, has to be careful in the face of others, not because these others will murder them, but because this fatal force will show itself. The witch will emerge. The witch emerges despite the will of the person who bears the witch inside her. But when she sees "They hate my dad," which means first of all, "They hate," it is they who are the witches. That they murder confirms it. Thus, a reversal: the witch is the murderer of so-called witches.

This exchange of the place of hatred and lethal force precedes any named agent. The people who come to the house are not, in her account, even "the *massa*." Nor are they neighbors, nor are they people with a grudge. They are merely numerous; so numerous that they are not identifiable: "There were lots and lots of people who came to the house. I couldn't see them all. I was afraid, I couldn't look at them one by one." Their numbers and their violence ("they threatened to whip me") make identification impossible. They are not merely anonymous, in the sense of having no name which might be later discovered. In their incoherence, they are without a name, for the group or for the individuals who are part of the group. These are the *massa* but before the name was invented. We would say that they are literally anonymous, except that the literal fails; language does not apply.

I thought it strange since the police later arrested her neighbors and thus they were recognizable to others, that she could not recognize even one. She insisted that she could not. Perhaps it was through fear of reprisals, though I do not think that is the case. One might think that large numbers offer the chance to find one or more people who give clues to their identities. But for her, numbers meant that she was overwhelmed. She could only see them in the aggregate, as a force. No "one" did the awful deed. They were the appearance of violence with nothing and no one behind that appearance. Sheer lethal force itself manifested itself to her.

Later, the *massa* appear under their collective name. Should these people who hate try to act again, she will report them to the authorities.

They are *bodoh*, which means "ignorant." This is also the usual characteristic of the *rakyat*, whose need of leadership is predicated on being *bodoh*.
Once she understands that "they" are *bodoh* and that she can simply report
them, the "they" here are somewhere between the *massa* and the *rakyat*.
They are the *rakyat* insofar as they are subject to control by the authorities. They are the *massa* insofar as they are not. In either case, the killers, in
her discourse, have a defined place on the Indonesian political scene. She
knows about them.

She has given hatred a place. It may be spontaneous and lethal in its
expression. But it is subject to control. There is spontaneous hatred and
it reveals itself in those who are inhabited by it, despite their wishes. But
there are also authorities who know it and who keep it in place. Within
this structure, "they," the murderers, have it in them and she does not.

At that moment, she learns to speak. She does not have to fear, as
she did initially, that she might be a witch, as her father might have been
a witch, too. In that case, she, like any witch, would reveal herself without
her knowledge. She knows this, not merely through the change of places between those charged with witchcraft and those who killed, but also
through the authorities whose presence in the relationship locates witchcraft in the *massa* and keeps it in place and harmless. She is thus sure of her
knowledge. Being certain, she speaks without hesitation. "Witchcraft," a
possibility of everyone, herself included, has been ruled out in her case.

Suppose she were a witch. How would witchcraft reveal itself? With
the man we have discussed who thought he might be a witch it was a
question of the rays of his face, visible only to certain experts, themselves
often thought to be witches. These women do not fear distant experts.
They speak of those they meet who live nearby. When Atmoyo's daughter
thought of the dismembered corpse of her father, she was overcome by her
identification with her father's corpse. She tried to say what she had in her
mind. Her mouth would not open, but she emitted noises nonetheless.
She tried to emit, to exteriorize, the dead inside her. If witchcraft is lethal
power that must be passed on, she was at that moment a witch herself, albeit a failed one. Witchcraft announced itself in the noises that her mouth
held back.

At that moment, could she only speak, surely she would have called
out "revenge." But her failed words issued as broken sounds. It is not mere-

ly that she could not formulate what she felt. It is rather that she was without words but with something else that I have betrayed by saying what she would have said. In retrospect, after the fact, there can only be a betrayal of a moment of nonrepresentation. And yet, past that moment, in retrospect, "revenge" would seem the only word possible. But no word was possible.

One could say that Atmoyo's daughter was divided against herself; the mouth being the living daughter and the noise the effects of her mutilated dead father. In that case, "she" was overwhelmed by death. In the other instance, the mouth opened, sound issued, but it was stuttering and babbling, not words nor anything that could be mistaken for language. What came out was violence, not because it was deliberate aggression against whoever was present with her, though it must have been unbearable for them to hear and watch her. It was violence because it was energy that overcame, one can say, annihilated, whatever it worked on rather than transforming it into a product: speech. She, too, was a witch at that instant. She remained so until she could say, "They hate me" and "They hate my father," when they, the killers, become the witches.

There is nothing in these women that can withstand the violence of the corpse. In the battle between themselves and hatred, they are overpowered. To regain themselves and exteriorize their lethal hatred, they need a source of themselves which they find only outside themselves. Atmoyo's daughter finds it in the aparat; the other woman, in the vaguer "eyes" she imagines have her in view. They can see themselves seen, once the government intervenes, in the scenes and prescriptions of the authorities. These women gain a place in the confines delineated by authority. Then they can say—and it is precisely their saying, their speech, that is, of course, at stake—"They hate me." The pronouns of that sentence, then, have referents. The "me" or "I" that was overcome by death comes back into existence. Not by the sheer opposition of "me" and "them," because the "them" before that point was only murderous force. It was an absolute other, a confrontation with something which could not be "faced," which offered no face of its own and so took no cognizance of one's own face; whose appearance offered no reflection of oneself. ("There were lots and lots of people who came to the house. I couldn't see them all. I was afraid, I couldn't look at them one by one.")

The experiences of these women might form moments in a logic of the sublime: "I almost died, I survived." But their identification with the corpse is so complete that instead the "I" disappears, so one can not even rewrite their experience afterward as "I was almost a corpse; I almost died." "I," here, has no referent in Javanese when it refers to the time of death; the gap between the two states is not formulatable. Instead, there is a sequence; first one is in the same state as the person killed, one is annihilated. This state is not named or conceptualized. It is followed by a denial: "I am not a witch," meaning, "I am not dead. I do not have death in me. Death will not betray me. I am alive. I belong to a certain society and a certain polity." The time of identification with the corpse is left without value for the present, unlike the logic of the sublime.

These women are without pathos; they do not speak about the possible loss of themselves. They insist instead on their living participation in their society, which is to say, that they are alive and were never dead or close to it. In the absence of a tradition of the sublime there is no attempt to say what it is that they "almost" experienced. Instead, they speak of a violence that they faced and which remained foreign to them. What they learn later is that "They hate us," which is to say that "they" are filled with violence and we are not. Before that point, when they might speak about their own possible deaths, they are so closely identified with the corpse that they cannot speak. When they recount their own experiences afterward, it is to say, in effect, that they were faced with actors they could not recognize and by something they could not name. They tell us of a moment of no recognition. They speak instead of numbers. We are brought as close to a description of absolute violence and an other who is totally other as perhaps we could ever be taken.

The mythologizing that usually accompanies death begins not with dyadic confrontation—me/death—but with the political "aparat" and one's connection to it. This mythology is, of course, that of political authority. The myth is that only political authority and only that particular political authority will do. It is just here that one sees one of the great crimes of the New Order: it left intact, pristinely unchanged, the idea of "the people," whether under the name *rakyat* or *massa*, as speechless and needing leadership to speak for it or to confer the right to speak. Nonetheless, it was the eventual assertion of authority that stopped the survivors of witch hunts from trying to take vengeance themselves and so stopped further murder. This, however, took time.

There are historical conditions for the outburst of witch hunts, though they are inadequate to entirely explain the events. Witch hunts broke out in East Java at the moment when established political structure seemed to no longer take notice of village life. At that time, in the absence of the ability to rely on the "aparat," as the local authorities—the police, the military, the civilian officials—are called, witches appeared in the world. It is not that there was chaos in the political realm and a real breakdown of authority. Things worked as well as they had. But with the end of the long, long Suharto regime, it seemed to villagers as though the state was no longer in touch with them. When, for instance, Asari's daughter says that her report to the military about the attack on them was lost and that she and her family had no connection to power but others had, she does not complain that authority should not work through connections. She complains that she and her family had none. Again, the complaint is not how the regime used power but that it did not use it, at least for "us," it being understood that this "us," those without access to political authority, have to be added up to form the village population.

The idea that security depends on connections to those in power is at least as old as the Indonesian republic. Connections had been established well before independence between members of the political class and those outside it, though what patterns of prenationalist culture they might have drawn on has still to be established.[21] No doubt, under the pressure of the economic stress of the time, they had practical consequences. In the Suharto period, with the end of populism, "networks," for lack of a precise term, became widespread. Through them, one had what was for most the only access, real or imaginary, to the state. The policies of the regime, which took little account of the general welfare, were thus sometimes ameliorated for a few, while many others had the illusion that they too could find their way to authority.

These "networks" should not be confused with the patron-client relations one finds in one form in the Philippines, in another in Thailand. They rest not so much on a sense of obligation as on familiarity. One "knows" someone, who knows someone, even if the starting point is only knowing someone by reputation. The basis is recognition; one is somehow familiar with a person who is, directly or remotely, connected to the government. Far more frequently than for a political gain or a furthering of interests, the ritualized recognition through which these networks are established is a denial of the opposite: "I do not recognize," or perhaps "I seem to recognize but I do not know how." Not to know someone who knows someone is tantamount to feeling excluded from the nation as conceived by its members. One is all too aware that powerful forces exist in the state and that without connections to them, one is at best unprotected and at worst their victim.

Connections to the state occur in the idiom of the family. Kenji Tsuchiya pointed out that the Boedi Oetomo, an early nationalist organization, instituted the use of kinship terms, "Father" and "Mother" in particular, as terms of address and reference equivalent to the English "Mister" and "Mrs." among its members, and thus established them in national society.[22] As Benedict R. O'G. Anderson pointed out, during the revolution the terms meaning "sibling" and "comrade" were used; then, after the transfer of sovereignty, these were slowly replaced by "Father" and "Mother."[23] These terms were, then, part of the Indonesian national scene practically from the beginning, as, indeed, were questions of the family: the authority of fathers, in particular. At the beginning of Indonesian nationalism there was both a fear that the authority of fathers would disappear and a hope that this would mean the end of traditional systems of authority considered antithetical to the modernity nationalists aspired to. The use of "Father" and "Mother" indicated a conservative tendency in the face of the fear of the weakness of authority. At the same time, it inscribed kinship in the context of nationalism. In English, "Mother" and "Mrs." are not interchangeable, indicating the difference of the realms public and private. In Indonesian, the equivalent kinship term is used as a general term of address, indicating a certain conflation of realms. The history of this confounding is still to be written. What is clear, however, is that, from the beginning, it was made to bolster the authority of nationalism and weaken that of traditional kinship structures by displacing the authority of the latter from the family and from ethnic unities to the nation.

To call the set of connections that linked one with the state "networks" is to reify hazy imaginary connections. One can best understand the idea of such linkages by thinking of them as familial or, more accurately, genealogical. The person who traces his genealogy knows at the start he has ancestors; his task is to find them. In the same way, someone like Asari's daughter knows that she knows people in the local aparat. She expects to find them when she has need. To discover that they, in return, do not know her has certain consequences which can be understood in terms of the history of the New Order.

The New Order began with an enormous massacre. Under the pretense that Communists had attempted a coup, hundreds of thousands were killed in 1965–66. The army encouraged local groups to do the killing or did it itself. After the establishment of the new regime the government declared itself always vigilant against further uprisings, which means it suspected a segment of its own citizens. When, by the 1980s, Communists were no longer part of the lived experience of young people, the regime killed thousands of people with tattoos, on the grounds that they were criminals. They might have brought such people to trial, but, as with the Communists, under the pretense of urgency they were massacred. Thus, the government verified its suspicions: there is an element interior to Indonesian society which by its very nature, as opposed to its deeds, is violent.

The effects of this in popular political assumptions were double. It was generally believed during the New Order, and still now, though to a lesser extent, that there was danger from within Indonesian society and particularly from its lower strata. Communists and criminals were endowed with a mythical power to regenerate themselves, and with a force of social disruption that seemed all the greater because it was so little evident in the world. At the same time, it was also recognized, this time with all too much evidence, that the state, through its army, could and did act with great violence against Indonesians.

Indonesian society was thus riven. On one side were good citizens and on the other were those who threatened violence and massive political and social disruption. The difficulty, particularly if one belonged to the lower strata, is that it was not clear who was on which side of this rift. The elimination of Communists did not end the threat of Communists. The elimination of "criminals" did not end criminality. The source of the menace is not evident. Recognition by the state, therefore, is reassuring, because it means that one does not make up a part of those who the state, in its omniscience, finds menacing.

The Indonesian experience is the inverse of the usual European notion of totalitarianism. In the latter, to be seen by the state is to be vulnerable; the state is a source of terror. It is the Indonesian genius to make the state at once the chief source of murder and also the means of granting not merely immunity but innocence to its citizens. But for that one needs to be connected to it. Those whom the state attacked were, of course, also recognized by the state, but as being without the connections that made one a part of the large community and therefore without the social definition that precludes the definition of oneself as violent and disruptive.

The perceived ending of state surveillance thus produced suspicion, first of all of oneself. Someone else knows one better than one does oneself. When this agent of recognition disappears, the reassurance it gives of one's innocence goes with it. It is possible that one is guilty. Guilty of what is now the first question. Guilty of being a witch, meaning that one has a capacity for hatred and that one might have done anything. One cannot draw on one's own experience of oneself to know one's own nature. This situation pertained during the revolution, when nationalists were afraid of being known as traitors even though nothing objective justified that claim. After Suharto fell, the aparat, which knew who one was, was felt to be temporarily out of commission. Nothing prevented the most heinous thoughts about oneself from being credible. In a hierarchical tradition, the impulse toward hierarchy does not end with the collapse of government. Peasants still looked to authority. Not finding it, they assumed they were seen by another power, this time one that penetrated them and that was dissociated from extant political structures, in fact, unlocatable and devoid of benevolence. From this arose the possibility of being oneself a witch.

The first defense was to find someone else responsible. "Witch" rather than "Communist" or "criminal" was the form that accusation took. For the general menace within Indonesia to have a name, it had to be part of a particular scene. Within the national context, that name was "Communist" or "criminal." But, for the moment, the local was severed from the national; indeed, this supposition is critical to our explanation. Menace had thus to be formulated within the immediate context. The menace was national but its appearance was local. "Witch" localized malevolent agents in the way that the *selamatan* put Muslims, "Javanists," Hindus, and so on, on the local scene, though of course without the same capacity to institutionalize their appearances. Seen from the place of those possessed or obsessed by feelings of overwhelming catastrophe, those closest were the unrecognizable face of malevolence. "Witch," with the subsequent witch hunt, offered a means for local control of general--or national—malevolence when state control failed.[24]

In colonial Africa, witchcraft beliefs were sometimes understood as efforts at social control, and thus might be interpreted as the internalization of the authority of the colonial state and the local application of the state's wishes.[25] In Java, witchcraft accusations arose in the absence of the state. They were an attempt to reassert social control, which at that moment meant control over phantasms. These phantasms were not the ghosts of Java but fears that arose within a national context. I will argue that they were new to Java and were a legacy of the New Order rather than a reassertion of a traditional practice. The witch hunts were a conservative movement, in that they wanted to put back into place an order feared to be vanishing. But they had the potential for revolution. They tapped a source of energy available not only for the murder of individuals but for the destruction of institutions, particularly the police, which stood in their way, and because the order they wanted to put back in place had, for them, vanished, leaving them without models for action. But to the degree to which they succeeded in assuaging uncanny sensations, they wrought no change. And, as we shall see, to the degree that their deeds reaffirmed notions of popular action as the savagery of the masses, they had reactionary effects. But though the witch hunts began with murder, harnessed to more advanced political thinking one could imagine a development in which the release of imaginative possibilities could have been used for radical change, as happened during the revolution. As it was, the movement for "Reformasi," a notion which left the idea of the savagery of the underclass untouched, saw in the *massa* only inchoate violence. Those who took on the rubric *massa* for themselves seemed to agree.

In the view of the survivors, the government (generally confused with those with education and standing of some sort: "those who count") understood not merely that survivors of attacks were innocent victims of hatred. It saw who they were. It understood that, contrary to their inner promptings, they were not witches. Violence and hatred, here, has one source; innocence, establishment of legitimate being, another. Justice in this system is in no way abstract. It is tied, much too closely tied, to a particular political system. It leaves a source of injustice, hatred, arising from sources unknowable except to "those who count," incapable of being understood. And what is thoroughly unintelligible was thought to have no other possible outcome than violence. Its presence rests as the justification of a regime which had the keeping of order as its primary excuse. In this way, the state became the point of reference for oneself. Justice here, meaning retribution for the killing of the innocent, is reserved to it.[26]

Where does the violent aggression inherent in suspecting that one might be a witch originate? One might start with unnatural "death." Its symptom was most often swollen bodies, which suggest hysterical symptoms, of course, as they also suggest the decay of corpses. What are the fantasies (which is not to say that these fantasies might not be based on real events) behind them? The grand massacre in this area happened in the prelude to the New Order, in 1965–66, when precisely Ansor, the youth branch of Nahdatul Ulama, along with others, particularly the Sakura, whom we will see in the next chapter, slaughtered Communists. At the time, there were numerous reports of bloated bodies floating in the river. The retention of water reported by a woman who would have been a young adult at the time of the massacres, the assertion that a man, who would have been about the same age in 1965, died because he could not stop urinating, the flow of water or its opposite that accompanied these bloated bodies, recalls those terrible earlier scenes.

Another repeated element of that time is the statement, "If we didn't kill them, they would kill us." Its original enunciation refers to Communists; its second, to witches. There is also the recurrence of stories of lists of those targeted for death. A figmentary version of this circulated widely in Indonesia in 1965–66, where in Aceh as well as in Jakarta and other places people repeated that lists had been drawn up by Communists and that their own names were on them. Though no such documents have ever been produced, aside from a blank sheet of yellow paper which proved that the Communists used disappearing ink, these lists justified the idea that if they did not kill the Communists they would themselves be killed.[27] Just as Muki's killers said that Muki and his family had to die if they, his fellow villagers, were to survive.

This, again, argues for repetition of an historical event, one never assimilated and therefore repeated. But if it is this, it does not begin with 1965. There were similar events during the revolution when nationalists were afraid that they would be slain by revolutionaries, though, to their knowledge, they had never been anything but supporters of the Republic. As I have already said, they felt that, unknown to themselves, they might be less than loyal, and that they could therefore betray themselves to revolutionaries who were keeping them in view.[28]

It is death and identification with the dead that begin these events. But actual, current death cannot be the cause of the identification, given their geographical scale and limited time span. Swollen bodies, representations of the dead from nearly fifty years earlier, that is, imaginary dead or the dead returned not as ghosts but as those who were never made into ghosts, give us the identificatory object. Certainly, these dead came to mind after Suharto's fall. Abdurachman Wahid, head of the N.U., president of the nation, apologized for the massacres. He incited protests for having done so, protestors claiming that an apology was uncalled for and threatened the return of Communists to power. There is no greater mass of unmourned dead in Indonesia than the Communists killed in 1965–66—none more fit to return with the lifting of state repression.

In the context of Java, the mere return of ghosts is not unexpected, as we have seen. The problem comes rather with the formation of national rather than Javanese ghosts. The hundreds of thousands of people massacred because they were suspected Communists were held in memory by the Suharto regime precisely as those who might return. And return, as we have said, in uncanny forms. Political disruption was frequently blamed on Communists and their descendants. The fear was that Communist ideas would prevail even without Communists. And so, in various disruptions, their traces could be made out. It was an example of "O.T.B" (*organisasi tanpa bentuk*) or "organizations without form or bodies" in the formulation of the time. Communists, defeated once during the revolution, came back again in the Sukarno regime. Massacred at the beginning of the Suharto regime, it was feared they could rise again through some unknown process, meaning without formal organization, but saying, also, "bodiless," just as specters lack bodies. This myth was widely subscribed to. In my opinion, its origin was not 1965 or 1948, but earlier. Indeed, it seems inscribed in Indonesian nationalism itself.[29]

We need not go further back in tracing these phantoms. It is enough to realize that one is preceded by another without reaching a definitive origin, though they are contained within the history of Indonesian nationalism and not within the regional traditions. These phantasms are not at all of the sort that prevail in the Javanese spirit world. Those, we have seen, are controllable by ritual means and through counter-sorcery. Control of national phantasms was claimed by the government itself. Their ghosts were not recognizably ghosts, from the perspective of the village. They required another sort of expertise to bring under control. It was precisely this source of control that was thought to disappear with the fall of the regime. We need merely seriously consider the threat of the Suharto forces—that without them there would be violence whose agents are subterranean—to see the effect.[30]

The clearest effect are the ninja, the term used for the killers who wore masks covering their faces which recalled figures seen on television.[31] Java is rightly famous for its masks. But these portray the features of the Javanese drama, adopted from the Mahabharata and Ramayana. To don such a mask was to take on the attributes of the character, but in the context of the theater. And though it was a ritual theater which sometimes featured possession, it was still theater. The ninja mask in illustrations is merely a wrapping over the whole of the face. The ninja mask does not merely obscure identity, as a robber's mask does. Ninja served samurai and developed, one Japanese told me, "hidden powers of personality." In their representations on Indonesian television, they are extraordinary fighters and have hidden weapons. No doubt the idea of possessing such heightened powers impressed the *massa*. Derived from television, the ninja masks in East Java embody powers that come from a distance. But this distance is neither that of the spirit world nor that of the person with "special powers of the personality." Unlike traditional Javanese masks, with their many characters, there is only one ninja. The ninja is merely an undifferentiated power, as opposed to the characters of Javanese drama, many of whom have particular strengths, or to the Japanese ninja who served particular masters. The nature of ninja power in Indonesia is never made clear. The mask designates a supernatural power, but which supernatural is not evident. It thus obscures what it also designates. We can speculate that during the witch hunts to wear a ninja mask was to hide two things: the face of the wearer and the power associated with it.

Ninja are sometimes also associated with the Indonesian army. Soldiers, it is said, wear ninja masks when they do particularly atrocious acts. But their representations in Indonesia belong to no particular world, neither the world of Java, nor of Indonesia or Japan. They are merely a power that operates in any world and that appear there without explanation. Lacking a particular origin, when they appear today, they are merely from "elsewhere."[32] They are, then, like the strange energy of television in the village, which brings figures from other worlds into the lives of villagers. Ninja are thus appropriate for the embodiment of spirits who do not belong to the Javanese spirit world; spirits who manifest themselves in bloated bodies rather than as corpses resurrected in their own identities, whether personal or political.

The *selamatan*, a ritual which localizes historical forces, cannot make a place for the unmourned dead of earlier massacres nor for the ninja, with their obscure origins. It has no place either for the violent revolutionary who is scarcely the one memorialized nationally. His violence remains at large. Javanese thus had to take on the enchanting power of these aggressive dead themselves, once the state was thought no longer to be there to keep them at bay. The ninja killers and the bloated bodies were that embodiment.

It is just at this point that the complex and even contradictory elements of the ninja mask can be seen. They come out of television; they are associated with a fear of the dead from times past. Figures out of mass-produced television serials are not known to embody deep fears. An educated Indonesian told me how surprised people he knew were to hear of ninja in connection with massacres. They were, to his mind, from the world of children. From one perspective, then, they are worn-out ghosts and the attributes of children's play—empty forms. But this merely left the fears they gathered together unexpressed and vague. They were fears of violence whose motivation remained unclear and which somehow came from below and from God knows where.

There is more to the involvement of the state in the witch hunt. We shall return to the topic in the next chapter.

Appendix: Political Effects:
Everything Back in Place

When witchcraft killings broke out in Malang Selatan, not far from Banyuwangi, the chairman of the local Nahdatul Ulama, Kijaji Hashim Muzadi, said that Malang Selatan was known to be a Communist area before 1965 and that if the situation was not brought under control, "Our government will collapse. What will happen will be a revolution in our country." For that fear to be realized, the witch hunters would eventually have to have acted in the name of the *rakyat* (the people). As it was, the results were conservative, leading back as they eventually did to the production of ghosts and the reliance on authority by the victims, which, of course, bolstered the aparat.

As it was, Kijaji Hashim's Nahdatul Ulama counterparts in Banyuwangi, site of the fiercest witch hunts, refused his diagnosis. They were afraid not of the *rakyat,* but of the *massa* as "provoked" by the army. Their fears were not simple, however; they are worth looking at carefully. Haji Abdul Rachman Hasan, the former head of the Nahdatul Ulama in the regency of Banyuwangi and, at the time I met him, the speaker of the regency's parliament, told me this:

Black magic? [*Ilmu santet*]. It means you are sick till you die. Many people here have black magic. But no supposition about someone is necessarily correct. The ones who know for sure are themselves sorcerers [*tukang santet*].

No supposition is necessarily correct. And, according to this distinguished leader of the organization headed by former President Abdul Rachman Wahid, to know with certainty would itself incriminate the knower. Everyone else must doubt. He, like the other Nahdatul Ulama religious leaders in this area, knows not only that magic exists and that the Koran affirms this belief, but that this area of Java has been known for centuries for its black magicians. With the exception of one religious leader, this time a supporter of Golkar, the former government party, who told us that there is no such thing as black magic, that if there was, the United States would have used it to send rockets to outer space, people time and again confirmed their belief in black magic. But black magic itself was not enough to explain what happened in 1998.

By chance, at that time, in this area, someone was using various strategies to cause trouble. They are using sorcerers. People were influenced to kill sorcerers. Who it is who was doing the influencing, we don't yet know.

In fact, as I have said, the general supposition, iterated by N.U. leaders who had more confidence in me, was that it was the army who was causing the trouble. It was not only reported to be so in the national newspapers; it was considered a fact in conversation. Certainly, there was a "konspirasi" (a word taken from the English or perhaps the Dutch).

After looking into the matter, it turns out that not all [the murdered people] were sorcerers. Among them were village teachers of Koranic chanting and mosque officials. As it turns out, most of them were members of the N.U. Out of 117 people killed, 84 were members of N.U.

The assumption seems to be that if the people killed were actually sorcerers, one would not have to resort to notions of conspiracy. There is witchcraft, and it is understandable that witches be killed. But, despite the fact that by their own thinking it is practically impossible to be sure who is a sorcerer, the N.U. leaders are certain that the majority of those killed were not witches. What makes them sure is that those killed were, according to them, often Koranic teachers. That such people often helped out their neighbors, for instance with white magic to make couples fall in love or to cure, is not disputed, either by them or anyone else. But that they were N.U. members makes them think that the movement against sorcerers was directed toward the N.U. That most of the killers were also followers of N.U. is accepted by them if it is brought up. But their answer to that objection is that uneducated villagers are susceptible to being incited.

The N.U. also report that when the masked men, or ninja, were arrested, not one of them was ever found to be from the army. This, rather than contradicting their supposition of a plot by the army against them, supports it. According to them, at the moment of their release from jail, they turned out to be madmen. And, they say, that at a certain moment in time, the number of mad people in Banyuwangi increased noticeably. There are several versions of this story, sometimes related by the same person. There is the simple story: the police substituted mad people for soldiers or for criminals hired by the army after the arrest of the latter. There is also a version that says that somehow the ninja turned into madmen.

And there is the further emendation that there were numbers of madmen who spoke with accents other than the one used in Banyuwangi. The evidence for this is that people suspected these madmen of being ninja (thus a reversal of the assumption that madmen were substituted for ninja) and therefore chased them. When caught, it turned out that they spoke with accents foreign to Banyuwangi and that they had the strong physiques common to soldiers. That soldiers posed as madmen and that genuine, though "foreign," madmen were substituted for soldiers was merely a complication. Their story, in any case, gained credence because the army is known to have instigated unrest in East Timor, in Aceh, in Jakarta, and other places.

To the charge that there were disputes in most cases where we could get information, and that the cases always involved local people, N.U. leaders felt that it made no difference. The wrong people were arrested; they may have participated in the killings, but they were not the "provakators." The latter were from outside the village, one could trace them ultimately to Jakarta, and they were from the army. They remain convinced that the leaders are not in jail

The N.U. leadership felt that the conspiracy ("konspirasi") against them had a planned trajectory. It began, they said, with "real witches," which means in the first place, with those not necessarily N.U. members. But it then continued with Koranic teachers who were N.U. members, and it was escalating to include themselves, the regional N.U. leadership. Many of them reported threats over the telephone. To protect their families, they often sent them away. Some of them circulated between villages every night, armed with whatever they could muster, both to protect the villagers and to protect themselves. One man, for instance, had a sword made for himself. They distributed charms to make themselves invulnerable.

So far as we could find out, no regional leader was harmed. The nearest to an attack that we heard about was a man driving with his family when a white jeep cut in front of him. The jeep is, of course, a reference to the army or the police, as, too, is the color white, since it is used by the military police. This man refused to stop, and he believes he thus escaped being murdered.

In the partisan politics that ensued, the regent, a military man from

Golkar, the party of the government under Suharto, was forced to resign. Blamed for allowing the killings to occur, his resignation no doubt validated the accepted and nationally publicized version of events distributed by the N.U. leadership, according to which "We are victims," or, more precisely, "we," the leadership, were almost victims. Victims, then, of whom? Victims, they say, of the army. But the army acted through the *massa*. And the *massa* here was composed of their own followers, adherents of the N.U. The army, they claimed, called up that force and directed it. This suspicion was without evidence, but it was credited in the mental and political climate that then prevailed. Credible because the army was clearly to blame for so much violence in Indonesia at that moment. But believable also because wishful. If the N.U. had not found the army to blame, that would leave only the *massa* and only N.U. followers, consisting of the same persons. Blaming the army diverted attention from this uncomfortable possibility. And it followed a pattern in Indonesia by which, once there is violence, someone in the center is said to have directed it. True or not, directed violence is less frightening than the uncontrolled aggression that arises from the *massa* alone.[33]

For the leaders of the N.U., once N.U. followers were transformed into *massa* the world was turned upside down. Rather than ignorant people for whom the N.U. could speak, it became populated with madmen and killers unreachable by the N.U. leadership. The target of this madness, deferred for a moment perhaps, was themselves. Witch hunts might be going on in the village, but the real target was "me." These unfathomable actions made sense to the N.U. leadership when they were considered as tactics and attributed to political rivals who, moreover, were famous for violence.

Among all the major political or religious organizations in Indonesia, the Nahdatul Ulama remained closest to its followers during the New Order. Precisely its decision not to be a political party left it free to have a closer relation to its membership, less influenced by the demands of national politics than the major parties. But, in the event, the connections between leaders and followers of the N.U. were as shattered as those between the aparat and villagers. The actions of the membership should have been first formulated for them. But in the wake of the fall of Suharto they were not formulated at all, or as little as possible. N.U. leaders were pressured to understand, to formulate, to speak what their membership felt. They could not do so once relations to the center had collapsed. They felt that pressure, therefore, as directed against them rather than, so to speak, through them, as would normally have been the case.

In the event, it was better to think of their people as being stolen by members of their own class if not of their own political persuasion. Here, we see the line between classes. On one side, those who are the repository of violence and in whom it can be awakened. On the other side, leaders of the people and those who would incite the mob. This way of thinking restores the political ideas of the Suharto regime, which depended on the firmness of this line and the threat that came from beneath it. That the N.U. leadership blamed the army did not mean that they denied that their own followers were part of the murderous *massa*. But their accusation gained them an advantage. Responsibility for violence rested with the army, who made *rakyat* into *massa* with their reckless incitation to violence. The N.U. leadership was on the side not only of the restoration of peace but also, and especially, of the reconstitution of the social and political body. They stressed how their followers needed the guidance and control N.U. leaders provided. Which includes, particularly, the need of this *massa* for the voice only their leaders can give them, and with it their restoration to the status of *rakyat*. Thus, the ending of the story is also the redrawing of the boundary between the enlightened classes and the underclass. On one side of that boundary, the same people took on the definition *rakyat* and "*massa*" alternatively. On the other side, depending on who was speaking, were either leaders of the people or inciters of the mob.[34]

Menace from All Directions

> "It will be said that the despot assures his subjects civil tranquility. Granted; but what do they gain, if the wars his ambition brings down upon them, his insatiable avidity, and the vexatious conduct of his ministers press harder on them than their own dissensions would have done? What do they gain, if the very tranquility they enjoy is one of their miseries?"
>
> —ROUSSEAU, *The Social Contract*

I. Power in Indonesian History

Indonesia in 1966, at the moment when Suharto took power from Sukarno, was a country invaded by fear. No Indonesian would deny that fact, as a massacre of hundreds of thousands of people charged with being Communists was underway. Indonesia was still called a "new nation," in the parlance of the social science of the time. Violent coups d'états were common enough in such states. One blamed the lack of firmly established democratic traditions. The ensuing repression of Indonesian Communists and the establishment of a rule based on force was nevertheless welcomed by those who supported U.S. policies, and ostensibly democracy as well, in Southeast Asia.

Whatever the role of foreign powers might have been in the massacre, the complications of the Indonesian coup indicate how deeply rooted the violence of that time was in the history of Indonesian nationalism. I have used the term "coup" to indicate the taking of power by Colonel Suharto from President Sukarno. But, at the time, "coup" referred not at all to that, but to the presumed attempted coup in which several generals and one of their aides were murdered. These killings were blamed on Communists and became the excuse for a massacre. The history of this massacre, and, along with it, the history of the change of regime, has yet to be definitively written. It appears increasingly likely, however, that Suharto himself had a hand in the killing of the generals, and it is well known that the army, under his command, instigated massacres locally. Suharto felt it necessary to implicate President Sukarno in the killings of the generals before he took the presidency for himself.

A coup in the style of Latin America would have been simpler. One leader replaces another by force. In the Indonesian case, a significant part of the nation had first to be called murderous and avid for power, and then massacred and imprisoned, almost always without trial. "PKI" stands for Partai Komunist Indonesia, the Indonesian Communist Party, but it increasingly came to mean anyone suspected of belonging to the party or having association with it, whether political or familial. Eventually, it meant simply people suspected of being opposed to the government. Finally, anyone at all might fear being labeled PKI and paying the consequence for it.

A logic was employed that made events seem inevitable. The generals were killed by Communists; Communists thereby revealed themselves as a threat to all Indonesians. Therefore we must kill them before they kill us. If such a logic was acceptable—"proof," as villagers of East Java said about accused witches—it must correspond to something already established. The supposed coup was taken to show how the Communists, who fought (other) Indonesian nationalists and were defeated during the revolution, were implacably violent and deceptive. The PKI was poised to win the forthcoming elections. Despite this, it was taken for granted by most Indonesians at the time that they were responsible for the murder of the generals. I will not go into the complicated politics of the murders of the generals, concerned as I am with the popular response to it. If these killings were easily accepted as the work of the PKI, it was ultimately because, as I have said, the particularly gristly murders of the generals evoked fears earlier established in Indonesian political consciousness from the time of the revolution.[1] The killing of the generals was understood, if that is the correct verb, in terms that came from Indonesian history rather than from an understanding of the politics of the time. It was not an analysis of contemporary political events that determined popular comprehension of the killings, but one at right angles, as it were, to those events, coming from the past.

Perhaps the bloodiest events in the memory of the revolution were the battle in Surabaya, against British forces who were trying to reestablish Dutch colonial authority, and the battle between Communists and nationalists already alluded to and referred to by the place where it occurred, "Madiun." Certainly, Communists alone were not thought to monopolize violence. But in 1965–66 and throughout Suharto's New Order, the assumption was easily made that their violence was disruptive to the point of creating pervasive disorder. Underlying this prejudice was a fear of the release again of revolutionary force, the residue of the revolution which was finally only an anticolonial revolution, the social revolution remaining incomplete in most areas of the Republic.

The nation's first president, Sukarno, followed a policy of populism which dealt with these fears. He claimed to speak for the people in a more literal way than that phrase is taken in American political rhetoric. The people, the Indonesian term is *rakyat*, were *bodoh*, which means "uneducated, inarticulate," the result of three hundred years of Dutch colonialism. Sukarno claimed the title of Extension of the Tongue of the People for himself. Via massive rallies broadcast over the radio he formulated what the *rakyat* could not say for themselves. After he spoke, they, presumably, understood what they had previously been thinking and could identify themselves with Indonesia.[2] Claiming also to speak for the revolution, Sukarno aimed to unify the nation, stressing the inclusion of all of its peoples, and to make his ideas theirs. In the name of the revolution, he effectively blocked the multiple roads taken by revolutionaries, who, in various places, had various ideas of what Indonesia should be.

In 1965 Indonesia suffered catastrophic inflation. The state was impoverished. It had no choice but to rely on cultural means to integrate its peoples, given its lack of resources and the inadequate development of the state bureaucracy. Benedict R. O'G. Anderson showed that during the Sukarno years a notion of power, Javanese in origin, inflected thinking about the presidency. Anderson pointed out that modern Western ideas of power stem from the time of the origin of the modern state. Power in those terms is discrete: there is economic power, military power, and so on. In Javanese thinking, power is a substance which the ruler gains through ascetic practices. He concentrates it in himself, with the effect that people attach themselves to him. The indication of power is precisely the numbers of people who show the ruler loyalty. The indication of weakness is the use of force. Ideological differences matter little, since the ruler is able to hold together various ideas. Thus, Sukarno coined the anagram "NASAKOM," standing for "Nationalism, Religion, and Communism." The more conflicting the ideas referred to by each of these terms, the more evident the power of the ruler.[3] The ruler, then, made every attempt to be inclusive. In the early days of independence, under the threat of separatism and conflicts of interest and without the resources to support much in the way of a state or military apparatus, such an idea had its purpose.

If their origins were premodern and prenationalist, they were not entirely reactionary, as the attempts to return to feudal ideas in the West were. The modern Indonesian state was not originally an instrument for the emergence from feudalism but for the imposition of colonial power. To infuse the independent nation with indigenous ideas was also to popularize the state that was to be the means of national expression. It made the state acceptable to its diffuse population rather than bolstering the privileges of diverse, feudally derived authorities. But such ideas were nonetheless antirevolutionary, stressing as they did centralization of legitimacy in the presidency and in the person of Sukarno and thus claiming the energy of the revolution for the state through its president.

Sukarno's "romanticism of the revolution," as he himself termed it, defined the energy of the revolution and left those who displaced local lords, for instance, in the province of Aceh, vulnerable to being seen as acting wildly. Seen locally, these were without doubt revolutionary and nationalist moves. Though never condemned by Sukarno, they were examples of actions which were undirected from above and whose limits of disruption were not at all clear. Such revolutionaries were later displaced from the state offices they gained.[4]

Suharto was as deeply Javanese as Sukarno, born of a Javanese peasant family. Taking power from Sukarno, however, he had to find another basis for power. He had none of the capacities of Sukarno for public speaking, and though he fought in the revolution, he lacked the authority that long and prominent participation in the nationalist movement and in the revolution conferred on Sukarno. At the same time, the Indonesian state was still weak in 1965, and state and nation were not sufficiently distinct to allow the simple replacement of one head of state by another. Control of the apparatus of the state alone was not adequate to control a nation whose people speak hundreds of languages and are distributed over an area extending over thousands of miles. Whoever replaced President Sukarno had either to be able to make his claim to speak for the people and to draw on the remnants of the integrating ideas of the early kingdoms, or to find another basis for authority.

The massacre of 1965 drew on the underside of the political culture of the Sukarno period. The control of the revolution promised by Sukarno was, in effect, said to have failed, while Sukarno himself was accused of being complicit with the PKI. Where, before, "the people" were the energy behind the articulations of their president, turning revolution into nationalism, they now were implicitly identified with the uncontrolled forces of revolution. The word used to refer to them quietly changed: *rakyat* became *massa*, or "masses," a word that once was used by the Left to refer to "the people." In the New Order, it came to be understood as the locus of unfocused and unpredictable disruption, the vehicle of the PKI, which was said to be continuously trying to win its way back to power even though, taken by surprise in 1965, it did not resist the massacre; the claims of the government during the New Order of Communist operations were the purest propaganda.

Under Sukarno, "Indonesia" had indicated a power of assimilation, the capacity to make anyone born in the archipelago into an Indonesian. An Indonesian was more than the citizen of a state; he was a person with a certain trajectory of development, one that depended on an orientation toward the center. In the face of large influxes of peasants into the cities, assimilation could not stop, but the idea behind it was no longer the union of diverse peoples finding their commonality in "Indonesia" but in ideas of a nationalist family, headed by the president.[5] Central state authority, for its part, displayed its might as it promised to control disruptive forces. Where there had been the claim to articulation of the voice of the people, there was now the suppression of expression.

The massacre of 1965 displayed superabundant destructive power throughout the archipelago. It based itself on the fear that if the Communists were not eliminated once and for all, Indonesians, meaning those who were not Communists, would lose their lives. It was a national fervor turned against other Indonesians. But if this destructive power had its source in national myths that centered on the transformations of the idea of the people, it was aroused and directed by the army under Suharto. There thus came into being a power associated with the leader of the nation directed against members of that nation.

Opposition was claimed to be subversive and to indicate the remounting of Communist power. In the face of a mythical claim, no force could be enough to assure security. There were a series of displays of governmental force, of which those occurring in 1983 in particular revealed the strategy of the government. At that time, thousands of "criminals" were murdered and their corpses left in public places, usually with multiple wounds, as though one could not be certain they were definitively slain. Victims were visited at night by soldiers in mufti, their faces masked, and taken away in jeeps, to be discovered on the roads and in the rivers as corpses the next morning. On the one hand, this was an attempt to show the power of criminals themselves, simply by the numbers of those killed and their ubiquitous presence as well as by news reports which emphasized their "criminality." On the other hand, it showed the superior and extra-legal power of the state. Criminals or, for that matter, anyone else might have been arrested, and in a system in which the police and the judiciary were under political control, easily convicted. Instead, the authority of the state was deliberately left unclear. One interpretation of these events claims that the government deliberately displayed itself as having a power comparable to that of criminals. Those slain were criminals not because they were known to have broken laws, though some had done so, but because they belonged to a category, "kriminalitas," that, as elaborated in the press, was as much a quality of their persons as a matter of their acts. The state, for its part, though it showed it had a power superior to that of criminals, showed also that, like them, it was outside the law, and, like them again, that it acted savagely. It used its power not simply instrumentally to do away with those who broke the law, but for display.

The killings were at first said to be the work of "mysterious shooters," though some victims were stabbed to death as well. It was soon admitted that soldiers were the murderers. In the first edition of his "autobiography" (written by someone else), Suharto boasted of having directed these kill-ings. The "mystery" (the word *misterius* was borrowed from English) of the killer's identity was soon solved, but the "mystery" of their force remained. Precisely because these killings were done blatantly, without pretense to legality, without even the invoking of a state of emergency, the relation of the government to power was unclear. When Indonesia turned against itself, what limits were there on the power concentrated in the hands of President Suharto and exercised by the army? Anyone could be a victim. At the same time, the New Order regime met remarkably little resistance of the sort one found in totalitarian regimes in the West. It is not only that the regime continued to kill, and therefore to terrify, citizens. It was also that the state continued to proclaim itself to be practicing preventive vio-lence and this was believed in. No other picture of the regime was gener-ated within Indonesia, which, with a few exceptions, lacked, for instance, the samizdat literature of the old Soviet Union or the powerful critiques of the Nazi regime written by German exiles. That Indonesians were afraid and relied on the state to protect them has a certain logic. But that the state resorted to extralegal means in exercising its force raises the question of how its power was understood. The effect of displaying itself as equally criminal as those claimed to menace it is unclear. The contradiction in its posture, however, is evident. On the one hand, the state claimed to uphold order. On the other, it showed itself to be criminally violent.

Suharto was incapable of implementing Javanese ideas of power in the manner of Sukarno. He may well have had it in mind, however, in one respect. The traditional Javanese ruler is himself outside questions of legiti-macy. Here is Anderson:

Since all power derives from a single homogenous source, power itself antecedes questions of good and evil. To the Javanese way of thinking it would be meaning-less to claim the right to rule on the basis of differential sources of power—for ex-ample, to say that power based on wealth is legitimate, whereas power based on guns is illegitimate. Power is neither legitimate nor illegitimate. Power is.[6]

The idea of power had changed during the revolution. The sheer force of the revolution against which its leaders set themselves had nothing to do with the Javanese idea of power. Sukarno did not gain the presidency through mystical practices or popular belief in such. But Javanese ideas of power centered on him for the reasons I have just given, with the result that the violence of the revolution was obscured. Suharto, by contrast, identified himself with massacres. His notion of power was modern, but his idea that power alone conferred legitimacy was Javanese.

What, then, could the signs of power be? It was no longer the assimilation of peoples and the coherence of the nation. It was the division of the nation itself, one part of which was called savage and violent, and just for that reason exemplified force or power. Massacre was the way in which Suharto established himself as superior to this force, in the sense that he controlled it or it worked through him, and at the same time he was of the same nature as it.

There is a famous photograph of Henri Cartier-Bresson, taken in the Governor-General's Palace after the transfer of power.[7] Two servants carry out a large canvas, a portrait of a Dutch Governor General. This photograph has been reproduced many times. It pictures the equivalent of the decapitated enormous statues of Stalin or the notorious pulling down of the statue of Saddam Hussein in Baghdad. It refers to the end of one era and the beginning of another, to the transfer of authority that accompanies it, and to the violence, symbolic and real, that goes with it. But the Cartier-Bresson photograph differs from the other examples. We do not see enthusiastic crowds eager to do away with the symbols of hated earlier rulers. Instead, there are two palace servants, acting on the orders of constituted authority, no doubt, doing their job without fuss and, for that matter, in exactly the same deferential way they acted when their boss was white. Moreover, one has the impression that Cartier-Bresson surprised them in the act of doing something out of sight, like maids on the back stairs. The violence, the mass movements, that accompanied the change from Dutch to independent rule are missing.

The violence of the revolution was hidden from the time of the independent Indonesian state up until 1965–66. With the so-called coup it was put on display, but in another form. The massacres of 1965–66 and the continued violence by the military after that drew on notions of the violence of the masses and showed the might of the military in containing it. The state sought an enemy, which it found first in the PKI even though it offered no resistance, and after that in mythical criminals. These were presented as violence itself, justifying the military's use of force but also showed Suharto's power to be what they were. As criminals acted outside the law, so too "we," the military, faces hidden, without uniforms, kill. Were the state to have followed its own laws, the extraordinary force on which the regime rested would not have been so clearly evident. It needed a version of power, which it then claimed to master, to express itself.

As I have sketched it, power in New Order Indonesia was immeasurable, unlimited by legality or notions of legitimacy. It represented nothing but itself. Its claim to be preventive of disruption was itself mythical and a secondary effect. Such a notion of power scarcely translates into the construction of a state. Indeed, it was early noticed that the Indonesian state had become separated from society and acted in its own interests.[8] But Suharto's demonstration of power went beyond even its use for himself and his family or for the state The New Order endured for over thirty years. It was unlikely to have done so if its savage power was without institutional effects of some sort.

It is here that we return to the familialism of Indonesian society; to the connection Indonesians felt with those in office, not on the basis of common political opinions but simply because they knew someone who in turn knew someone else, until, in an imaginary chain, one reached Suharto himself. The usual means of communication between society and the state were closed in New Order Indonesia. There was no genuine political representation, civic organizations were organized by the government, and the press was controlled. Nonetheless, Indonesians did not seem to feel they were without means of communication. There was always someone who knew someone.

To speak of this as a real chain of communication is a distortion, however. It was, rather, the illusion of one, an apotropaic reaction against the power of Suharto. One had a choice; one could be a victim of Suharto or one could be in the chain of persons that led to him or close to him. If the latter, one was a member of the national family, prepared to play one's role as such by acting rightly, meaning inclusively, with others. If one was unknown, one was merged into the savage masses, without means of expression. And as such, one potentially played a part in the mirroring of power I have described.

Many, perhaps most, Indonesians could not be sure where they stood.

As we will see, even those with lifelong histories of membership in groups opposed to the Communists were afraid of being accused of being such, particularly when they came from the lowest social ranks. Such uneasiness was expectable, given the underlying political menace. By the end of the Suharto regime, Indonesian society was remade, or perhaps hollowed out, by this relation of power. The structural change in Indonesian society came with the "gap" (the term was used by Indonesians at the time) between classes as the market expanded. With it came the fear of the inability to contain relations within the workings of national-familial recognition. Indonesians used the term "gap" to express the fear that the bonds between Indonesians had lost strength. Without the ability to assimilate the impoverished masses, without the capacity to bring them into the national family, they feared violent uprisings.[9] They felt that their fears were confirmed when, just after Suharto left office, major riots broke out in Jakarta, followed by various types of violence in many places in the archipelago.[10]

It is with all this in mind that we return to the witch killings of 1998 and later.

II. Massa, Army, Witch

We want to understand the place of the massacres and the exercise of power as Suharto understood it on the formation of witches. We give the example of Muki's village, where to understand the sense of "PKI" we turn to local history. Muki's village was founded during the Japanese period. There had been a coffee processing plant in the area which, in Dutch times, furnished housing for its workers. The Japanese ordered the workers to build houses for themselves in the area that became the village. The village, Harjonegaran, is said to have been named after a foreman from the factory who often stood up for the workers. During the revolution, as part of their scorched earth policy, nationalist forces asked the local people to cut down the coffee trees in the plantation about a four hours' walk from the factory. They were then entitled to the land they cleared. Many settled there. In 1979, during the New Order, the army ordered the workers off the land which had belonged to the coffee estate, reclaiming it for the estate, now under government control. The village took in the displaced farmers, taking a proportion of the land of each villager to make room for them.

(When it was discovered that the village authorities had not sacrificed any of their own land, there were demonstrations, which led to the replacement of these officials.) To this day, villagers have been pleading with the army for the return of their land. The army has on previous occasions agreed but then reneged. Today there is the possibility of a settlement, which will yield each villager barely enough for his subsistence. The total land to be returned to the villagers is considerably less than that confiscated in 1979, but villagers feel happy that they might get anything at all.

The result of taking in the settlers from the coffee estate is that there is not enough land to support the inhabitants by agriculture. Nonetheless, the village does not look poor. This is the result of the efforts of women who have worked abroad in Saudi Arabia, Malaysia, and other places. On their return they often use their savings to build a new house. It is claimed that the style of these new houses reflects the styles of the countries where they worked. Included among the women who have worked abroad is one of Muki's daughters-in-law, married against her will to a son of Muki, who worked in Malaysia. She gave her wages to her husband, who was in the process of building a new house, presumably for Muki, when he was murdered during the witch killings. The house stands empty today, just as the small field Muki worked stands unused, since his grandchildren will not claim their inheritance and villagers will have nothing to do with the property.

In 1965–66, in Hardjonegaran at the time of the massacres, only one person was abducted from the village. He is said to "be still away," though it is obvious he was killed. One person, a supporter of the Nahdatul Ulama, the religiously conservative organization that produced Abdul Rachman Wahid as president after the fall of Suharto, took part in rounding up those accused of being Communists. He was twenty-seven at the time and "went along" (*ikut*) in hunting down the PKI. "If they were not killed, yah, we would be killed," he said in the phrase which was and is repeated throughout the archipelago.

We cooperated [the "we" here being the army and local people] in hunting down important figures who were to be taken away. It was tense. There had to be officials. It couldn't have been done otherwise. Like a team. Everyone acting alone, that doesn't go. Here in this area, it wasn't like that [i.e., it was organized and orderly]. It wasn't wild, each one doing his own thing, no, it wasn't like that at all.

Otherwise people might have used it [i.e., they could kill whomever for whatever reason]. There were places [*lokasi*] set aside for the killings. There were pits.

There are two elements in this paragraph. There is the insistence on "organization" and working together, which is typically Javanese. And there is the fact that organization was led by the army. This association between local people and the national military had various meanings. It lent the killings a certain legitimacy for people such as the speaker, a teacher of Islam in the public schools. And it associated the force necessary for the killings with the center, not only for him but for others as well.

He goes on:

I could not have acted by myself. I almost died, I was almost killed. The local army commanders came around [and said,] "Those who supported the PKI, round them up now." I was twenty-seven. I was almost killed; those PKI, if you did not kill them, you got killed. I was almost struck. Going on the "operations" [*operasi*] they could attack. . . . I wasn't brave enough to do it by myself. . . . The local people dug the pits, the government told them where.

Asked who the executioners were, the speaker responded:

They were from here and from outside too. But they had to register. There was an administration. And it was Koramil [the local military commander] who prepared things. It was not wild. Not like demonstrations today.

His force was added to that of the military. By himself, he would have been weak. That should be distinguished from the statement that it was organized and not wild—that, therefore, only appropriate people were targeted. And it was led by the army. Taken together, this meant that the killings were legitimate, an expression of the will of the people. The killers acted in the name of "Indonesia," which was at once strong, organized, and appropriately led. The killings, even though done locally, were effected by the center, in this view.

Most villagers today say that during that period they were afraid, but, unlike the man above, not of the Communists. Despite the fact that they were not Communists and that the majority of them were Muslims not only by religion but by political activities as well, they thought that they themselves might be abducted. They were particularly afraid of Sakera. Sakera was not precisely an organization, but a style of dress, black in color, after the dress of Madurese. It is in defense of Sakera members that the man above insisted that there was nothing "wild" about the round-up and that it was all under the control of the military. Sakera members, he said, were from various villages and were ethnically Madurese, as are a significant portion of the people of the area.

There are various kinds of Madurese. There are Madurese who act like Javanese. But there are also Madurese who let their Madurese character show. [Madurese have a reputation for taking vengeance and for being violent.] It was these [the latter] who made up Sakera. Sakera was a group, like Banser [the paramilitary arm of the Nahdatul Ulama].

It was in speaking of Sakera that various persons expressed their feelings at the time of the killings. Thus, two men I will call "S" and "Y":

S: Yah, I kept worrying about the wife. The thing is, I was afraid the wife and kids would be abducted by the Sakera.

JS: What exactly was the Sakera?

S: They were thieves, robbers. People who took others because they wanted vengeance. There are always people like that.

Y (objecting): Here it was peaceful enough.

S: That's what made the guards here thin. [That is, it was peaceful because local people guarded the village at great effort.]

JS: Where were they standing guard?

S: Here in Hardjokuncaran. They circulated throughout the village . . .

JS: Where were the Sakera from?

Y: There wasn't anybody from here.

S: I don't know. I don't know where they were from. No idea. Here the only people out were the guards.

Y: Sakera was an organization like organizations nowadays. Like the Satgas [local watchmen]. Along with the local military and the police [i.e., like the Satgas, they were, in effect, an arm of the military and the police]. But they wore uniforms, like Sakera. [The Satgas have uniforms.] They were from Karang Asem [a place nearby]. They all spoke Madurese. But lots of people, thieves, copied Sakera clothes. They were false Sakera. Now, dressed like that, they made trouble . . .

S is asked if he ever met any Sakera. He says no. He is then asked what would happen if he did meet them.

S: If it had been me who was standing guard, the Sakera would be the ones to run away. Those who guard their friends don't run. . . . The Sakera were from outside the area [*kecamatan*]; they weren't supposed to come here. They had to report to the police and the local military because they had weapons. But the thing is, we who stood guard were determined. If there weren't coordination between the Sakera and the government officials, there would have been fights between groups. In the daytime, everything was clear. [He implies that it was different at night.]

The Sakera, in this view, were thieves and robbers. S might have added, "murderers," since they are said to have abducted people who disappeared forever. They were unwelcome in the village. During the daytime, there was order. But at night, had they appeared, they would have been opposed, even though they were supported by the army. Opposition to them was not in the name of supporting Communists or supporting fellow villagers. It was rather that they were understood to be a "wild" force who threatened everyone. And at the same time, they acted with the knowledge and even the authority of the government.

Y, in the face of S's statements, is forced to make a distinction between real Sakura and Sakera in disguise. The latter were the thieves and murderers, the former, presumably, were people like himself, namely those doing their duty as good Indonesians. Furthermore, in Y's view, none of the Sakera were local. S, however, is convinced that he does not know where they were from or who they were. They were, to his mind, anyone at all from anywhere, including his own village. Nor, it seems, does he accept the difference between real and false Sakera.

S and others stood guard at night, as people in villages all over Indonesia did at that time. But they did not always know whom they were defending themselves against. Rather than a fear of Communists, there is a fear of marauders, who were at once anonymous and associated with the military. Their fear began with Communists as its agents, but as events continued, they feared figures hunting Communists, or disguised as those hunting Communists, as well. Once the killings started, the fear was simply of killers. The actual killers were the army and the local people who acted with them. Anyone could be taken for a Communist, abducted, and killed. Those who presumably opposed Communists formed bands of murderers and, as these accounts testify, were feared to act indiscriminately. Villagers conflated Communists, the army, and anyone at all, until there was a single, unclear category. From the point of view of villagers, there were not two or three opposed forces; they were mentally conjoined into a single force, linked by the fact that one feared them all. One could be killed and for no reason at all and by anybody.

Later, an old woman spoke of 1965–66, saying, "In the daytime everything was alright. It was night when they took people away. Lots and lots of people stood guard." At night, Sakera in black clothes and false Sakera in black clothes could not be told apart from neighbors, military, and whomever else. A time when anyone could be anyone, and when this was a matter of life and death, repeats a psychic state that existed during the revolution. Come across, found out, by someone whom one cannot distinguish in return, one could die.

Under the New Order fear was consolidated. Anyone could be a victim. To guard against this, there were the forces of the government. But the government remained conflated with those they violently suppressed. Here is the statement of a woman from another village speaking of the events of the year 2000, when witches were killed in her area. After the killing of one of them, the police and the army arrive in front of her small food shop:

At the time of the killings, lots of people came to the shop. But I was afraid. Because it was the army, ABRI [an acronym for the Indonesian armed forces], the police and all in full uniform. There weren't just one or two, but trucks full. Because of that I was frightened. I sweated like wartime earlier. Then, those people rounded up people and then killed them.

The scene starts with the roundup of people accused of killing a presumed sorcerer. The woman is a believer in sorcery and told us that the man killed had been a sorcerer for years. She had nothing against his death. But seeing the soldiers come she thinks of "wartime" earlier. She might have been old enough to have known the Japanese occupation, but I rather doubt it. "Wartime earlier" seems, rather, to conflate that period with 1965, about which she had been speaking to us; periods of violence are mixed together. "Those people," in the last sentence, manages to refer to the soldiers at the moment of the witch killings and the killers of 1965 and those of "wartime." Seeing the soldiers arrive, she is no longer afraid of witches; she is afraid of the soldiers. Once again, opposing forces are conjoined into a single fear and that fear is given the name "military."

That the soldiers and police here are said to be both numerous and in "full uniform" is also significant. She does not recognize individuals; only soldiers. Here we see the value of knowing the local military and civilian authorities. When one recognizes them as persons and when they know one, they are no longer blind force. One can speak with them, ask them for help, and so on. At this point we see the familialism of the New Order. In the face of a regime which relied on displays of violence and which intentionally showed itself to exceed intelligible, not to say legal, limits on its own violence, the best guarantee of security is not retreat and avoidance but personal connection. One knew someone who knew someone and eventually one had access to the very center of power. What one feared most was held at bay. Familiarity, "familial" connections, neutralized violent force. Of course, that force could always show itself again. This, indeed, is what the woman quoted in the previous chapter complained about. "They" have connections, "we" do not.

Meanwhile, villagers perceived the military as a force potentially directed against them. Asked why the peasants driven from the coffee estate did not resist, and why, after the fall of Suharto, they did not take back their land by force (as was done in other places in Indonesia), a man replied, "The problem is, we were up against the army. The army, as they say here, has rifles." This is the same man, quoted above, who told me how he cooperated with the army in the 1960s.

This man went on to say that "the local officials are afraid of the people [*massa*]; and the people are afraid of the soldiers' weapons." As an activist trying for years to get back the land confiscated by the army, he identifies himself with the anonymous people, themselves thought violent, who are opposed by an equally violent but more powerful force. It is, moreover, a force which takes no account of who they are, and which sees in them only potential and past violence. He sees himself seen as violent in their eyes, and therefore their target. He told us the story of how he was arrested. It was during the 1980s when he was teaching in a school some distance away. Soldiers stopped him in Harjonegaran because of his militancy in trying to win back confiscated land. He tells the soldiers that it would be "disrespectful" of them to arrest him without first informing the principle of his school. He draws on the assumptions of familialism. They, the soldiers, should respect those who have government positions. Telling the soldiers this, he tells them that he is "known," recognized by someone in authority. He is therefore not just "anyone," an element from out of the *massa*. With this, he was released. Caught in the conflated memories of Indonesian history, the poor woman seeing trucks full of soldiers sweats again. She is deprived of such connections, or at least fears herself to be, and therefore feels that, unrecognized, she too will be a victim.

In this context one understands another man, T, with more education than many, a member of the committee negotiating for the return of the confiscated land. He claims that, in fact, there were no PKI in the area in 1965. "Here, we are all firm believers [*fanatik agama*]," Y adds. T gives the example of a man who lived next door to the PKI headquarters. This man did not understand who the PKI were; he was a practicing Muslim, as were the speakers. Once, sometime before 1965, the PKI had a meeting and needed chairs; he lent them some. For this he was rounded up and has had to report to the authorities ever since. "There were no PKI, just people called PKI," T says (apparently forgetting the PKI headquarters and its lack of chairs). "They were afraid of being called PKI. At that time, it was the same as being called a 'terrorist' [*téroris*]. No matter what one was or, for that matter, what one is at the present, one can always be called 'PKI' or terrorist. They have the force to call one whatever they chose."

One accepts this possibility. One might be PKI no matter what one knows oneself to be. One has the authority of those with superior force who embody the Indonesian state poised to so identify one. The defense against this superior force is to become known to it, to exit from the anonymity of the *massa* and to be familiar to those who matter. On one side, the need to be known, even though it was not and is not a possibility for many, if not most. On the other side, an acceptance of the possibility of being what one might be called, with possible lethal consequences. In face of the confusion of identities, in which "*massa*" and "army" and "army" and "witch" are conflated, one might be anything. One strives to have a reflection of oneself for what one is; but the risk, and even the major possibility, is that one will be reflected back in some other, foreign guise. Here we see why people were not sure if they were witches or not, just as they did not know if they were PKI or not.[11]

This, however, does not speak to the question of how the witch is formed. But we are closer. There were witches before, we have said. They were, however, tolerable. At best, they were made to leave the village. Killings were rare. It is only when Suharto fell from power that those accused of witchcraft were killed, most of them within months of one another. Why should the category "witch" change its character? It was a national event that made the difference, and so we look for a solution in the national sphere. It should be clearer now that the uncertainty about connections with government officials that pertained at that moment was important. It meant that one feared that, once again, one might be found out by an overpowering force, for anybody or anything at all. One could be a witch oneself. Why a witch and why not PKI? In the first place, because "PKI" was usually reserved for incidents of public disruption while witchcraft accounted for personal misfortune. But also because the question of familiarity rested on the transformation of one's possible murderer into someone one knew and who knew one. The political restlessness attendant on Suharto's fall (and his incipient fall, for that matter, since the killings began before Suharto left office, though not on a large scale) meant that menace showed itself through the familiar. The earlier, tolerated witch was someone one knew and therefore someone one could deal with. Now, even those who were not considered witches before, but were merely one's neighbors, could be thought to be lethal menaces. We see this in the conflation of epochs and in opposing forces brought forward in such indications as swollen stomachs recalling the dead PKI. The uncanny emerged, as it does, from the familiar. One opposes the military in the name of something or someone—as a Muslim or an Indonesian, for instance. But those beset by fear at that moment might have been anyone to themselves. Gripped by fear, they had no consolidated identity. In that (in)capacity, they stumbled on someone who seemed to reflect their incoherent shape.

Thus, the witch took a new shape. He had been well known. The Javanese witch had been present in the way of the Azande oracle; one could always look to him to explain misfortune. Suspicion had its place. If nothing can explain death, yet still there was an explanation. But with the fall of Suharto, the witch as he had been known to be was insufficient to his task. Suspicion was now generalized. It was no longer a question of a certain misfortune that needed to be explained. It was a matter of feeling that one no longer was recognized because the person to whom recognition referred was no longer there. In that situation, symptoms appeared, signs of something inhabiting one; signs of another self, unrecognizable to its possessor, but vulnerable to being recognized by any power that might appear. Anyone could be a witch, beginning with the accusers. The witch could no longer separate misfortune from the world. Instead, the accusation "witch" indicated that misfortune was present everywhere, potentially in everyone. One would be picked out and one would die.

Who, then, was the witch? The witch, a force affecting anyone at all on any occasion, bringing a generalized catastrophe, was the form Suharto took when he vanished from the political center. Suharto had been both the source of violence and the person toward whom recognition was oriented. Without him in that second capacity, he appeared in the first. All transaction with him risks being abnormal. One does not appear, in his eyes, as one presents oneself. "You are PKI," "You are a criminal," and it is true even if factually it is false. But, also, his recognition via his soldiers and officials, can confirm one's normality and that one belongs to the nation. Thus with Muki, one's neighbor. But with Muki, recognition of the ordinary fails, though one keeps trying. One sells to him and he pays in death. He does not recognize one in one's usual state but in some other capacity, and this recognition brings catastrophe. The same is true of the person who earns money mysteriously. One cannot deal with him. Catastrophe ensues.

With the end of Suharto, there was a (temporary) failure of denial. The denial I refer to is, of course, the denial of the power of Suharto that comes through familiarity. The object of acquaintanceship, if one can use that term, is gone, and with it the force of denial. Indonesian witchcraft at the end of the twentieth century and into the present constructs an other *en face* of whom one cannot be recognized for what one is. The witch is Suharto as nightmare; he is power that is exercised without the protection against it that was offered through being recognized by authority.

One might consider the other possibility. It might be that one could complain to one's neighbor that one is bewitched, that one is certain that Muki is a witch, and that one has narrowly escaped death. This would be the condition for the sublime. One has come in contact with an overwhelming power and one has barely escaped. It offers the possibility for what Kant called a negative pleasure.[12] The sublime, said Kant, rests on one's powers of judgment, which, in the face of what is later to be called sublime, are inadequate. One tries to say what it is one faces nonetheless: "If something arouses in us, merely in apprehension and without any reasoning on our part, a feeling of the sublime, then it may indeed appear, in its form, contrapurposive for our power of judgment, incommensurate with our power of exhibition, and as it were violent to our imagination, and yet we judge it all the more sublime for that."[13] It is the escape from what overwhelms us that makes the sublime what it is. With this escape one has a sense of renewed intellectual vigor. One can now congratulate oneself that one has regained one's powers; they now seem even greater than one thought before this experience.[14] One could define oneself as someone who has faced a great danger and survived, hence is enhanced by the experience. It would be a way of subtly appropriating the power of death, the hidden and transformed power of the state. It would therefore establish oneself in a position of resistance.

But this is not what happened. Instead the power that one came up against was overwhelming, and there was no escape. The East Javanese witch, as of 1998, was the outcome of the attempt to reconstruct Suharto and thus to account for the lethal power that came with the failure of self-recognition. If the construction of such a figure had been successful, one might have dealt differently with the witch. He might have reverted to the useful figure he had apparently been earlier, an equivalent of the Azande witch: not entirely successfully integrated, but sufficiently so that a certain gain might come from escaping his power. But no such figure could be successfully constructed and that is because of the contradiction inherent in the attempt. Suharto, embodying the power of the nation, terrorized but also guaranteed the social through his power of recognition, and thus guaranteed the familiar. The witch was a composite of the neighbor, Muki, for instance, and Suharto with his powers. But the embodiment of terror canceled out the power to confirm the familiar, and so Muki was murdered. Had Suharto been brought to trial for his murderous atrocities, perhaps Muki would have lived. As it is, Suharto's fall from office has scarcely diminished the fear of him.

The witch, after Suharto, was someone in face of whom one could find no reflection of oneself. To say this, of course, is not simple. It is not that one merely met a blank. It is rather that each time one encountered Muki, instead of what one expected from normal exchange, one had the threat of death. Which means that each version of oneself reflected from him meant that one saw oneself missing. One cannot be missing unless one has a view of oneself as that which is absent. It is this oscillating picture of oneself as there and as already inhabited by death, therefore as not there, that issued from exchanges with Muki.

The sublime is not available to everyone. It depends on the cultivation of those involved. Kant postulated that one who lacks a certain culture might not have the intellectual force to recognize that one cannot comprehend or defeat this power. It is not that Javanese are uncultivated and so not capable of a sublime reaction. Our idea of the sublime rests on a distinction between life and death that differs from the Javanese notion, as I have already explained. In any case, Kant does not tell us what the capacity to recover ourselves from the overwhelming of our intellectual powers depends upon. It is clear that for these Javanese to tell each other of the menace of the witch was not to confirm that they had evaded his power. What was lacking was the ability to reassure each other. The social nexus within which they could find their normal selves reflected once again had eroded. Each saw only that the other too was menaced. The witch offered no gain. Theirs was a cultural failure which one might attribute as much to the extraordinary decline of Indonesian culture under the New Order as to ideas of death embedded in Javanese thinking. Their reaction, which we will reconstruct in the next chapter, was a certain panic, inside of which one can trace a process that culminates in the naming of the witch. It was a weakness of the cultural and the social in general that allowed panic its place.

East Javanese witchcraft begins as a profoundly conservative, even reactionary, movement as it tries to reestablish the mythical power of the state. But at the same time it is potentially revolutionary as, all complications accounted for, it does away with Suharto in his disguised form. The exit from witchcraft was the entry of restored Indonesian familialism. In between, the political consequences, such as the burning down of the police station, go unnoticed. Whatever stands in the way of the elimination of the witch becomes a target. But precisely because it is blind, witchcraft contains in it the possibility of another future, one not at all necessarily conservative.[15] When the murderers of Atmoyo called themselves "the *massa*," and thus called for recognition by the state, they too were conservative. But they need only have applied an older meaning to that term, one used before in leftist thinking, to put themselves on the path to revolution. Independent Indonesia has guarded itself against revolution, but in doing so it has also stopped up the opening to the future in favor of a progressive hardening of class lines. One hopes that there is still a future for that nation. One finds that hope in the same forces that produced witchcraft.

6

No Witch Appears

Early in the 1980s, after Suharto had been in power for a dozen or so years, I was riding in a Jeep outside the city of Cirebon, in Java, going back to Jakarta with a friend, an Indonesian educated in the West. His wife and his younger sister were with us. The asphalt road was narrow, just two lanes raised above the rice fields, lined by occasional trees. It had been drizzling and my friend was driving. A motorbike came toward us, driving on the wrong side of the road. R, as I will call my friend, swerved to miss him. The Jeep began to skid, turned around twice, headed into the ditch, crossed it, continued into the rice field, and then tipped over, tossing the four of us onto the soft earth. We picked ourselves up, in various stages of bewilderment. There was some blood on R's wife, but she seemed all right. Looking back, we saw that the cyclist had crashed into a tree. A crowd materialized and we learned that the man had been seriously hurt and that someone had gone for help. In the event, he was taken to the hospital.

From out of the crowd a young man in shorts without a shirt, dressed as farmers do when working in the fields, appeared. He demanded to know what we were going to do now. A car stopped. A middle-class type emerged and said to the young man, "We don't gang up [*keroyokan*] on people here." We have encountered the term *keroyokan* previously. "Gang up on," here, from the point of view of the man making the demands, could as well be translated as "take vengeance," something perhaps understood by the middle-class type when he added, "The police have already been called," meaning perhaps, both "Don't try anything" and "The police will take care of things for you." Indeed, the ambiguity of the police plays an important part in this story. In any case, the region was known to be dangerous to anyone who got in an accident with local people who, we say in English, "take the law into their own hands" (there is an often-used Indonesian equivalent) and are known to have killed drivers from the city who injured them.

With the help of the middle-class type, we righted the Jeep. Two policemen arrived on a single small motorbike and then left without doing very much. The middle-class type also left. There were still a few villagers, some of whom helped us turn over the Jeep. But one of the youths threatened us again unless we did something about the accident. We assured him we were going to do something. I told him, however, that we had to get the women to a clinic, as they were bleeding, and therefore had to leave. They agreed. Looking down the road I saw a crowd rapidly approaching us. We got in the Jeep and left, followed by the crowd. The latter, to our relief, receded as I accelerated, but two youths on motorbikes kept up with us. We got to a police post and stopped, but there was no one there. We left again and the youths caught up with us again. We explained that we were not trying to evade the consequences of the accident. We were taking the women to the clinic further up the road. But, they pointed out, the hospital was in the opposite direction. We knew that, but going that way would have meant heading back into the crowd. We pointed out that we had stopped at the police post, and they were appeased by this. We reached the clinic followed by the youths. The police appeared, angry with us. Why had we left? And why had we gone to this clinic when it was out of their jurisdiction? They were not worried that we would escape the law, but that they, the police, would be left with the villagers to deal with. Villagers hope the local police will look after their interest. But the difficulty was that these police agents, as they themselves explained, were Balinese, not from the region, and therefore not confident of their ability to control the villagers in this situation.

We could not rely on the local police, part of the aparat, any more than the villagers could. The police were not acting with the law in mind but rather with the idea of keeping peace. At that point, they did not care who had caused the accident; they only wanted there not to be trouble. The point at issue at that moment was not who was at fault, but whether, regardless of fault, we would compensate the victim's family or would we escape to Jakarta, out of reach of the family. The police were willing to speak for the villagers, and the villagers wanted them to do so. But it was evident from the statements of the police that the local people did not entirely trust these particular agents. The idea, shared by the police, was to settle the matter outside the law with the villagers. Precisely because the settlement was outside the law, it had to be made right away. The only sure hold the villagers had on us was while we were present.

Here we see the "aparat" of which we spoke earlier at work. Connections to the aparat are valuable because if villagers are to be heard at all, it is through them. The law was a separate matter. Settling with the villagers would be only the first step. After that, the question of legal responsibility could be dealt with. The police here felt an obligation to prevent violence, no matter who had broken the law or in what manner. Villagers assumed that there was a correct way to behave; that they should be compensated by those who injured them, regardless of fault, as a way of recognizing the obligation of those with education and means toward their fellow Indonesians who are less fortunate. This is also the understanding of the police agents, though it is not a legal matter. Not to do so often means that villagers attack those they think are not fulfilling their obligation. This is not a question of primordial vengeance but of a certain nationalism, which, however, may also draw on earlier forms of justice.[1] The aparat appear here as those who understand this practice.

I have presented the story as if, were the police not to act, villagers were prepared to take matters into their own hands. This, however, is not the correct formulation, at least not for most villagers. They did not wait for the police to do something, and, once the police failed, decide to act themselves. The interval between the accident and the chase was barely sufficient for us to right the Jeep and for them to mobilize themselves. The police felt in the middle. They feared retaliation from the villagers against themselves if we left without making compensation. We ran off because we feared violence from the villagers. We were first threatened, then chased, and we had no protection from the police or from anyone else. The police feared that if we were seen running, it would provoke the villagers. But they had already indicated their intentions. We might have headed them off if we had begun to negotiate with the youths, but R was not at that moment in a position to do so and I could not speak for him, even if I knew then what I later learned about how to deal with such incidents.

The police were not, in the first place, concerned with us as guilty of a legal infraction. Nor were they concerned with our safety. Had either been the case they would have stayed with us. What concerned them was what the villagers might do. If we left, they might hold the police responsible. They might burn the police station, or at least demonstrate. From their point of view, we were not criminals according to the law nor citizens requiring protection. We were individuals whose actions were sure to stimulate violence if nothing was done to stop it. Nor were villagers, in their eyes, possibly wronged citizens whose complaint had to be considered. Villagers here were becoming a mob and threatened violence of some kind: against them, the police, or against us. This agent of this violence did not fall under the categories of the law, at least not at that moment. They were the *massa*, the mob, and as such they were figures out of national mythology, associated with violence, and in their capacity as *massa* likely to be outside normal forms of communication. The police wanted to prevent this entity from coming into existence and, if they could not do so, they wanted to be out of the way of whatever might ensue. If they could do so safely, the police would take on the roles of spokesmen and mediators; if they couldn't, they would vanish, as, in fact, they did. However, they still hoped that we would remain within reach to prevent a diversion of violence against us toward them.[2]

We stayed overnight across from a police post some distance from the place of the accident, outside the area of the local aparat. The next day, an officer from the regional police office arrived and questioned us and then let us return to Jakarta by bus, the police retaining the Jeep as evidence for an eventual trial. This marked another change of register. From that point, and for some time further, the question was not "the law," but the legal bureaucracy. It was not a question of building a legal defense, but of extracting R from the officials of the local prosecutor's office and the police.

After we returned to Jakarta, we learned that the man on the motorbike had died. I am unable to say what emotional impact this had on R, who had been in a confused state since the accident. I suppose it left him, like me, amazed at one's own capacity to kill no matter what one's intentions. Practically, it made more urgent the overwhelming question of how to deal with the prosecutor's office. No one was certain whether R would be charged with a crime. Furthermore, the Jeep belonged to the organization R worked for and was still held by the police. The question concerning the prosecutor's office, from the beginning, was how R, with the help of his organization, was going to prevent any legal action from taking place. The immediate problem was how to find out how the accident was going to be dealt with by the police and prosecutor's office. In the usual Indonesian way, it turned out that someone from R's office had a brother-in-law who was a prosecutor, retired from the section of the office that would handle the case. A team, including R and several people from R's organization, most prominently the man with the brother-in-law, was formed to return and find out what was happening. I went along as well. I will not go into details, but this reconnaissance mission resulted in finding out facts in several different registers, the least of which was perhaps the legal register. The police had found traces of white paint, no doubt from the Jeep, on the pants and the helmet of the dead man. This evidence was enough to show that R was responsible for the accident, according to the brother-in-law. There was, of course, in the minds of everyone, the possibility that the evidence had been fabricated and that the man on the motorbike had skidded into the tree just as we had skidded into the paddy field. I had pointed out to the police officials at the time that there were no marks whatsoever of a collision on the Jeep. But the former prosecutor dismissed this; the police might not have been able to see them because it was dark (though it was four o'clock in the afternoon). The point here is that no one worried about the evidence. It only confirmed what we already knew: that the prosecutor's office could act against R. Whether the evidence was fabricated or not would never be an issue. Most importantly, no one worried about whether or not R was actually guilty. No one, including R, asked whether he had actually caused the accident by, for instance, driving unsafely, or even whether he had actually hit the man. These questions arose only for me. In the context of the law as it operated, or rather did not operate, they were irrelevant. In the context of the way a settlement was eventually reached, by an agreement between families, the law was also irrelevant. From the latter point of view, relations which, in fact, had been brought into being by the accident but which, in ideology, had existed since the beginning of the nation were disrupted, and it was up to both parties to negotiate a settlement.

The practical question was to find those who could be influenced. Influence took two forms. There were bribes. But bribes cannot be simply offered to anyone. One has to know who controls what and who will take bribes. The heads of the offices involved, the police chief and the head of the prosecutor's office, for instance, could not be offered bribes. One had to find out who controlled the flow of paper to make sure that the case fell into the desired hands. Those paid off were middle officials. With the help of the retired prosecutor, we got the necessary information; certain payments were made. However, it took months and there was no definitive resolution. Aside from the release of the car, the only result was that no action was taken. But no document ever confirmed that the case was closed. The effort was always to forestall the legal apparatus from working. And the form this took was to see that the documents concerning the case moved through certain channels and not others. No one bribed had the authority to definitively terminate the proceedings; or if they did, these authorities did not do so. They only moved the case on or refused to act. The effort, then, was to see that the legal machinery was set in motion in such a way that it would very slowly run down.

The other form of influence was menace. Whether threats were actually made or not I cannot say. But the boss of R's organization promised that if R were *peras*, "squeezed" (the term used to mean made to pay or to pay the consequences), which might include being brought to trial, the prosecutor would be moved to a *daerah kering*, a "dry district," meaning a region where there is little money to be made through corruption. Indeed, the city where all this took place was already "dry"; but the menace was that he would be moved somewhere with even fewer opportunities for graft. The menace, that is, was the use of influence to deprive a corrupt official, in a corrupt manner, of the chance for more lucrative corruption. And this in case our initial means of corruption did not work.

In all of this, there was not one place where one can say that the law functioned. But one can also say that without the threat of the law in the background, there would have been no game, not no menace that the legal apparatus would take R in its grasp and squeeze him. Everyone wanted the law not to work. The legal authorities would be deprived of financial opportunities. R and his colleagues, for their part, dismissed the possibility of proving R's innocence in a court of law, no doubt because it is well known that judges sell their judgments to the person who pays the most. Considerations of guilt or innocence, from the point of view of the law, were almost irrelevant. The actual operation of the law was limited to the fact that the prosecutor had enough evidence to keep hold of R. The idea of the law persists, even given its almost total lack of proper functioning, as an idea of punishment that descends from the state without regard to merit or justice. One is not entirely helpless before it if one has money and connections.

Actions in the legal register had no effect on R that I could perceive. Perhaps because the operations of the law offered so little chance of proving innocence, thinking through the events to determine who, if anyone, might have been at fault, never happened. And, not happening, the legal register offered no chance to formulate a version of the events that might have assuaged the turmoil besetting R. Had R had to occupy himself with the determinations of guilt according to the law, it might have prevented him from being captivated by the feelings and memories that arose in him after the accident. Instead, there occurred the beginnings of a trajectory from accident to the explanation of misfortune that Evans-Pritchard would have recognized.

A short time after the accident, R was convinced he had been, indeed, at fault. This had nothing to do with the facts of the accident. On the way back to Jakarta on the bus, he told me he had been certain that something terrible was going to happen. He had had a strong premonition the day before the event. We had visited the holy grave of one of the persons reputed to have brought Islam to Java. There were many beggars there. R had refused to give to one of them, who, he said, then warned him catastrophe was on its way. He became convinced the beggar was being truthful when he saw me buy some *jimat,* or amulets. These, he said, are dangerous because one never knows if the man who wrote them was good or evil. He went on to say that he did not believe in superstitions. He comes from a family that for a long time have been modernist Muslims who eschew such beliefs. But his grandfather, a strong modernist, had nonetheless once told him that their house was full of spirits. R himself had never seen them, but he had been shaken to see that his grandfather, despite his modernism, acknowledged such superstition. Another time, he said, his brother fell ill and no doctor could cure him. They brought him to a magical curer and he recovered. R said he could not entirely free himself from such beliefs.

The story of the *jimat,* in particular, bothered him. A few days later he told his wife that he was the only one who, after praying at the grave, had refused a *jimat* from the person in charge. He was convinced that in some way malevolent influence was at work against him. But not any sort of malevolent influence. Rather, it was precisely the type which his parents and grandparents had believed in despite themselves. When R invoked curses, omens, and amulets, he linked himself with those whom he believed in, his familial authorities; but they were a failed authority, from his point of view. They, too, did not believe in superstition; they, too, at critical moments succumbed to it. At the point where they failed, "superstition" appeared as a real force. Or, more likely, one can say that where superstition arose within him, so did memories of his father, his grandfather, and his mother. He became guilty because he brought the catastrophe on himself in various contradictory ways. He did not buy a *jimat* from the man in charge of the grave; he did not give to the beggar. His guilt stemmed from giving in to a belief that he held despite his attempt to reject it.

There was magical power at work, but it was not magical power in the first degree. It was magic that had been banished and then reappeared. And not merely banished by him, but by his ancestors, who themselves, however, could not rid themselves of it entirely, despite religious injunctions to do so. Injunctions they believed in. Beyond their conscious and sincere beliefs, and beyond R's, there were other beliefs under whose influence, and, he thought, control, he had fallen. He was, one might say, possessed by beliefs to which he could give no credence. And therefore against which he had no recourse.

By chance, R's mother came from the provinces to visit him in Jakarta. She had not known about the accident. He had a long talk with her, after which he was calm for the first time. He told me how marvelous it was to have a mother. How she, though she was a simple women without education, understood. She had explained to him that he should "do the right thing." This set in motion preparations for reaching a settlement. When we returned to call on the prosecutor and the chief of police, R explained, and with genuine eagerness, that he wanted to apologize to the family of the dead man.

The way to negotiation followed a particular path. First, there was the sense of impending doom that appeared after the fact of the accident. With this, the accident is not an accident at all, but something planned in advance. As I have had said, had the law operated, the event could have been put in another register in which magical believes were excluded and in which the accident as mere chance was also excluded. Instead, the sense of catastrophe, not entirely reducible to the actual events (R might have thought himself fortunate to have escaped with his life, for instance) prevailed. That sense of catastrophe, directed by an implacable power against R, is, as we have already said, close to a sense of guilt. But it is closer to a feeling of being in the control of powers beyond oneself. The contradictory stories—that it was R's fault for not giving to the beggar, that he behaved incorrectly by not buying an amulet at the grave, that it was my fault for buying an amulet, have in common a recourse to magical powers. Because he no longer believed in this power, none of the established ways of dealing with it, such as visiting magical curers, were open to him without a radical revision of who he was. As it stood, he was split. There was the modernist Muslim, Western-educated person on one side. This person felt overwhelmed, as every important authority in his life, beginning with his mother as she existed in his memory, was unavailing. Some of these authorities had themselves been in his situation. But he had not lost his belief in them, for all that. Giving in to magic was not a solution, unless he were also able to give up these authorities, the very ones responsible for placing him on the side of the enlightened as opposed to the ignorant masses who had attacked him. The difficulty was to acknowledge the forces that overwhelmed him. A difficulty compounded by their association, in his discourse, with particular social types. They were the forces of the Indonesian world that had not yet been encompassed in modernity.

Had the law operated he might have continued to play the educated person who knows how to resolve a situation, involving him with the law on one side and with less fortunate villagers on the other. He then, as a responsible Indonesian, could have invoked procedures that he, by contrast to those who had attacked us, understood. He would then also have "done the right thing" much earlier. That opportunity was taken away from him, and other views of himself prevailed. The accident was not a matter of a slippery road or ways of driving. It became a question of "why" it happened to him just at that moment.

Had he kept the thought that someone, perhaps me, since I bought the amulets, or the beggar, or the seller of the amulets, had malevolent intentions against him and had used supernatural means to further them, he would then have been in the situation of those who called Muki a witch. He would have found a reflection of unwonted and hitherto unperceived forces in himself that he could rid himself of only by doing away with the witch. That is, only by doing away with a figure who consolidated his own undesired powers to take life. To have taken this path, however, would have sunk him even deeper into the strata of Indonesian life which he and his family had left behind. It would have taken him past identification with his parents and left him entirely estranged from the person he knew himself to be up until the accident occurred.

The chase did not figure in R's accounts to me. He did not speak of how we barely escaped. Neither did he talk about the way in which the accident occurred. He apparently did not repeat the scene of the accident in his mind. He said nothing about the rain, the slippery road, the way the Jeep had turned over. He concerned himself not at all, so far as I could know, with the people involved in the accident. He only wanted to speak of the uncanny cause of the accident. In this, I believe he repeated the behavior of Azande when they were on the route to finding the witch. He was no more interested in the slipperiness of the road than the Azande were in the termites that caused the granary to fall on them. The question was the uniqueness of the event. And the uniqueness of the event could not be accounted for by knowable factors. He thus escaped the usual form of traumatized speech in which one speaks repeatedly and inadequately of what has happened. He was, instead, traumatized, if that is the right word here, in the register of magic. But the magic open to him did not result in the easy transition to narrative that we have seen among the Azande who applied to the oracle.

It is remarkable in the light of how the incident was settled that the people involved did not register in R's mind during the time he was obsessed with the accident. He was not concerned with the identity of the man on the motor bike, nor with the members of his family. His concern with knowing how at that time and place he could have been involved, a concern answerable only by magic or some similar idea, equally inexplicable, such as "fate," blinded him to them. A settlement, by which I mean, a settlement of R's mental state as well as of the conflict between him and the law and him and the surviving family, was made only when he could begin to recognize these people for who they were in the thinking of others. And here he had two choices. They could belong to the *massa*, blind savage force, incapable of ordinary communication, or they could be part of the *rakyat*, the people. In the latter case, he would be obliged to recognize them as fellow Indonesians in a sense which, as we will see, is familial and national at once, and thus to help them, regardless of who was responsible for the accident. But whichever the case, they had to enter his mind as actors in the scene. As it was, they were simply unrecognized, with the result that he was closed in upon himself in a world in which only those with magical powers figured. Social figures had to replace magical ones for him to regain himself.

One can return to the witch for the beginning of an account of how this happened. His occult power belongs to him as witch. As neighbor he is recognizable; as witch he has to be divined by special means. The witch is always a dual personality. One can say that the witch is the other of the self as it goes ordinarily unexpressed. Precisely for this reason, he is unacceptable. Witchcraft is the "proof," when the possibility is pressing, that one cannot take the place of the other. That one is not oneself what one accuses the other to be; one is not him and one cannot find oneself in his place. Once the witch is expelled, the world works again as it should. One's neighbor pays for his soup; one does not fall ill. One is oneself, which means that one is reassured by the reflection of oneself in the other. The accusation of witchcraft says that whatever it is that one sees of oneself in the witch is not true, abnormal and incompatible with normal social intercourse. Which is another way of saying that the multiple accounts of "oneself" one has when one can find no reflection of oneself are all repudiated in favor of the unitary being of everyday life. This is to say also that communication with the witch works abnormally, outside the equivalences that pertain when, for instance, one exchanges a bowl of soup for Rp.3,000 in the ordinary way. In the other case, one sells a bowl a soup and is paid in illness and death.

From inside witchcraft itself, however, we can see this incapacity differently. If R had found a satisfactory magical explanation for the accident, he would have been cured of his moroseness and his obsession. Had he done so, he would have been relieved of finding in himself elements that he had not recognized before. Because, indeed, R was someone else after the accident. Before, he was like the man who stopped to help us and warned villagers not to take the law into their own hands. He knew his place and he acted in those terms. He lost that capacity with the accident. He was now involved in another scenario in which his own part was unclear to him. To find the central character of that scenario, as it were, would be to take the next step and to see why he was really himself but affected by something from outside himself. But he could not do this. Nor could he take the normal step of settling the affair in the way that convention outlined for most Indonesians. He was caught in something he felt to be beyond himself, but which he could not understand. The problem, indeed, is that the "he" of this paragraph had no identity.

He was deprived not only of an identity and with that of his capacity to be social. A way out, an exorcism of some sort, would then have been possible. As it was, he lacked the ability to narrate satisfactorily. He could only say things which appeared to him as inadequate, which is why he invented so many different explanations. We should note that the variety of explanations he gave were not different possible reasons for the event, among which he could chose. Rather, they simply appeared one after the other because of the inadequacy of whatever he had said previously. It was not a puzzle that concerned him. What he lacked was a word which would justify the stories he gave, a word such as "witch" that, once accepted, would make things impossible to explain seem explicable. The dilemma he found himself in called for a magic word, but none was available to him. He knew one existed—it might have been *santet* (witch), for instance. But when he found it, he rejected it for the reasons we have seen above. His explanations were each plausible in their own terms, but the terms changed, oscillating as they did between the words of magic—"amulet," for instance—and the devaluation of these terms in modernism.

The magical word, in that sense, still seemed to him to exist, but he could not find it. He did not know what to focus on. He needed a word to interpret in the way that the Zuni warriors wanted magical feathers.

The function of such a word or such an object would be not to stop the creation of stories but to show that they were linked to one another as aspects of a certain power. The word would thus be a copula of sorts. As it was, there were associations without linkages, governed by nothing in particular. The Zuni sorcerer created stories and displayed a power, "proof" of sorcery, and would have been put to death for doing so, the "just" reward for the destruction of the social. R's creation of stories, one displacing the other, was the creation of memories whose references to the past did nothing to stabilize his narrative stream. They did not leave him in a position, even, of someone able to be judged.

The stories were told by himself to himself. I was there because I was in the vicinity, someone overhearing him, an excuse for R to talk to himself rather than being a true interlocutor. At best, I existed as a foreigner who, as a friend, was benign, a neutralizing version of the third person, perhaps. It was not until, years later, after I had asked his permission to publish an account based on the notes I took at the time, that my status may have changed. R, however, was generous indeed in allowing me to do so, all the more so in that the Indonesian political situation was not yet settled and he was justifiably worried about how he might be viewed were his identity to be revealed. It is to acknowledge his generosity that I interrupt my narrative at this point.

His mother's advice saved him. Yet she only told him to do what everyone had expected of him. It was in his power to bring the situation to an end. But it is obvious that he was incapable of doing so before he met with his mother. He was obsessed with the magical causes of the event, but he had found no one he thought reliable who could confirm his thoughts about magic. Everyone recognized in him only the person who, educated and with a good position, would automatically behave correctly. Finding no one to confirm thoughts of himself that seemed now to define him, he could do nothing.

If his mother's advice worked where nothing else would, it seems likely that it is because she restored to him a sense of the familiarity of his old self. No one knew that self better than his mother. What was at stake, then, was familiarity of himself to himself, which demanded the driving out of the possessed other of himself. This, in his case, could be done only through the authority of his mother to assure him that he was who she, the first ever to know him and therefore someone who knew versions of himself that he was necessarily unaware of, knew him to be. It was a question of acceding to familiarity in order to, or with the consequence of, putting into the background an overwhelming volume of shreds of thoughts and memories.

This was done in the double register of kinship and of nation. The widow, he told me after he had apologized and given the family a large sum of money, was his "mother." She could become so because he had behaved by a nationally defined standard, though one probably derived from Malay or Javanese kinship. If she had not been Indonesian, if the accident had not happened in Indonesia, the change of registers would not have been possible in the form that it took.

As it was, the putting of overwhelming power into the background in favor of a relationship given in terms of kinship followed a general tendency in Indonesia which, though not beginning in the Suharto period, developed on a wide scale during those years. It duplicated the pattern by which one had a relationship to the center, perhaps to President Suharto himself, because one had an acquaintance who knew someone who knew someone and so on. And this, just during the time when Suharto demonstrated that as president he was bound by no restraints in law.

Recognition is the end of singularity. One sees in terms of something that already exists and one then "knows" it. R could not recognize in the man who had the accident himself as he had been—the foreign educated, the person who knew how to make his way and how to behave correctly. Nor could he recognize the widow as a version, for instance, of his mother, or her children as his putative brother and sister. He had, in effect, to allow himself the possibility of having two mothers, one the duplicate of the other, or one the standard by which the second was recognizable. It was a question of the singular and the plural. He needed to make use of duplication and, until his mother arrived, he could find only singularity.

After his mother arrived, singularity was forgotten in favor of convention. But this transition should not conceal its logical impossibility. That it happened nonetheless has everything to do with his mother. Her power was to see in him what she knew him to be but he did not. She could do this, I believe, because her authority did not depend on the categories of the nation, nor did they depend exclusively on ideas about what "mother" means, either from an Indonesian national or a strictly genealogical point of view. One's mother knows one before one knows oneself. She therefore knows one and knows about one in ways that have force and yet are not subject to confirmation by appeal to memory or convention. In ordinary circumstances one leaves this special authority aside. But in the circumstances that prevailed, R found his mother convincing. He believed that she knew something about him that he himself did not know. There was no necessity to the outcome of their encounter. From out of the privacy of this relationship, its irreducibility to other forms of relationship, a form of recognition was somehow generated. His mother, in effect, consented to being doubled. She authorized the possibility of finding another like her for her son. It was a concession granted by the familial to the nation.

Witch and Violence

In the anecdote just related, "magic" without accepted magical discourse figures as the singular and thus the unrecognizable. The movement away from magic into categories generated by nationalism illuminates the fear of the people. This fear is the result of the incompleted revolution, of the reappearance of revolution, and it can be seen also as an effect of the foundation of nationalism and the break with the colonial order, as I have argued elsewhere.[3] There can be no doubt of the political use of this fear in the New Order. But the fear of the people cannot be entirely reduced to political strategy. It is inherent not only in the historical forces I have just mentioned. Rather, the movement from magical singularity to the recognition of "the people" (*rakyat*), of the kindred of Indonesians and especially of "the mob" (*massa*), bears within it the traces of the magic that it obscures. The impossibility of the relation of self/other and the fear of death are concealed but nonetheless felt in the menace of the lethal mob. Magic, in that sense, has not been banished, merely sublimated or buried.

In East Java, when relations to the state were feared to have been broken and national categories felt not to apply, witchcraft emerged. Wherever one turned, there was lethal menace rather than consolidated conflict. Anyone could be a witch. The fear of the people consolidates fear and attempts (without being entirely successful) to give it a social and political definition against which the state can organize itself. When Indonesian categories failed to hold, this fear splintered to reemerge in, it seems, practically every human being of the rural region where witch hunts began. Witch hunts attempted to consolidate fears again. The witch hunts were the work of men usually from the same village. But they were not the work of "the village." They were carried out by men who felt themselves all to be in the same position in regard to the menace of death. Differences were obscured in favor of a common anxiety which defined the members of the group. We see this, for instance, in the case of the boys who joined in killing one of their friend's father. They did not do so in their capacities of friend or enemy, but as those who "went along," as they put it, with others, and who acted to save their own lives. Banding together, they reached for political recognition through the use of the word *massa*.

R represents another path. In him, we see fear as an aspect of the person, hence private and psychological. This was, however, ambiguous. The ambiguity reflects the place of magical belief in Indonesia. On the one hand, Indonesian nationalism brought with it modernity for the Indonesian people and hence a rejection of "superstition." But on the other, the generation of an idea of "superstition" which occurred in Europe as a result of the division between elite, literate culture and popular belief did not happen with the same clarity in Indonesia.[4] There, as we have said, with the replacement of Dutch rulers by educated Indonesians, Javanese "feudalism," with its complicated forms of etiquette, was disowned. But the beliefs of the courts retained their prestige. Presidents of Indonesia regularly consult soothsayers. R, as a modernist Muslim, did not share in this. But neither could he find unambiguous opinions which would have helped him reject his fear of being cursed.

At the same time, the way to social reintegration was not through psychology, therapy, and so on, but, as we have seen, through the reassertion of nationalist categories. Witchcraft, or at least its elements, was not disowned, merely reburied. Its violent potential was not eliminated, any more than nationalist thinking eliminated it. But could it ever be? As the presence of witchcraft and the accusations of child abuse that go with it in America show,[5] witch hunts are a potential of human relations, or, more precisely, of their breakdown. They cannot be entirely reduced to historical circumstances.

R's magical explanations tried to show how the events of the accident were linked together. He invented ideas about the workings of the world which expressed the world's abnormality, searching as he did for something that would connect events—or words—which otherwise remained disparate. Had others shared what he said, the conventional magic word would have been reinvented and a witch might have been named. But in the end his accounts were instead displaced through the words of his mother. He recovered his "own" words; convention reappeared. No witch presented himself; possible magic evaporated. Witchcraft, that is, needs not only accident as the pure gift and with it the collapse of social relations; it needs also the mediation of foreign words eventually accepted as such. Through the magic word, the invisible trace (in the Derridean sense of this word) of the provenance of the pure gift offers itself for discourse if not for interpretation, making the gift less than pure and making the naming of the witch seem to be possible. "Witch," during a witch hunt, is thus a word with two sides. On the one hand, it indicates the impossibility of naming the provenance of the pure gift; on the other, the very existence of this name obscures this impossibility.

7

Naming the Witch

I. Lévi-Strauss Again

Witchcraft, held responsible for the insupportable and inexplicable travails of the world, says that society is innocent. "Witchcraft explains unfortunate events," once formulated by ethnographers, makes witchcraft explicable, as it rightly describes the mythological function of witchcraft. One is innocent, one is a good neighbor, one has children, friends, kinsmen, and yet one suffers and one dies. No one can help. This failure of the social is hidden from view by the witch. Normality is not fundamentally inadequate when death is the work of witchcraft. This would be the profit of the exchange of justice for truth when witchcraft works as Lévi-Strauss claimed, bringing the worst suspicions into expression.

According to Lévi-Strauss, the marginal social types that exist in every society express what in normal terms cannot be said. They may be handicapped, unable to fully participate in social life. But it is persons from this category who articulate what cannot be articulated by the reason that pertains to a society. Thus, the witch.

In his *Introduction to the Work of Marcel Mauss*, Lévi-Strauss says what is necessary in order to be sane:

For, strictly speaking, the person whom we call sane is the one who is capable of alienating himself, since he consents to an existence in a world definable only by the self-other relationship. The saneness of the individual mind implies participation in social life, just as the refusal to enter into it . . . corresponds to the onset of mental disturbance.[1]

To alienate oneself, as Lévi-Strauss understands it, means to accept that one is defined by one's relation to the other; one is not self-sufficient or self-defined. This necessarily means a split in the self; one identifies oneself with the other and at the same time one is whoever one was before the identification took place. "Sanity" is the capacity to manage this division. Those who cannot do so live disproportionately, either in the other or within themselves.

The implication of this passage, taken together with the statement about the language of the curer as we discussed it in chapter 1 is that some people, those who cannot manage this split in identity, will have a special access to "pure" language, to language with little concern for reference to the world. This enables them to speak as the Zuni sorcerer spoke, caught as he was in the words which carried him forward even against his interests, without regard for the reality of those in front of whom he spoke. Neither common sense nor verisimilitude governed his discourse, but a possibility suggested to him by the suspicion of his audience which they themselves could not bring to expression.

People so situated are necessary to society, in Lévi-Strauss's thinking. Lévi-Strauss thought of culture as a series of systems which are only imperfectly translatable into each other. Inadequacy of translation is made up for by persons who emerge from the social margins:

Any culture can be considered as a combination of symbolic systems headed by language, the matrimonial rules, the economic relations, art, science and religion. All the systems seek to express certain aspects of physical reality and social reality, and even more, to express the links that those two types of reality have with each other and those that occur among the symbolic systems themselves. (16)

There are reasons that the relations between systems are always inadequate. First, because, as "a result of the conditions of functioning proper to each system . . . the systems always remain incommensurable" (17). For instance, one cannot translate music into language; the systems are different; the terms of their functioning prevent such translation. Furthermore, whatever equilibrium there might be between systems, history disrupts. There is the impact of other societies, for instance, and even if there were not, translation between systems depends on "values external to the two systems" (17). If we take the example of translation between languages, we understand that translations have to be remade because the values that govern the establishing of the equivalences between them come to seem inadequate.

Lévi-Strauss rephrases his hypothesis into terms that apply to witch-craft:

Instead of saying that a society is never completely symbolic, it would be more accurate to say that it can never manage to give all its members, to the same degree, the means whereby they could give their services fully to the building of a symbolic structure which is only realizable (in the context of normal thinking) in the dimension of social life. (17–18)

Only certain persons are capable of completing "the symbolic structure." The demand on these persons can be seen, for instance, in the Zuni interest in truth. There is a suspicion that something has been left unsaid or unnamed. And there are people "who find themselves placed 'off system,' so to speak, or between two or more irreducible systems." Such people have "apparently aberrant modes of behavior" (18). They might be ill. They might seem to be abnormal, but these very people make the system work. "The group seeks and even requires of those individuals that they figuratively represent certain forms of compromise which are not realizable on the collective plane; that they simulate imaginary transitions, embody incompatible syntheses" (18). They may be "peripheral," but they are nonetheless "integral parts of the total system" just because of that. Placed as they are between systems, and therefore unable to fully participate in the normal way in social life, they feel the differences and therefore articulate them. By definition, their articulations have to take special forms and this is all for the best. "It can therefore be said that for every society, the relation between normal and special modes of behavior is one of complementarity" (19).

Lévi-Strauss thus accounts for those considered abnormal, their very abnormality being the condition for their usefulness. Such a theory is not improbable on the face of it. Those on the social margins are more likely to say what others would not think of saying. The test of Lévi-Strauss's explanation is the acceptance by others of what the marginal person says. Lévi-Strauss finds it reasonable and even necessary that it be accepted.. People feel their lack of symbolic capacity, and the witch or his equivalent provides them with it. The Zuni witch, who at the beginning of the episode is not known to be a witch at all, admits to being one and says what people suspect. When he does so, he imaginatively remakes himself in order to fit the incoherent impressions of others. Their suspicion marks their "lack of symbolic capacity." The boy, taking his clue from it, makes up for their inability to formulate. He makes up a story, the central figure of which is himself, and it is accepted.

Before this, suspected of being a witch but without the satisfactory articulation of that possibility, he would not be "capable of alienating himself," to put it in the mild terms of Lévi-Strauss. "Mild" because being accepted by others means he figuratively, and thus within the reality of discourse and with the implications that implies, becomes a murderer. He "consents to an existence in a world definable only by the self-other relationship," in which "self" means "witch/murderer." "The saneness of the individual mind implies participation in social life," says Lévi-Strauss, and this man participates as one who killed his neighbors rather than live with them. The hearing of his confession excuses him to the community because just such a figure lends coherence to a culture where it otherwise lacks it. Misfortune and accident are then comprehensible. Murder may be condemned, but incoherence is worse because it shows the limitation of the social. When the Zuni witch confesses, incoherence is converted into expression and the social dominates.

We might think that the admission of murder as a route to social acceptance is aberrant or that it is a transvaluation of values. But this is not precisely what Lévi-Strauss says. It is not the inversion of social values, which is perfectly within the possibility of articulation as such, nor the simple bringing to the surface of a suppressed wish, but something structural that accounts for the exchange of truth for justice. The incommensurability of systems of thought itself creates suspicion. The pressure to articulate, the thought that something is hidden, is built into the nature of culture and of language and becomes intolerable for everyone. The story of murder by witchcraft would be the release of this pressure. Its very improbability satisfies the feeling that something inexpressible needs to be expressed nonetheless. There is a maleficent power; it exists. Its revelation is the restoration of mental coherence. One forgets about the damage caused by the sorcerer out of relief at having suspicion confirmed.

There is nothing in Lévi-Strauss's formulation that makes stories of murder and violence necessarily the subject of the witch's discourse. But at the same time, confession to murder as a route to social acceptance could be taken to indicate how difficult it is to represent what is otherwise un-

representable. The eager acceptance of the accusation "murderer/witch" is
the effect of the pressure to speak in the presence of suspicion. As such,
it needs the lurid and unusual, which is usually also the socially harmful.
But, once again, in Lévi-Strauss's explanation, real murder, the hanging of
the sorcerer, is avoided by the telling of the story.

In any case, Lévi-Strauss does not say that the relief of the pressure to
articulate is always lurid. The articulation of discrete systems results sometimes in the naming of the sorcerer and sometimes in art, poetry, and "every mythic and aesthetic invention," as he remarks when he comes to his
idea of the floating signifier which is the means to this linkage (63). For
Lévi-Strauss, what is important is the "equilibrium" generated by these
activities. Without sorcerers and other marginal types, "the total system
would be in danger of disintegrating into its local systems" (19). "The
group seeks and even requires of those individuals (who are 'off system')
that they figuratively represent certain forms of compromise which are not
realizable on the collective plane; that they simulate imaginary transitions,
embody incompatible syntheses" (18).

Presumably, they would not be able to do so without the means provided by already existing systems of signification:

A fundamental situation perseveres which arises out of the human condition:
namely, that man has from the start had at his disposition a signifier-totality which
he is at a loss to know how to allocate to a signified. . . . There is always a non-
equivalence or "inadequation" between the two, a non-fit and overspill which divine understanding alone can soak up; this generates a signifier-surfeit relative
to the signifieds to which it can be fitted. So, in man's effort to understand the
world, he always disposes of a surplus of signification. . . . That distribution of a
supplementary ration . . . is absolutely necessary to ensure that, in total, the available signifier and the mapped-out signified may remain in the relationship of
complementarity which is the very condition of the exercise of symbolic thinking. (62–63)

The mark of this "signifier-surfeit" is the magic word which links domains
and insures a degree of cultural coherence. The "imaginary transitions"
and "incompatible syntheses" have their sociological locus in marginal figures and their cultural locus in language. Thus, the incompletely symbolic is incipiently symbolic, while the marginalization of social types results
in their social usefulness. Where is there room here for the witch, as we

have seen him among, say, the Murngin? Is the sight of the dripping killing stick, of the "half dead" who exceed cultural categories, the result of an
overwhelming power to symbolize? We have rather treated it as the near
opposite; as an effect of the inability to bring the "half dead" into a symbolic construction. When, as with the Azande, witchcraft as an institution
depends on the oracle, is this not an indication of the workings of Lévi-
Strauss's notion? But it is not the oracle as such, but rather the convention
of acceptance of what it says, a convention linked to a political structure,
including the authority of the princes' oracles and the injunction of the
British that forbade the killing of those accused of witchcraft, that made
witchcraft seem a viable institution. Furthermore, as we have seen, the oracle produces suspicion as much as it resolves it. Which is to say that it produces a "signifier-surfeit," validating as it does the power of witches, at the
moment that it indicates the guilt of any individual of being a witch.

The pursuit of certain cases, at least, of witchcraft does not show that
making symbolic is the means by which the sorcerer is named, nor necessarily, were it to be so, that it provides coherence. Not only the killing
of the witch, but the repeated killings of witches, indicates incoherence.
In place of the comfortable denial common to witchcraft—that death is
caused by witches, that eliminating the witch repays him for his lethal efforts with the satisfactory exchange thus established—the "equity" of exchange is an illusion established by political arrangements. One sees this
in the complaint today that colonial power, which prevented the killing of
witches, did not protect Africans from witchcraft.

Everything thus points to witchcraft as a power different from that
which results in political structure. To put it differently, the authority of
the witch is questionable. The fear he stimulates is not socially integrated
or integrating. It would be if the entire interest in naming the witch was
to confirm suspicion, and if this interest was always realizable. Different
systems would thus always tend toward the compatible; there would always be incipient coherence and thus a possible basis for the exchange of
truth for justice, to the profit of political arrangements. Then, no matter
how terrifying his message, the coherence produced by the witch would be
translatable into authority. The power of the witch would be appropriable
by the Zuni warriors, either because they shared in it or because they protected against it. They, however, were fascinated by a power which, with-

out Mrs. Stevenson, they would have tried to banish, only to have it autonomously reappear.

Killing the witch is not exactly killing the enemy. The witch, it is true,
threatens political power. But "witch" could be the basis against which a
polity is formed only if the witch could be identified and thus built into an
ideology. The fear of witches as we have seen it, however, is directed against
something unnamable. The word "witch" galvanizes attention only when it
is charged with the uncanny, and that is not always the case. When it is, it
remains outside the possibility of recognition, which would be the basis for
making "witch" the equivalent of "enemy" and thus the basis for a political
system. Which is to say that the authority of the Zuni warriors is not based
on their ability to defend the community against witches. By the same to-
ken, the people of East Java who murdered Muki and his family, though
they claimed to save their village, could not transform their deeds into the
recognition from the state which they thought they merited. Those who
murdered in the name of the *massa* tried to take on a recognizable political identity. They succeeded, however, only in confronting a state apparatus which was concerned to reassert its authority and did so without clas-
sifying them as "witch murderers," or perhaps "saviors from witchcraft,"
rather than simply "murderers." The best that could be done was for local
political leaders to think of the lawlessness of their actions as proto-revolutionary, where "revolution" had an unrecognizable source different from
and threatening to the national revolution claimed by the regime.

For Lévi-Strauss, the witch integrates not because he is an enemy but
because he unifies a voice which has been dispersed among contending individuals. This unification is the condition for the expression of truth and
thus for the putative exchange of truth for justice. In reality, the confessing witch does not possess an integral voice. Like the shaman, he speaks in
another persona. Even this characteristic is inaccurate, however. The curer
who goes into trance can be said to have a second persona, usually with
identifiable sources for the voices that issue from him (or, often, her), such
as spirit familiars. Such voices can be appropriated, albeit by complicated
means.[2] But the witch is inspired from no one knows where in the cases we
have examined. He or she speaks from elsewhere, in the voice of a nameless
other. In the Zuni case, the accused person's confessions are rejected up till
the point where he overawes his listener. At that moment, no one replies

to him. He is unanswerable, speaking, finally, in a voice which is as close to being entirely foreign as possible while remaining understandable. Such a voice cannot be appropriated or mimicked by others; it is uninhabitable.[3]

The Zuni witch is named by the community, assumes the name "witch," and convinces others he is a witch by his speech. He is first called a witch and then he proves it by speaking as one. As we have seen, his capacity to speak as such is central to Lévi-Strauss's argument. The accused can embody suspicion; he makes its supposed substance issue forth from himself by his power to recount. The warriors are fascinated with the power displayed by the witch. They forget the original charge against him as their attention is taken by the artifacts of his magical force. Their fascination with that power indicates their desire for it, but not their ability to appropriate it. The Zuni witch is the analogue of the Azande oracle. He turns suspicion into certainty by eliminating other suspected possibilities. But he does it by saying what other Zuni cannot imagine. This consists of inventing events in order to show that impossible connections can be made. Up to this point, we confirm the interpretation of Lévi-Strauss.

Everything depends on a man being named a witch while that naming, to be effective in the Zuni case, has to designate someone who can speak as the witch. But their naming of such a person only shows that they themselves cannot say the same thing. They, who ordinarily are the powers in the community, meet a power to which they have no access. Whatever foreign power it is that speaks to the witch overcomes them. They become the addressee of the accused, but in so doing, they are no longer who they were as warriors. They meet a version of themselves, or of their power, which is greater than themselves. And then the witch is murdered by the warriors in their capacity as warriors. They reassert a social power in the face of a power of discourse that they cannot contain. The witch, then, is the opposite of an enemy because the enemy is always an equivalent; someone recognizable who offers the possibility of being conquered. The witch, however, asserts a nondialectical possibility; he cannot be assimilated. The witch merely indicates that there is a power, in effect a power of discourse, that is outside control even of the person who is accused.

One might argue that the witch, nonetheless, becomes the voice of the community, saying what they cannot say. But is this an accurate formulation? Voice implies that the sorcerer says what is intended. He is the "voice of the community" because the intention belongs to the community, integrating its individual voices. It is they, the warriors in particular, who suspect and who want to see power. But the boy was not a witch before he was called one. He had to invent his own witchcraft. Or, rather, he had to be coerced to do so. "His" words are not his. Initially, they are forced onto him by the community. He is carried away by them to the point where he becomes, through them, someone he surely would not have recognized earlier. His is a strange voice, not belonging to himself. It is the voice of a ventriloquist or of a puppet and at the same time the voice of a man, a voice alien to the Zuni repertoire. It is not the voice of the community but rather the expression of what the community fears set in a form of expression unavailable to them.

We might think further in Lévi-Strauss's terms. The sorcerer, telling his account, feels his eyes change to blue, the color of American eyes. We can speculate that he incorporates American power. That power is immensely destructive, going far beyond the harm he is accused of doing to the girl initially. Lévi-Strauss can account for an impossible synthesis of systems, in this case, incompatible political systems. "We can see quite well how and why a witch doctor is an element of social equilibrium" (19). If so, it would be because the power of the witch would domesticate American power. It would make it an element in Zuni ideas. But it is evident that this "equilibrium" did not hold at that moment. Zuni ask Mrs. Stevenson to take the feathers the Zuni sorcerer has produced as proof of his power to the president, to show him that sorcerers do exist. The conclusion is evident: Zuni should be allowed to protect themselves by hanging the witches they discover. Incompatible systems are conjoined through the narrative of the witch, which ends in producing proof of itself. But this conclusion does not hold. There is not a balance of powers, but either the conquerer's imposition of his peace or the conquered's symbolic and temporary riddance of the victor.

The Zuni conclusion is that the witch be killed. Mrs. Stevenson had an ethical objection to this. I share it, but it is not the basis of my criticism. Unlike Mrs. Stevenson, I do not dismiss belief in witches as superstition. I merely ask whether an equilibrium between systems is generated, as Lévi-Strauss would have us believe. The witch confesses to murder. It is around this pristinely asocial act that Lévi-Strauss wants to say that social equilibrium is achieved. One sympathizes with Africans whose fears are real, regardless of whatever it is that gives rise to them. The recognition of their terror by the state, however, does not banish it. Without the sharing of the equivalent fears among the Murngin, the fear of the "half dead," there would be no voodoo death. If the Azande were able to manage witchcraft, it is, by contrast, ultimately because political power—that of the British and the Azande princes—forbade the consequences of the recognition of witchcraft. The inability to appropriate the strange power of witchcraft is evident, however, in the persistent imbalance of exchange and in the suspicion which accompanied it. One sees here the inability to integrate the voice of the witch.

One understands a fascination with murder and the attempt to appropriate the force that motivates it. No one familiar with the history of the twentieth century will fail to recognize this possibility. The murders of East Javanese witches approach it; even more so the murders of Indonesians suspected of being Communists in 1965. Narrative and phallic power are conjoined in the Zuni witch's testimony to produce something inappropriable. The argument depends on how the witch is named. On whether culture assimilates the inassimilable and by that means tames violence. Or whether the naming of a witch is a step in a process which tends toward the elimination of elements thought unsupportable because unassimilable, and therefore, at times at least, leads to a divisive violence.

II. A Strange Performative

There are other approaches to the subject. "Witch" is the effect of a speech act. Like the famous promise of Austin, a witch does not exist until he is pronounced. Austin insisted that a promise is the result of an intention. The witch, however, is a strange creature from this point of view. Can one say that when Muki was called a witch, it was with the idea that, out of their own volition, villagers decided Muki was a witch or intended him to be one, in this way inventing him? Without "proof" would such an accusation have any meaning? Was it not because their stomachs swelled, because their wounds would not heal, because they fell sick for no reason, because some died, and, above all, because they were convinced that they were next to die that they called Muki a witch? It was not that they wanted to, or that they decided to. They felt that they had no choice. They had to call him a witch because they sensed death near to them and even already within them. The Javanese witch of 1998 was thus a witch not in the first place by a belief in witchcraft or by convention. He came into being by a coincidence of factors which compelled villagers to accuse, that is to say, to speak.

What stimulated the Javanese witch hunt was the intuition that one was possessed by elements strange to oneself. It is easier to say that what we name the "self" here is split. There is the normal self which responds to everyday conventions; one knows without thinking about it that one is the same as one was yesterday. And there is another whose swollen belly designates another person (for lack of an appropriate word), unknown to the first, but intertwined with him. At that point one does not know with whose voice one speaks.

Pronounced, announced, the witch accounts for this splitting within one. It names the foreign within oneself as the effect of an alien force hidden under the guise of one's neighbor. What one suspected but could not name takes shape. One thus accounts for strange behavior. One sells Muki soup but he does not pay. One duns him only at the cost of suffering an infection. Ordinary exchange becomes extraordinary. One gets a swollen belly in place of Rp1,000. Muki does not pay; he is a witch; one cannot expect him to pay. But one still deals with Muki, giving him soup in the hope of evading disaster. If one does so, one assumes that one is vulnerable; that Muki has a power over one for some reason that one does not know. It is not an ordinary power, of the sort one knows from the experience of seeing, for instance, a gun. It is one based on "proof," which is to say that it depends on what one knows already from knowledge lodged in oneself, although inaccessible to one's own scrutiny and critical faculties.

If Muki is a witch, then, confronting him, who am I? There is another being in the place not only of the neighbor but of oneself. The ordinary reassurance of oneself one gets when dealing with one's neighbor is missing. And one cannot extricate oneself. As witchcraft explains misfortune it also reflects oneself back to oneself as strange but as understandably so. It is why acknowledgment is central to witchcraft as an institution. The accused Azande excuses himself. He did not know he was a witch. He has no malevolent intentions. The matter ends there. What is suspected but not heretofore expressible has become expressed. The witch is established and with his establishment the doubleness of oneself becomes reasonable. This we could call the successful witch, the one through whom truth issues and who makes revindication, if not exactly justice, secondary. But the question is still open whether the path to this institution runs simply from suspicion to accusation to acceptance. With the Azande and the Zuni, this occurred only through the coercion of colonial power, which forbade the killing of witches.

The witch confirms something within oneself unknown to oneself. Since the witch often does not know he is one, he looks for evidence about himself. It was the case with the Zuni sorcerer. It was not only feathers and other implements he sought and found. He noticed (but how?) his eyes change color. The witch was powerful, was actually a witch, when his eyes were those of foreigners, perhaps of Mrs. Stevenson herself. To call someone a witch and to find the evidence for it is to find the foreign present within Zuni society. And not any foreigner, but the conqueror. To accuse someone of witchcraft is to find in them a power to which one has to submit. It is to find the foreign power that one senses at work in someone near at hand. If truth is ever more important than justice, it is because to call someone a witch is to try to incorporate this power, if not into oneself, into one's own cultural terms. Even if it works malevolently, the "truth" here is "our" truth. It belongs to the Zuni repertoire.

But we have seen that the Zuni witch was only tolerated because of Mrs. Stevenson's threat. Perhaps it was foreign force that stimulated Zuni witchcraft, but that same force also allowed the accused witch to continue to live. But whether the witch is killed or not, witchcraft is not eliminated. Which means that even when foreign power is incorporated in the witch, the references of witchcraft are not complete when one sees the witch as Zuni-American. The reference of witchcraft cannot be wholly assimilated through the figure of the witch. Behind American power there is another, still greater force, that remains unnamed.

Through the concept "witchcraft," there is an attempt to assimilate power alien to a cultural system. Witch killings seem to begin when this attempt at assimilation fails. "Witch," rather than being an understood concept, then, in given historical circumstances points to a limit or an alterity which cannot be accepted. If one could acknowledge the other, there would be no witchcraft. There would be instead, for instance, the acceptance of the possibilities closed off to oneself. However, when the other reflects death within one, it is not surprising that there is no dialectical movement.

If witchcraft were merely a conception, enlightenment might remove it from history once and for all as mere superstition. Superstition is excessive credulity, in the West usually thought to be the result of cultural lag. It is thus unjustified belief; what reason cannot establish has to be left unexplained. But witchcraft does not go away, no matter how convincing the explanations are of its lack of basis. It might be better not to understand witchcraft as ignorance to be banished through explanation, but as based on a credulity which forces itself on people in certain situations. Witchcraft would then not be founded on ideas or stereotypes of witches but on the uncanny which appears without regularity. To say this is to take account, for instance, of the fact that where witchcraft beliefs prevail, they are not activated on all occasions. It is only when a combination of historically given factors occur that some have a sensation of the uncanny.

Freud, the most important explicator of the uncanny, gives an example of an experience of his own. Riding in a compartment of a train, the door flew open and a stranger entered for whom Freud felt antipathy. The door had opened by itself and Freud had seen his reflection in a mirror attached to it, but without recognizing it for what it was. As a consequence, a version of himself produced antipathy which Freud thought was perhaps "a vestigial trace of that older reaction which feels the double to be something uncanny." If there had been no reference to himself at all Freud might have found his unrecognized reflection neutral. However, facing a version of himself in which he could not find himself was unsettling.[4]

Freud does not elaborate the reasons for his uncanny sensation. In his essay, he attributes the uncanny to the return of something seen earlier and then forgotten. The return of the repressed accounts for the sense of déjà vu. But this may be secondary to seeing oneself freed, for an instant, of one's usual view of oneself as reflected back by others. For Heidegger, "Uncanniness is the fundamental kind of being-in-the-world, although it is covered over in everydayness."[5] *Dasein*, being-in-the-world, heretofore sunk in worldly preoccupations, is delivered over to itself through the working of anxiety. Realizing it is not at home in the world, freed of absorption in others, no longer *en face* of anyone but itself, *dasein* finds itself uncanny. The uncanny, which Heidegger terms a "mood," is thus a result of a removal from the world of the daily, a moment when everyday definitions of oneself no longer hold. The moment when one loses one's everyday definition of oneself can also be the moment when one loses one's everyday "I," the "I" who speaks as well. The connection between oneself and signs is lost.

This brings us close to the witchcraft cases we have looked at. When the Murngin is faced with the "half dead," neither dead nor alive, he finds himself as one of them and unlike every version of himself he had previously known. His fellows shrink from him. So, too, in East Java, what I have mildly called the "unbalance" of exchange means that the assumptions one brings to exchange with others do not hold. One cannot find a recognition of oneself in the reactions of the other. One is other to oneself and therefore calls the other "witch." *En face* of the witch, one finds a version of oneself entirely unlike the everyday self one had assumed and which had been heretofore verified in daily life. These moments are uncanny and, we will argue, are not recuperated for the self by a retelling of the event.

The removal from the daily, however, is scarcely a simple matter. In East Java, we claim, it occurred when it was felt that connections with authority had ceased. This amounts to saying that there is someone who before kept me in view and who no longer does so. I was seen by the other, but I am no longer. Where the double of myself was, in the eyes of the other, there is now "nothing." This lack of myself, however, is not a blank. One cannot imagine it without at the same time imagining an impossible double. One which has to be posited in order to think that it is no longer there. Both the other and the self disappear at the same time without, however, disappearing definitively. A paradoxically substantive "nothing" now reflects itself back to me.

This would be the nearest we could come to the place of the true gift, the gift which never occurs and which is therefore never repaid. It is the point from which something issues to which we feel compelled to react. But this point is not a point since it is both "nothing" and something; both me and not me. It is the absence of a place. In the face of this ambiguity people wanted to speak. What they said was "Muki is a witch." These were not their words, as we will see, but words that came from others.

There is no way to predict how it is that in the same historical circumstances some are affected by the uncanny and others with the same cultural beliefs and the same experiences are not. But the uncanny is always unexpected and seems inexplicable, these being also the qualities of accident. It happens for a reason which can only be irrelevant, as, when the door flies open to produce a mirror, one speaks of chance. Suffering such an accident, one finds oneself jerked out of the imaginary registers that ordinarily carry one through the day. It then is a question of restoring oneself.

This process can begin by saying "I." The attempt to do so can produce the symptoms of trauma, as we have seen. Or it can lead to an attempt to normalize the events through the use of the conception of witchcraft. With the Murngin, the Zuni, and the Javanese as we have interpreted them, it is not the production of the witch that leads to murder. It is the failure of such a production to restore a normal situation by attributing the events to the work of someone whom one thinks has not only supernatural powers but usually also interests contrary to one's own. The failure to normalize can be expected because what is involved is the transformation of one thing, accident, which by definition cannot be normal, into something ordinary. Such a transformation cannot be complete. What Lévi-Strauss would call a discrepancy between registers results not in the automatic restoration of reason and the workings of symbolization but its opposite.

How does one get from the uncanny mood to the accusation of witchcraft? It does not follow automatically, as the divergent paths to trauma or to witchcraft or to no lasting effects at all, attest. Trauma and witchcraft have linguistic difficulty in common. The traumatized person, we repeat, may not be able to inhabit his voice. This may also be the case with the person who feels bewitched.

The witch is the result of a performative, but, I argue, of a peculiar one. In the usual performative, "I" is the subject. The performative depends on a particular verb ("promise," for instance) directed at the second person. As Austin described it, the performative required the sincere intention of the speaker. The person who said, "I promise . . . " had to mean it. The witch, however, does not come into being with the speaker, the first person, but with the third, or more accurately, with multiple third persons. One does not say the equivalent of "I promise . . . ," namely, "You are a witch," unless "He is a witch" has already been said, particularly in the cases of communally produced murder. The speaker repeats what others have already said. The characteristics of his words are thus far removed from those of the promise. They are not his words, filled with his feelings, but others' words, filled with their sentiments which he comes to share. The authority in the first instance for knowing that Muki is a witch comes from the "they" of the "they say," "Muki is a witch." But this third-person plural is confounded with whatever it is that has delivered the "proof" that Muki is a witch. The swollen stomachs, the infected wounds, the deaths come from somewhere or someone. The force of the performative is the force of its provenance. But its provenance in witchcraft is infinitely recessive. It refers to the "they" of "they say," but it refers as well to the unknown force that has produced symptoms or proof. To repeat what one has heard is to try to gain the force of those words for oneself, in a way similar to the Zuni accused witch when he confesses. But the constant circulation of such rumors attests to the inability to satisfactorily attach words to referents. Instead there is the continual assertion of "proof" that a force exists. "Proof," in this context, we recall, means finding an object for what one feels one already knows. It is the attempt to find a consolidation of the force of words in the world.

For Lévi-Strauss, those "off system" are endowed with a capacity to symbolize that normal people lack and that some, such as those who fall into near complete passivity, lack almost completely. The mere coincidence of these divergent types seems to be enough to ensure that the symbolic is restored, though in "The Effectiveness of Symbols" Lévi-Strauss evokes transference and abreaction as the mediating factors.[6] But the person named "the witch" is not exactly "off system." Rather, the system itself has changed. When the fear of the breakdown of social order occurs, as it did with the fall of Suharto, the finding of a reflection of oneself in everyday discourse ceases. When exchange means that now in return for whatever one offers the witch one receives death, it is not only the witch who is wholly "off-system," it is oneself as well. Everyday social definitions no longer hold. Another system pertains as the person who, feeling in himself the symptoms of death, accusing another of being a witch, speaks outside of ordinary discourse. To change the idiom, the subject who accuses at that moment is not exactly the speaking subject. He uses words, but he cannot credit himself for them.

He is already dead in his own mind. Like the bewitched Murngin, he might attempt to say "I am dead." But is there an "I" here? "I," noted Benveniste, "is the individual who utters the present instance of discourse containing the linguistic instance I."[7] "I" must therefore always be present at the moment of speaking. But the first-person singular of this sentence is only ambiguously present. If he is dead, there is no true first-person singular. The utterance has no provenance, coming as it does from another realm altogether, not only an "elsewhere" but a "nowhere." Historically speaking, in East Java this "nowhere" would come about through the perceived break in connections with authority. Following Derrida and putting this in linguistic terms, the speaker, considered as dead, cannot present himself in his sentence. The "I" here lacks a double of itself assured by social recognition. The "I" that is pronounced is hollow; the speaker is unlocatable. The recognition by others of such a speaker can only mean the inability to communicate with him normally.

The "am" of "I am dead" must also be put in the context of the predicate which in this sentence makes the speaker into someone other than himself. He is not the first person but the third, the nonperson. It is not a matter of "I is an other" but of "I" being incapable of being a recognizable other and thus both being "totally other" and not other at all. There is no doubling, no "ipseity," as Derrida uses this term, which allows "I" to mark a place where speech emerges into linguistic symbols, leaving behind a singularity which would then be necessarily lost. There is a failure to inhabit one's own speech because in a sense, there is nothing (or no one, no defined entity, yet still someone from whom speech issues) to do the inhabiting. When, then, in uncanny circumstances, one speaks to Muki the witch, language still functions since it begets a reply, but it works too well, transcending the social and yet reaching no one extant but rather another "person" who is also in a certain sense dead or, in the idiom of his neighbors, someone who must pass on death in order not to die himself. His response, regardless of what he actually says, is lethal, attesting to its (lack of) provenance.

For Derrida, in *Monolingualism of the Other*, the language of the other is the source of speech, but it is not appropriable.[8] Whatever it is that gives rise to speech remains alien. The urge to speak is a true gift. Something given whose gift nature is hidden because it appears already to belong to "oneself" though not yet to "me"; it is what one wants to say, even though it would be impossible at this stage to say what that would be for lack of linguistic signs. One does not know who gave or even that it is a gift. There is merely the accident which gives rise to the feeling of having something to say.

The Javanese who felt himself bewitched, like the Murngin in the equivalent situation, might try to say "I am dead." But not only is the "I" of this sentence no longer stable, each word of this sentence is distorted. "Am" or "is" then means both "exist" and its opposite, "is not," the person being incomprehensibly both dead and alive. The sentence we have just parsed makes its appearance in full strength only at a certain historical moment. One in which an indiscernible limit has been reached, on the other side of which is nothing definite or definable. Nothing, that is, which can make itself represented except by the deformation of language we have just seen. The person who feels himself *en face* of a witch, who is bewitched, who in effect says, "I am dead," finds that his words have been inverted and that they revert to their original sense and back again without ever gaining stability. This is the reaching of a limit, as Blanchot had it. Out of the confluence of circumstances such as occurred after Suharto left office, the defined other disappeared. There was no longer a second person who could mark the reception of one's speech and so confirm the existence of the "I" of the speaker. At that point language was not delimited but unlimited, so that it meant everything and its opposite.

In these circumstance, the word "witch" itself is deformed. It is no longer part of ordinary vocabulary. It is, rather, in one respect like Lévi-Strauss's floating signifier. It is a word that is called upon when signification is not effective. "Witch" thus, in certain contexts, does not designate a social type, even that of the outsider or the person somehow "different." (Remember here Muki, a poor peasant not different from his neighbors; but becoming "different" after he was called a witch.) "Witch" rather becomes a symptom of the failure to signify, of the distortion of whatever it meant when "witch" was part of easy conversation. As such, unlike the floating signifier, it does not make up for discrepancies between registers nor does it draw on the power to signify rather than signification itself. It is, at best, a projection of an intransigent negativity inhabiting the speaker, commanding but not defining him, causing him to speak to someone else without, however, that other being recognizable. It reflects a singularity of intention, insofar as one can use the word "intention" here at all, that is warped into a conventional sign but which conveys not a meaning but the facts of deformation and a sentiment of inadequacy.

"Is" becomes hyperbolic at the moment that it tries to designate something it is incapable of bringing into expression. In witchcraft, the copula "is" links anything with anything. Association at that moment is not limited by similarity or contiguity nor by the conventions of magic. "Is" in its ordinary form, as it exists in the conventions of Azande magic, when the oracle says, "X is a witch" and "X is harming you," is limited in the associations it makes. It is this very limitation that is the power of the oracle. It substitutes certainty, or a single idea, for suspicion, which contains many possibilities. But Azande society, we claim, was uncannily charged. Any Azande might be a witch, and the certainty of any particular accusation was soon enough replaced by suspicion and more accusations. In East Java, accusations followed by murder arose with great rapidity without the conventions of magic to limit them, however ambiguously. Nothing prevailed against the uncanny produced by the circumstances of the moment.

The hyperbolic form of "is," trying to say what cannot be said, is alien to understanding. It becomes a foreign word, allowing a judgment, as Mauss showed, that is neither analytic nor synthetic. Foreign words are central to magic, Mauss claimed. They connect their users to the alien source of magical power. One hears, "Muki is a witch," but from where— a person, a dream, an intuition—is not clear. One says to one's neighbor, "Muki is a witch." The neighbor agrees. The provocation of a response depends not on previously constituted agreement about witches, about Muki, or about common experience. It depends rather on the power of the verb to sum up and communicate, indeed provoke, the strangeness felt within the speaker and his auditor. When "is" can establish by the very power of pronunciation the foreignness of myself to myself and my neighbor to himself, Muki becomes a witch by agreement. Witchcraft accusations succeed as poetry does, summoning up a word before there is a thing. The word "witch," no more than the word "is," is not usually uncanny, but in these circumstances it becomes so.

Language by its nature might be foreign to its speakers, as thinkers from Rousseau through de Man to Derrida have it. The working of society depends on making it conventional nonetheless, and this depends on the certainty of the first and second persons. Witchcraft arises at a moment when this certainty fails to take hold. At that moment language is alien to us. The conventions of magic words try to give a place to this foreignness. To say "witch" is to make this attempt. But in some circumstances, naming fails. Even when a person is accused of being a witch, the uncanny remains at large, not fully identifiable with him. Witchcraft in its lethal form is the failure to recognize the foreign as such. Witchcraft, we said in the introduction, is the effect of a pure gift, one which is not recognized as such and produces no gratitude. It is the arrival of something, let us call it an accident, from the point of view of the analyst, whose provenance is never established. Which is to say that the third person of the gift is not named. There is no *hau*, no *mana*, no witch, even when the words are used because the uncanny and the words of this series remain separate. The uncanny remains at work even when the witch is killed. The third, the power of the gift, remains unnamed even when it is given a name.

Naming means ordinarily finding the name that already applies. One learns this name from others; like all names, it is established by convention. But the name "witch" is conventional only as a signifier and not in terms of its application to an object. Its usage has to be established each time. And each time it depends on the agreement of others of a strange sort. "Strange" because its referent is not the knowledge one has without usually being aware of it as knowledge, but the discovery that others also feel suspicion. Only agreement can establish the "reality" of the existence of something truly foreign: "We are right to be suspicious," is a statement that in no way depends on finding what makes one so. Hence the imperative to find an interlocutor. What passes between people when they say to each other, "Muki is a witch," is a communication whose force rests, tautologically enough, on the simple ability to pass from person to person rather than on reference to a meaning. This is an ability to communicate what is really nothing at all.

But this communication passes between people who, knowing there is a witch, feeling themselves already or incipiently bewitched, are no longer "themselves." It was not a community, "the village," who killed Muki. It was a collection of people who lacked a definition and who wanted to retrieve one.

The person to whom the term "witch" is applied is the object of an unsuccessful naming. The uncanny contained in the designation is insufficiently accounted for. Thus, after dispatching Muki and his family, villagers stood guard against the return of ghosts, Muki's and others, each night for months and perhaps even at the moment I write this sentence. With each accusation, the speaker hopes to regain for himself his normal identity, his ability to say "I" as he was accustomed to. Failing that possibility, he tries again. And again. He repeats a sentence someone else already pronounced, never making it his own, as one does when one retells a joke one has heard. A joke in almost all cases ceases to make us laugh after we have heard it several times because, with repetition, our defenses against it are raised. Accommodation to the sentence, "Muki is a witch," is not so rapid. Accusations continue, witches are murdered and perhaps one day they are forgotten.

Four-year-old children have jokes which invariably incite them to laughter, no matter how many hundreds of times these jokes are repeated. In France, for instance, the child says "caca boudin," meaning "sausage-shit," or simply "caca," "shit" or sometimes "caca-pipi," "shit-piss." She may even say it to herself and make herself laugh. The failure of the joke to wear out is the inability to believe that a part of one's body can be alienated from oneself, particularly at the moment when the image of the body is being formed and its wholeness is at issue. Shit, said Freud, was the first gift.[9] If so, it is not a partial object. The child gives itself; nothing is left behind. The origin is contained in the gift, which is to say that it arrives by itself, in itself, from nowhere. "Muki is a witch" was an infantile joke, a gift of the same sort. The speaker, unable to find himself, gave himself in his speech. But instead of releasing the energy of laughter, his communication let loose murderous aggression. The teller of this joke was history and language and "finally," accident. History and language that humans in a certain condition, a certain place and a certain time, were incapable of defending themselves against. This joke took months and years to fade as the deplorable normality of the New Order could not fully reestablish itself nor be replaced with another. Thus the murderous retelling of this humorless drollery.

There might have been further consequences in Indonesia. When there is no definitive second person, when language is directed to anyone and to no one in particular, the way is open for revolution, as was feared by leaders from the educated class. In 1998 in East Java there were no models for action, as there are not as well in a true revolution. But to develop further, of course, other historical circumstances would have to have prevailed. As it was, the identities of the New Order, reestablished by the succeeding regimes, eventually absorbed the witch hunters, obscuring the compelling origins of their actions and reducing them to contemporary figures, sometimes the *massa*, sometimes horrible murderers. They were thus left uncomprehended by the world outside their villages as well as by themselves. So, too, were most of the survivors of these massacres, caught as they were in the mentality of witchcraft and thus heard only ambiguously by the authorities to whom they turned for help.

There is another possibility. We saw it in Atmoyo's daughter, who, after her father was killed as a witch, could not speak. Identifying with the dead so close to her, she suffered the contradictions we have seen in the sentence, "I am dead," and therefore stammered rather than articulated. No stable "I," and no "you," formed. This poor woman issued incomprehensible noises until the moment when, for whatever reason, she felt recognized as not being a witch. Perhaps all speech begins as did hers, without given first and second persons. If we rarely stammer it is because we find the acceptance of others and thus of ourselves almost instantly. But we have experiences like Atmoyo's daughter, even without witchcraft or trauma, as Freud illustrated. Glancing into a mirror or at someone else, we find our double; but for an instant it is alien, unrecognized, and therefore no one at all; nonetheless it demands a response. For a second, we are stifled, with an unrealizable desire to speak. It takes effort to recall such moments because they remain insignificant. But it is the insignificant that inaugurates witchcraft, a fact obscured by the important historical circumstances in which it manifests itself.

Acknowledgments

The Prologue is excerpted from "Some Views of East Javanese Sorcery," *Archipel*, no. 64 (June 2002). Chapter 1 was first published in *Cultural Anthropology* 18, no. 2 (May 2003), while Chapter 4 first appeared in *Indonesia*, no. 71 (2001). The latter two articles have been modified for inclusion here. All are published with permission.

The Cornell Southeast Asia Program furnished my travel expenses to East Java. I thank them for their support throughout my career. And I want to acknowledge the generosity of the Graduate School for Asian and African Studies of Kyoto University, which provided me with a fellowship while I worked on this study. I am particularly grateful to Professor Tsuyoshi Kato of that institution for his kindnesses.

Michael Meeker offered me a detailed analysis of the manuscript, which provoked considerable revision. His analytic ability, his openness to a variety of intellectual approaches—one more indication of his infallible generosity as a person—and his extensive knowledge of anthropology have furnished me much of what I lack. Petar Bojanic gave me the warnings and criticism I needed as I strayed into the works of people he knows so much better than I do. Richard Klein and I taught a seminar on Witchcraft and Jean Genet, in which I learned much of help in writing this book. Arief Djati's knowledge of East Java was indispensable to me. Filtered as it was through his intelligence, initiative, and humor, East Java became a place larger and much more attractive than its grim magic might indicate to the reader. He leaves me with the ambiguously tinted feeling that East Java is much greater than my capacity to understand it. In the end, I am grateful. Once again I thank Ben Anderson for his comments, this time on Chapter 4, unique in my experience because they are invaluable both for their detail and for their generality. John Sidel generously gave me not only references, but books and photocopies and his own thoughts and trenchant remarks, some of them stemming from his extensive knowledge of East Java. Tom Keenan offered me very important criticisms of Chapter 1. Ben Abel of the Cornell Library, on his own initiative, found items for me in the Echols Collection. I want to acknowledge the stimulating conversations about East Java with Roland Bertrand. I thank everyone warmly.

Anne Berger commented on several chapters of the manuscript. She pervades my words, even those she has not read and, for that matter, those I have not yet uttered.

Notes

INTRODUCTION

1. George Bataille, "The Notion of Expenditure," in *Visions of Excess: Selected Writings, 1927–1939/George Bataille*, ed. Allan Stoekl, and trans. Allan Stoekl with Carl R. Lovitt and Donald M. Leslie, Jr. (Minneapolis: University of Minnesota Press, 1985), 117; see also Georges Bataille, *The Accursed Share: An Essay on General Economy*, trans. Robert Hurley (New York: Zone Books, 1991), pt. 1.

2. Georges Bataille himself exposed the inability to appropriate death in Hegel's speculation on the master and the slave. In place of a communication that creates social structures, there would be, instead, a certain laughter in the face of what one cannot represent but still cannot avoid being affected by (see Bataille, "The Notion of Expenditure"; and Jacques Derrida, "From a Restricted to a General Economy: A Hegelianism without Reserve," in *Writing and Difference,* trans. Alan Bass [Chicago: University of Chicago Press, 1978]). A certain form of communication would result, but it could not be incorporated into social structure, much less become the basis of the latter. Allan Stoekl points out that Bataille had conflicting ideas about the nature of this communication, not merely wavering between opposed points of view but expressing both during the same period in different places (Stoekl, Introduction to *Visions of Excess*).

3. Bataille, *Visions of Excess*, 122–23.

4. Jean-Luc Nancy, "Exscription," *Yale French Studies*, no. 78 (1990): 47–66.

5. Rebecca Comay, "Gifts without Presents: Economies of 'Experience' in Bataille and Heidegger," *Yale French Studies*, no. 78 (1990): 66.

6. Marcel Mauss, *The Gift,* trans. W. D. Halls (New York: W. W. Norton, 1990), 3.

7. Jacques Derrida, *Given Time. 1, Counterfeit Money*, trans. Peggy Kamuf (1991; reprinted, Chicago: Chicago University Press, 1992), 13.

8. Ibid., 24.

9. Ibid., 7.

10. Ibid., 13.

11. Ibid., 14.

12. Mauss, *The Gift,* 11. The passage has incited much commentary from an-

thropologists who have sought the reference of the *hau*; see, in particular, Marshall Sahlins, "The Spirit of the Gift," in *Stone Age Economics* (New York: Aldine de Gruyter, 1972).

13. Mauss, *The Gift*, 10.

14. Ibid.

15. Ibid., 10–11.

16. Ibid., 39.

17. E. E. Evans-Pritchard, *Witchcraft, Oracles, and Magic among the Azande* (Oxford: Oxford University Press, [1937]), 63.

18. Lucy Mair, *Witchcraft* (New York: McGraw-Hill, 1969), 7.

19. Ibid., 10.

20. H. R. Trevor-Roper, *The European Witch-craze of the Sixteenth and Seventeenth Centuries* (1967, rev. 1969; reprinted, Penguin, 1990). Says Trevor-Roper:

> Thus the genesis of the 16th-century witch-craze can be explained in two stages. First, there is the social tension. Just as systematic anti-semitism is generated by the ghetto, the aljama, not by the individual Jew, so the systematic mythology of the witch-craze was generated not by individual old women casting spells in scattered villages—these had always been tolerated—but by unassimilable social groups who, like the Jews and Moors of Spain, might be persecuted into outward orthodoxy but not into social conformity, and who therefore became, as others did not, objects of social fear.
>
> It was out of this tension that the frustrated evangelists began to manufacture the new mythology of Satan's kingdom." (Ibid., 52)

21. Trevor-Roper also says that the Jew and the witch are interchangeable. "In its periods of introversion and intolerance Christian society, like any society, looks for scapegoats. Either the Jew or the witch will do, but society will settle for the nearest" (ibid., 34). Thus, the Dominicans' search for Jews in Spain and witches in the Alps and Pyrenees. But why others suddenly appear intolerable when before they were not is not a question to be answered simply by historical methods:

> Why did social struggle, in those two centuries, invariably revive this bizarre mythology? We might as well ask, why has economic depression in Germany, from the Middle Ages until this century, so often revived the bizarre mythology of antisemitism: the fables of poisoned wells and ritual murder which were spread at the time of the Crusades, during the Black Death, in the Thirty Years War, and in the pages of Julius Streicher's Nazi broadsheet, Der Sturmer? The question is obviously not simple. . . . We have here to deal with a mythology which is more than a mere fantasy. It is a social stereotype: a stereotype of fear.
>
> Any society is liable, at times, to collective emotion. There is the exalted "messianism" which is common in rural societies in medieval Europe; in southern Italy, Spain and Portugal in early modern times; in modern Brazil. There is also the undefined "great fear," such as ran through rural France at the beginning of the revolution of 1789. And these emotions tend to take stereotyped form. (Ibid., 93)

22. See, e.g., Cyprian Fisiy and Peter Geschiere, "Witchcraft, Violence, and

Identity: Different Trajectories in Postcolonial Cameroon," in *Postcolonial Identities in Africa*, ed. Richard Werbner and Terence Ranger (London: Zed Books, 1996); and Peter Geschiere, *The Modernity of Witchcraft: Politics and the Occult in Postcolonial Africa*, trans. Peter Geschiere and Janet Roiman (Charlottesville: University of Virginia Press, 1997), 169–97. For cases of the state acting against witches directly, cf. Ulrike Sulikowski, "Eating the Flesh, Eating the Soul: Reflections on Politics, Sorcery, and *Vodun* in Contemporary Benin," in *L'Invention religieuse en Afrique: Histoire et religion en Afrique noire*, ed. Jean-Pierre Chrétien, C. H. Perrot, G. Prunier, and F. Raison-Jourde (Paris: Karthala, 1993), 379–91; Karola Elwert-Kretschmer, "Vodun et contrôle social au village," *Politique-Africaine* 59 (1995): 102–19; and Emmanuelle K. Tall, "De la démocratie et des cultes voduns au Bénin," *Cahiers d'Études Africaines* 137 (1995): 195–209, all cited in Geschiere, *The Modernity of Witchcraft*.

23. Jean Jacques Rousseau, *The Social Contract and Discourses*, trans. G. D. H. Cole (London: J. M. Dent and Sons, 1913), 15–16.

24. Biko's words appeared in *Biko*, by Donald Woods (Harmondsworth: Penguin Books, 1978), 166, 167, and are cited in Isak Niehaus, *Witchcraft, Power, and Politics: Exploring the Occult in the South African Lowveld* (London: Pluto Press, 2001), 183. Biko's statement is taken from his testimony at a trial in which the ideas of black consciousness were examined. They appear as part of his answers to the meaning of the word "black," which led to the question of "black magic." Asked by the judge if he justified the killings of those accused of being witches, Biko answered:

No, we do not. We do not accept superstition. We do not accept witchcraft. But all we are saying is that there are certain things within this whole sphere of black magic which can be usefully investigated. I mean, I would reject it as much as you do, because I do not believe in it myself, but I do not have disdain for the people who believe in it like most of society seems to have. I understand it from the cultural roots. This is through my education; my exposure to so much more literature and other, I would say, cultures in the world. I have decided that there is no place for this in my belief, but the person who believes in it, I can still talk to him with understanding. I did not reject him as a barbarian. (Edited trial transcript, in Woods, *Biko*, 128)

Thus, after defending superstition, Biko disowns it. But the context has changed. Witchcraft belief is superstition seen from the outside, traditional belief seen from within. Steve Biko was well capable of a double perspective. One sees him slide from one to the other when he speaks of his education, which includes both his "cultural roots" and his reading from other literatures and his experience of other cultures. His personal rejection of "superstition" thus did not mean his rejection of those holding beliefs he did not share. His rejection of witchcraft was a "decision," a matter of reflection. He held within himself, however, the power not merely to appreciate those with other beliefs but to communicate with them ("I can still talk to them with understanding"), as Donald Woods testifies to in the many stories of Biko in his book.

25. Of course, by no means all Africans and only a small minority of African states recognize witchcraft. For the policy of the ANC on the subject, see Niehaus, *Witchcraft, Power, and Politics,* especially chap. 8. Niehaus delineates the complications of political legitimacy that arise around the subject. In their important account of witchcraft in South Africa and elsewhere, Jean and John Comaroff summarize the lengthy report of the Commission of Inquiry into Witchcraft Violence and Ritual Murders in the Northern Province as revealing the tension between "civic rationalism" and "frank, even assertive cultural relativism" ("Occult Economies and the Violence of Abstraction: Notes from the South African Postcolony," *American Ethnologist* 26, no. 2 [1999]: 279–303). They see witchcraft as an effect of "millennial capitalism," which explains, in particular, the sufferings of those left out of capitalism's promises. Thus, their work is an important bringing-up-to-date of Evans-Pritchard's finding that witchcraft explains misfortune. It is similar in its assumptions, though not in its findings, to Peter Geschiere's understanding of Cameroon witchcraft, since the latter accounts for the new inequalities and powers of people in the independent state. According to Geschiere, witchcraft may or may not be malevolent power, but belief in witchcraft is an adjustment to the contemporary world rather than a nativistic reaction against it. In the Comaroff's analysis, witchcraft results from feeling the effects of something one cannot comprehend. A certain boundary is reached in which what occurs on one side has psychic and cultural effects on the other, without its being assimilated. Witchcraft, in their analysis, is a local manifestation of international phenomena; it exceeds the categories of present-day capitalistic exchange. They describe the setting of a limit across which effects are felt rather than assimilated or understood, and to that degree theirs is also the approach that I take (see also Jean Comaroff and John Comaroff, *Modernity and Its Discontents: Ritual and Power in Postcolonial Africa* [Chicago: University of Chicago Press, 1993]). In a very general way, one finds the same idea of a limit in the work of Michael Taussig, though the boundaries are different. Taussig recognizes that parts of the experiences of the people he studies are not reachable by ordinary methods. He dares to fill in the gap, explaining why he does so, rather than have recourse to misleading explanations (see Michael Taussig, *Shamanism, Colonialism, and the Wild Man: A Study in Terror and Healing* [Chicago: University of Chicago Press, 1987]; as well as his *The Magic of the State* [New York: Routledge, 1997]).

26. See, in particular, George Clement Bond and Diane M. Ciekawy, *Witchcraft Dialogues: Anthropological and Philosophical Exchanges,* Research in International Studies, Africa Series, no. 76 (Athens: Ohio University Press, 2001), along with the literature cited therein.

27. See, e.g., the Introduction in Bond and Ciekawy, *Witchcraft Dialogues.* For

a particularly insightful view of the moral and intellectual difficulties of studying contemporary witchcraft, especially in Africa, see Karen E. Fields, "Witchcraft and Racecraft: Invisible Ontology and Its Sensible Manifestations," in the same volume.

28. Geschiere reports one such statement: "As a Maka friend who was then municipal counselor of Abong-Mbang told me in 1973, 'With decolonization, all this is going to change. You whites, you think witchcraft does not exist. But now Africans occupy positions of authority and they know witchcraft is too real here. Soon we will change so that judges can confront the witches'" (Geschiere, *The Modernity of Witchcraft*, 170; see also Niehaus, *Witchcraft, Power, and Politics*, 146).

29. The problem is recognized by legal authorities in Cameroon, the difficulty being in the first place whether witchcraft really exists. Fisiy quotes a judge: "'. . . que la sorcellerie est scientifiquement non démontrable, que le recours á un médecin n'est pas determinant dans le cas d'espèce, que seule *l'intime conviction du juge* peut guider les débats objectifs à l'audience'" (Cyprian F. Fisiy and Michael Rowlands, "Sorcery and Law in Modern Cameroon," *Culture and History* [Copenhagen] 6 [1989]: 63–77; Fisiy and Rowland's italics).

30. "In nearly all cases, an accusation made by a witchdoctor, followed by the discovery of incriminating evidence in the compound or belongings of the accused, is the principal evidence used in court" (ibid., 77).

31. See, e.g., Elias Bongmba, "African Witchcraft: From Ethnography to Critique," in Bond and Ciekawy, *Witchcraft Dialogues*, 39–79.

32. Bond and Ciekawy, *Witchcraft Dialogues*, 7.

33. Christina Larner, *Witchcraft and Religion: The Politics of Popular Belief*, ed. Alan Macfarlane (Oxford: Basil Blackwell, 1984); and Christine Larner, *Enemies of God* (Baltimore: Johns Hopkins Press, 1981). Larner's view is that at the moment when feudal ties began to erode there was a necessity for an ideology that did not exist previously. Christianity became that ideology. The witch hunt was part of the process of Christianization that before this time had not been important among peasants. Christianity became opposed to witchcraft as a way of enforcing obedience to the king. Witchcraft was an alternative power—a power based locally. But through diabolism it was generalized to become the opposite of the Christian. To combat it was to combat this other power. On the role of the devil, see Norman Cohn, *Europe's Inner Demons: The Demonization of Christians in Medieval Christianity* (Chicago: University of Chicago Press, 1993).

34. Robert Muchembled, *Le Roi et la soriere: L'Europe des buchers, XV–XVIII siécle* (Paris: Desclee, 1993); and Muchembled, *Sorciéres justice et société aux 16e et 17e siécles* (Paris: Éditions Imago, 1987).

35. See "L'Extension sociale de la norme," in Michel Foucault, *Dits et ecrits: 1954–1988*, ed. Daniel Defert and François Ewald (1976; reprinted, Paris: Gallimard, 2001), 74–79 (quote is from p. 75).

36. Jean-François Bayart, *L'État en Afrique: La politique du ventre* (Paris: Fayard, 1989); and Michael Rowlands and Jean-Pierre Warnier, "Sorcery, Power, and the Modern State in Cameroon," *Man* 23, no. 1 (1988): 118–32.

37. Cyprian Fisiy and Peter Geschiere, "Judges and Witches, or How Is the State to Deal with Witchcraft? Examples from Southeast Cameroon," *Cahiers d'Études Africains* 118 (1991): 135–56.

38. "If one did not accept the initial premise of the debate and argument over the capacities of 'Africans,' as we never have, the book is logical but unscientific, a product of savage thought" (Bond and Ciekawy, *Witchcraft Dialogues*, 7). And yet, as an ethnography of practices surrounding witchcraft, the book is perfectly well constructed and intelligible to anyone who was not aware that Evans-Pritchard had taken up the notion of primitive mentalities earlier in considering the work of Lévy-Bruhl (see E. E. Evans-Pritchard, "Lévy-Bruhl's Theory of Primitive Mentality," *Bulletin of Faculty of Arts* [Egyptian University, Cairo] 2, no. 1). For this reason, one can conclude that by the time he wrote *Witchcraft, Oracles, and Magic among the Azande* the question was largely behind him. An astute reader of Evans-Pritchard thus remarks that the book centers on another theme: "He asked why any metaphysical system should be accepted" (see Mary Douglas, ed., *Witchcraft Confessions and Accusations* [London: Tavistock Publications, 1970], xvi).

39. Geschiere, *The Modernity of Witchcraft*, 2.

40. Wyatt MacGaffey, Preface to Geschiere, *The Modernity of Witchcraft*, viii.

41. Geschiere, *The Modernity of Witchcraft*, 1.

42. Ibid., xi.

43. Ibid., 1.

44. Ibid.

CHAPTER 1

1. The passage continues: "The defendant, who serves as a witness, gives the group the satisfaction of truth, which is infinitely greater and richer than the satisfaction of justice that would have been achieved by his execution. And finally, by his ingenious defense which makes his hearers progressively aware of the vitality offered by his corroboration of their system (especially since the choice is not between this system and another, but between the magical system and no system at all—that is, chaos), the youth, who at first was a threat to the physical security of his group, became the guardian of its spiritual coherence" (Claude Lévi-Strauss, "The Sorcerer and His Magic," in *Structural Anthropology*, trans. Claire Jacobson [New York: Basic Books, 1963], 174).

2. Ibid., 173.

3. Mrs. Stevenson tells us that the chief curer gave her the plume to give to the President of the United States as proof that there are witches in Zuni. They assumed, of course, that anyone would be convinced by such proof. They had a motive in making this gift. The U.S. government tried to suppress the killing of witches. If the President of the United States were given evidence that witches really exist, the suppression of the Zuni authorities who controlled witches would be stopped. The Zuni gift, meant to show that witches exist, was no doubt also a plea for allowing for their extermination (see Matilda Coxe Stevenson, *The Zuni Indians: Their Mythology, Esoteric Fraternities, and Ceremonies,* Bureau of American Ethnology, Annual Report no. 23, 1901–1902 [Washington, D.C.: Government Printing Office, 1904]).

4. Lévi-Strauss, "The Efficacy of Symbols," in Lévi-Strauss, *Structural Anthropology.*

5. Ibid., 197–98.

6. See "L'Efficacité symbolique," in Claude Lévi-Strauss, *Anthropologie Structurale* (Paris: Librarie Plon, 1958), 218.

7. Lévi-Strauss, "The Sorcerer and His Magic," 182.

8. Ibid.

9. Marcel Mauss, *A General Theory of Magic,* trans. Robert Brain (London: Routledge and Kegan Paul, 1972), 123.

10. Ibid.

11. Immanuel Kant, *Critique of Pure Reason,* trans. Norman Kemp Smith (New York: St. Martin's Press, 1929), IV:48.

12. Mauss, *A General Theory of Magic,* 122.

13. Kant, *Critique of Pure Reason,* IV:49.

14. Ibid., V:53.

15. Mauss, *A General Theory of Magic,* 124.

16. Kant, *Critique of Pure Reason,* 53.

17. Mauss, *A General Theory of Magic,* 124.

18. Ibid.

19. Ibid.

20. Ibid.

21. Ibid.

22. Ibid., 122–23.

23. Stevenson, *The Zuni Indians,* 392; hereafter cited in text.

24. Mrs. Stevenson sometimes spells this name as Nai'uchi.

25. For the interesting relationship between Mrs. Stevenson and Frank Cushing, see the remarks of Jesse Green, the editor of Cushing's correspondence, in *Cushing at Zuni* (Albuquerque: University of New Mexico Press), 7, 350 n. 31.

26. Mary Pratt pointed out to me that the changing of the color of the boy's

eyes from black to blue and black again indicates a relation between sorcery and colonial power. I take up this suggestion later. I thank Mary Pratt for her remark.

27. The translation of Lévi-Strauss's original French has been published separately from the essays of Mauss which Lévi-Strauss introduces (see Claude Lévi-Strauss, *Introduction to the Work of Marcel Mauss*, trans. Felicity Baker [London: Routledge and Kegan Paul, 1987]).

28. Mauss, *A General Theory of Magic*, 122.

29. Lévi-Strauss, *Introduction to the Work of Marcel Mauss*, 59.

30. The important passage is this: "Man has from the start had at his disposition a signifier-totality which he is at a loss to know how to allocate to a signified, given as such, but no less unknown for being given. There is always a non-equivalence or 'inadequation' between the two, a non-fit and overspill which divine understanding alone can soak up; this generates a signifier-surfeit relative to the signified to which it can be fitted" (Lévi-Strauss, *Introduction to the Work of Marcel Mauss*, 62). Lévi-Strauss comments that this is true of humanity in general, thus not merely in places where magic is practiced. Rather, "In our society, these notions have a fluid, spontaneous character [he gives the examples of "oomph" in American English and "*truc*" and "*machin*" in French]. The latter can stand for a range of objects not defined in advance of the word. Whereas elsewhere they serve as the ground of considered, official interpretive systems; a role, that is to say, which we ourselves reserve for science" (ibid., 55).

31. Mauss, *A General Theory of Magic*, 57.

32. Ibid.

33. Ibid., 57–58.

34. You will notice the congruence of Mauss's formulation with Freud's statement that the unconscious knows no negative. "Dreams have no means of expressing the relation of a contradiction, a contrary or a 'no'" (Sigmund Freud, *The Interpretation of Dreams* [New York: Avon Books, 1965], 361). Instead, "dreams show a particular preference for combining contraries into a unity or representing them as one and the same" (353). Negation in dreams could hinder the wish on its way to expression. A similar (il)logic is implied in magic. Nothing prevents the expression of statements, which if they were not magic would be untrue (ibid., 353). Freud later showed that dreams did have a way of expressing contradiction indirectly (ibid., 372).

35. Cited in Walter B. Cannon, "'Voodoo' Death," *American Anthropologist* 44 (1942): 169–81.

36. I, of course, do not mean to say that the magical word of any society is necessarily translatable outside of its magic usage by the English word "is." It is, rather, as Mauss says, that the function of the magical word is the same as that of the copula. If we had to translate the word in the context of magical usage, we would thus have to say "is," no matter what the meaning of this word or words in other

contexts. Whatever it might be, in magical usage the magical signifier means "is." It has also to be kept in mind that Mauss said that magical words were often from languages foreign to the place where they were used, implying that their sense was unknown and that, in any case, they were formulaic, meaning that their form was important, while their particular sense was disregarded. It is again a question of effecting a linkage, thus acting as the word "is" acts and so requiring us, in that context, to translate the word or words as "is." Though even this translation is inadequate if I am correct in what I say in the paragraph that follows.

37. Sigmund Freud, "A Seventeenth Century Demonological Neurosis," in *Standard Edition of the Complete Psychological Works of Sigmund Freud*, ed. and trans. James Strachey (London: Hogarth Press, 1962), 19:72–105.

38. One can object that I am confounding culturally grounded examples against the universal category of language. Which is to say that magical power is always linguistic and derives its force from within language. Given that, the idea of the floating signifier includes both the language of sorcery and of curing. But they remain distinct. The magical words that Lévi-Strauss interprets as floating signifiers are, as he says, vague in their reference. But, as he points out, they have a defined place: "They serve as the ground of considered, official interpretive systems; a role, that is to say, which we ourselves reserve for science" (Lévi-Strauss, *Introduction to the Work of Marcel Mauss*, 55). By contrast, the equivalent words in a society without the institutions of magic are, in the French case, *truc* or *machin*, which we might translate as "thing," and which have referents undefined in advance. Their very power to cause signifieds to appear make them equivalents of magical words. The language of sorcery is different. It has a power of reference which never produces particular signifieds at all, but which, instead, points to always different sources of itself that, so long as there is sorcery, remain uncontrollable. To equate these sources with "language," the general term, is both correct and incorrect. It is correct to the extent that sorcery is a linguistic phenomenon. But it is incorrect because the nature of that phenomenon is not necessarily to be a closed system such that the very nature of significations requires a consolidated system of signifiers on the one hand and a single source for them on the other. As Jacques Derrida has pointed out in many different ways, the idea of a closed system, whereby the lack that is in every signifier, that is filled in by its reference, and in general filled in by a singular place of reference, is tied to speech and ignores the written qualities of language that surpass this system and that are necessary to it.

39. Lévi-Strauss, "The Sorcerer and His Magic," 174.

CHAPTER 2

1. W. Lloyd Warner, *A Black Civilization: A Study of an Australian Tribe* (1937; rev. ed., New York: Harper and Row, 1964), 229; hereafter cited in text.

2. The white magician can diagnose a man whose soul has been stolen and who will therefore die. He can find out who is responsible, but apparently he cannot cure the man. Here is what one white magician said to Warner: "Sometimes when people steal a man's soul in the bush he comes here to my camp. I go look; he is empty inside. I say, 'I can't fix you up. Everything is gone. Your heart is still there, but it's empty. I can't fix you up.' Then I tell everybody he is going to die" (Warner, *A Black Civilization*, 204; see also 186 and 200–201). Among other groups, the man can sometimes be saved by white magic (see Herbert Basedow, *The Australian Aboriginal* [Adelaide: F. W. Preece, 1925]).

3. Emile Durkheim, *Suicide: A Study in Sociology*, trans. John A. Spaulding and George Simpson (Glencoe, Ill.: The Free Press, 1951), 241–76.

4. Ibid., 217–40.

5. The procedure is always the same, enabling Warner to give a synthetic account (see *A Black Civilization*, 184–88).

CHAPTER 3

1. John Middleton and E. H. Winter, *Witchcraft and Sorcery in East Africa* (London: Routledge and Kegan Paul, 1963), 4.

2. Ibid., 5–6.

3. Douglas, *Witchcraft Confessions and Accusations*, xviii.

4. Ibid.

5. Ibid., xvii.

6. Max Marwick, *Sorcery in Its Social Setting: A Study of the Northern Rhodesia Ceŵa* (Manchester, U.K.: Manchester University Press, 1965), 91.

7. See Mary Douglas, "Introduction: Thirty Years after *Witchcraft, Oracles, and Magic*," in Douglas, *Witchcraft Confessions and Accusations*.

8. See Trevor-Roper, *The European Witch-craze*, and Cohn, *Europe's Inner Demons*.

9. Largely, but not entirely. See the remark of E. H. Winter, who wrote in the line of British social anthropology: "Thus if the Amba [a people of western Uganda] are to believe in the existence of witches, they must also believe that each village contains within it a group of people who are secret enemies of the social order, a fifth column, which is constantly attempting to destroy the village from within. The damage done to community solidarity by focusing on witchcraft fears within it must be accepted" (E. H. Winter, "The Enemy Within: Amba Witchcraft," in Middleton and Winter, *Witchcraft and Sorcery in East Africa*, 296). Because witchcraft was destructive, it was also inexplicable: "What remains inexplicable . . . is the fact that witchcraft suspicions are so destructive in terms of group cohesion, when this need not be the case" (ibid., 291). For most social anthropologists, it was not simply a question of violence, but of putting aside the terrors of others in

favor of explaining how these terrors are useful. It would be interesting to look at the studies of anthropologists as attempts to displace the fears of Europeans onto another, benign, social scene. It perhaps is no accident that the most important studies of witchcraft were written after the First World War, when they stressed terror and violence, as in the account of Warner, or at least did not neglect it, as in the ethnography under discussion. After that, they stressed the usefulness of what then are referred to not as terrors but as beliefs, as though terror can be put aside. The cries of Africans for protection from witchcraft today are all the more difficult to hear in Europe (I include America in that term) because of that history.

10. Here, of course, one might consider the place of anthropology in the time of colonialism. Anthropologists, including Evans-Pritchard, advocated tolerance for the beliefs of those they studied, and saw in witchcraft both an expression of those beliefs as well as an instrument for the functioning of their societies. There is some irony, then, in the complaint of certain Africans that the colonial regime did not protect them from witchcraft. To do so, of course, they would have had to recognize its validity, but at the same time, the idea that witchcraft was the internalization of colonial authority suppressing African voices, an idea thrown off by Mary Douglas, who noted that anthropologists of the time were liberals and thus basically also in tune with colonial authority. One might also add that colonial authority did protect Africans against some of the worst results of witchcraft accusations which, in the time of independence, resulted in murder. The possibility of seeing conflict as benign rested on the suppression of violence by colonial governments.

11. Evans-Pritchard, *Witchraft, Oracles, and Magic among the Azande*, 76; hereafter cited in text.

12. See Maurice Blanchot, "The Narrative Voice (the "he" the neutral)," in *The Infinite Conversation*, trans. Susan Hanson (Minneapolis: University of Minnesota Press, 1993), 379–87; and Emile Benveniste, "The Nature of Pronouns" and "Relationships of Person in the Verb," both in *Problems of General Linguistics*, trans. Mary Elizabeth Meek (Coral Gables, Fla.: University of Miami Press, 1971).

13. Evans-Pritchard says this about consulting the oracle himself: "I never found great difficulty in observing oracle consultations. I found that in such matters the best way of gaining confidence was to enact the same procedure as Azande and to take oracular verdicts as seriously as they take them. I always kept a supply of poison for the use of my household and neighbors and we regulated our affairs in accordance with the oracles' decisions. I may remark that I found this as satisfactory a way of running my home and affairs as any other I know of" (Evans-Pritchard, *Witchraft, Oracles, and Magic among the Azande*, 269–70).

14. Blanchot, "The Narrative Voice (the "he" the neutral)," 379–87.

15. One wonders what the Zande word for "citizen" means. On it, it seems, depends the force of Zande ideas of politesse and sociality in general, so important

in the domestication of witchcraft.

16. Jacques Derrida, *The Gift of Death*, trans. David Wills (Chicago: University of Chicago Press, 1995), 82–83.

17. Lévi-Strauss, *Introduction to the Work of Marcel Mauss,* 18–20.

18. Evans-Pritchard, 271–80, especially 279–80.

19. The comparison here is with literature, the "strange institution," as Derrida names it, which, like the oracle, has no limits put on what it can say and which is both outside the law and makes its own law (see Derek Attridge, "This Strange Institution Called Literature: An Interview with Jacques Derrida," in *Acts of Literature*, by Jacques Derrida [New York: Routledge, 1992]).

CHAPTER 4

1. The killings in fact began earlier, when the Suharto regime looked weak. But their major incidence was after Suharto was no longer president.

2. Contrary to the usual practice of anthropologists, I have not changed the names of people.

3. "Bisa Kencing Sehari Penuh" [Able to urinate for a whole day], *Malang Post*, December 12, 1999, 1.

4. The word *massa* in its original sense meant "masses," as we shall see below. During the New Order, it took on the meaning "mob." It is possible that the original sense has returned, particularly given the proto-revolutionary quality of this witch hunt. The reader might want to substitute "masses" for "mob"; the writer would not object. But here, in particular, the qualifier *beringas* ("savage") makes me opt for "mob."

5. "Masya Allah, 2 Dukun Santet dibunuh Lagi" [My God, two more witches killed], *Malang Post*, December 21, 1999, 1.

6. For a description of these incidents, see my *Solo in the New Order: Language and Hierarchy in an Indonesian City* (Princeton, N.J.: Princeton University Press, 1986), 232–54.

7. "500 Polisi Serbu Kalipare, 25 Pelaku Diciduk" [Police descend on Kalipare, 25 scooped up], *Malang Post*, December 23, 1999, 1.

8. Clifford Geertz, *The Religion of Java* (Glencoe, Ill.: Free Press, 1960), 109; hereafter cited in text.

9. Koentjaraningrat, *Javanese Culture* (Singapore: Oxford University Press, 1985), 419–21.

10. Pramoedya Ananta Toer, "Dendam," in *Percikan Revolusi, Subuh* (1951; reprint, Jakarta: Hasta Mitra, 2001), 178–202.

11. Benedict R. O'G. Anderson, "Reading 'Revenge' by Pramoedya Ananta Toer (1978–1982)," in *Writing on the Tongue*, ed. A. L. Becker, Michigan Papers in South and Southeast Asian Studies, no. 35, University of Michigan Center for South and Southeast Asian Studies, 1989.

12. The failure of the social revolution is definitively treated in Benedict R. O'G. Anderson, *Java in a Time of Revolution: Occupation and Resistance* (Ithaca, N.Y.: Cornell University Press, 1972).

13. Benedict Anderson has generously given me the history of the word: "It is from the Dutch-German *Masse(n)* and I am sure came to the Indies via Sneevliet [the Communist leader] and the first modern radicals, meaning the Marxist idea of the masses, i.e., not the bourgeoisie, and not the aristocracy and political elite. It shows up positively and honorably in Tan Malaka's great 1920s pamphlet, 'Massa Actie.' In the revolution it was always there (used by the Left mainly) and competed with *rakyat* (which could also mean something populist and un-Marxist, and sometimes even "the nation"), *murba, marhaen*, and so on. In the 1950s liberal period, the parties increasingly (to win elections) thought they had to have *or-mas, organisasi massa* = mass organizations, or better perhaps, 'organization of masses'—as part of their weaponry. These *or-mas* were sectorially segregated: youth, women, farmers, fishermen, laborers, intellectuals, schoolteachers, and so on. This 'positive' idea of *massa*, connected of course to *organisasi*, did not disappear under either the Old or the New Order. But in the early 1970s Ali Murtopo's Opsus gang invents the idea of the *massa mengambang* ('floating masses'), i.e., deliberately 'not-organized' masses, which also were not sectorally defined. They were also designated as rural for the first time, i.e., outside *kabupaten* seats, etc. These floating masses were to be left to float, unmoored. Gradually this idea of *massa* as unorganized, floating, menacing, 'mob' emerges to compete with older meanings. This is why in the 1980s the meaning of *massa* is highly unstable, so hard to translate. Lefty groups like the PRD still used *massa* in the older sense, as well as some PDIP people."

14. This retrospective account of a youth who fought in the revolution is included in James Siegel, *Fetish, Recognition, Revolution* (Princeton, N.J.: Princeton University Press, 1997), 220.

15. Ordinarily the phrase is *main hakim sendiri* ("to play judge oneself"). But in East Java the word for "judge" (*hakim*) was often substituted for the word for "law" (*hukum*), as indeed I heard also in other parts of rural Java. While syntactically impossible, I retain it here both to record the strange usage and to open speculation about the reasons for this notation. We will see more of this phenomenon in the following chapter. For a history and analysis of *keroyokan* which also contains extensive bibliographical references, see Freek Columbijn, "Maling! Maling! The Lynching of Petty Criminals," in *Roots of Violence in Indonesia: Contemporary Violence in Historical Perspective*, ed. Freek Columbijn and J. Thomas Lindblad (Leiden: KITLV Press, 2002).

16. See Gillian Hart, Andrew Turton, and Benjamin White, eds., *Agrarian Transformations: Local Processes and the State in Southeast Asia* (Berkeley: University of California Press, 1992); and Hans Atlov and Sven Cederroth, *Leadership on*

Java: Gentle Hints, Authoritarian Rule (Richmond, Surrey, U.K.: Curzon Press, 1994).

17. Andrew Beatty, *Varieties of Javanese Religion: An Anthropological Account* (Cambridge: Cambridge University Press, 1999), 34; hereafter cited in text.

18. There has long been *keroykan*, which we have discussed above. This could be said to be the behavior of a mob. But "mob," in the new sense, is the group of people who appear not in a village identity but who adopt a term from national discourse, *massa*.

19. But not for not protecting her father. Why did the military not protect him? I do not know. Perhaps it was because they were afraid that they could not prevail against the mob, perhaps because it would have meant recourse to troops further up the chain of command, which they were reluctant to ask for. Perhaps they were convinced the man was a witch. It is evident that the military was not behind the events and that they tried to save the man's life initially.

20. We can speculate as to what language she might speak as the witch. It would not be Javanese but the language of elsewhere, a babble of the sort, perhaps, she uttered when she was still afraid.

21. On this topic, see Tony Day, *Fluid Iron: State Formation in Southeast Asia* (Honolulu: University of Hawaii Press, 2002).

22. Kenji Tsuchiya, *Democracy and Leadership: The Rise of the Taman Siswa Movement in Indonesia*, trans. Peter Hawkes (Honolulu: University of Hawaii Press, 1987. For the influence of these terms on the lives of children in the New Order, see Saya S. Shiraishi, *Young Heroes: The Indonesian Family in Politics* (Ithaca, N.Y.: Cornell University Southeast Asia Program, 1997).

23. Benedict R. O'G. Anderson, 'The Language of Indonesian Politics," *Indonesia* 1 (1966): 89–116.

24. The other limitation of widespread witch hunts is geographical. To my knowledge, on a large scale, witch hunts occurred only in Java (West as well as East). In my analysis, the fusion of Javanese and national hierarchies is central, and this, of course, limits the geographical area. Obviously, one would have to take account of other conditions where other kinds of violence broke out, as, for instance, in Aceh or in the Moluccas.

25. This, at least, is the interesting supposition of Mary Douglas (see *Witchcraft Confessions and Accusations,* xxiii).

26. It is not only the survivors of accused witches who thought this way. The inhabitants of Hardjokuncaran burned down the police station when the police refused to release prisoners who had been arrested for murdering witches. Their fellow villagers did not think they were innocent, but that they were justified in their actions nevertheless. Eventually, the villagers rebuilt the police station (Nicholas Herriman, unpublished paper in author's possession). They, too, eventually

recognized that the aparat knew who was guilty, even if the crime was, in their eyes, justified. It seems to be a question of different moments: at certain times, possessed by violence; at others, released from it, though, in my experience of this incident, without neutralizing the witch. In any case, the term they applied to themselves, *massa*, implicitly calls upon authority for containment. This is discussed in greater detail below.

27. Benedict Anderson and Ruth McVey, *Preliminary Analysis of the October 1, 1965 Coup in Indonesia* (Ithaca, N.Y.: Cornell Modern Indonesia Project, 1971).

28. See Siegel, *Fetish, Recognition, Revolution* (Princeton, N.J.: Princeton University Press, 1997), pt. 3, "Revolution."

29. This is the thesis I presented in a study of the massacres of 1983. Indonesian nationalism marked a break from the societies of the archipelago which existed before it. The national family was of a new sort, with a new morality, leaving the old society as a source of immorality and illegitimacy, which, it was feared, would emerge again in the heart of Indonesian society (see James T. Siegel, *A New Criminal Type in Jakarta: Counter-Revolution Today* [Durham, N.C.: Duke University Press, 1998]).

30. See Siegel, *A New Criminal Type in Jakarta*, for a description of the (non-) ghosts of the New Order. My assertion here assumes that there was widespread support for the New Order. No one will deny that only at the end was there significant opposition to it. Even the political prisoners released after as much as seventeen years without trial seldom tried to establish their own historical record, contenting themselves with a demand for the restitution of their full civil rights.

31. See Roman Bertrand, *Indonésie, la democratie invisible: Violence, magie et politique à Java* (Paris: Karthala, 2002).

32. They are not necessarily associated with Japan, as their purported use by the Indonesian army indicates. Their appearance on television confounds their origin rather than making it clear. An elementary schoolgirl I knew in Jakarta watched television daily. She knew that some programs were Japanese and others American but believed that what was from Japan was from America and vice versa.

33. On this topic, see James T. Siegel, "I Wasn't There But . . . Gossip and Politics in Jakarta," *Archipel*, no. 46 (1993): 59–65.

34. One could look at the *massa* in a somewhat different light. As the repository of violence, they play the role of banishing not merely violence but force as well from the vocabulary of Indonesian political thinking. Force is made unthinkable. Thus, the work of the army is made abstract. As I mentioned, the dioramas in the army museum show revolutionaries without showing their opponents. When, in another part of the museum, the bloody clothes of Indonesian victims are displayed, it is without their killers. The history of France can not be thought to be

without its conflicts with Britain, with Germany, etc. But Indonesian history has battles whose memory is only that of a unity not yet achieved, just as the histories of many other Asian countries are told without mutual reference. Conflict is discounted, leaving no place for hatred and violence. The idea of the *massa* shows how violence is banished from awareness and where. The *massa* are ephemeral. They are easily replaced in memory by "the people," and when they are, violence is almost forgotten. But not entirely. It comes back abruptly in ahistorical guise. The lack of sociological definition prevents an accommodation, thus an amelioration, of those who are said to be violent and who are therefore feared. One does not negotiate with the mob. One only controls it. The mob thus disappears and the people reappear. Presto, "they" become the *rakyat*.

CHAPTER 5

1. "Particularly gristly" as presented in government propaganda. The atrocities claimed to have been committed on their bodies were not verified by the autopsy reports (see Benedict R. O'G. Anderson, "How Did the Generals Die?" *Indonesia* 43 [1987]: 109–34).

2. James Siegel, "Revolutionary Stink and the 'Extension of the Tongue of the People': The Political Languages of Pramoedya Ananta Toer and Sukarno," *Indonesia*, no. 64 (1997): 9–21.

3. The ruler, able to hold together conflicting ideas, is himself exempt from questions of legitimacy:

Since all power derives from a single homogenous source, power itself antecedes questions of good and evil. To the Javanese way of thinking it would be meaningless to claim the right to rule on the basis of differential sources of power—for example, to say that power based on wealth is legitimate, whereas power based on guns is illegitimate. Power is neither legitimate nor illegitimate. Power is." (Benedict R. O'G. Anderson, "The Idea of Power in Javanese Culture," in *Language and Power: Exploring Political Cultures in Indonesia* [Ithaca, N.Y.: Cornell University Press, 1990], 23; this essay was first published in Claire Holt, Benedict R. O'G. Anderson, and James T. Siegel, eds., *Culture and Politics in Indonesia* [Ithaca, N.Y.: Cornell University Press, 1972] 11–69).

4. On the fate of social revolutionaries, see, in particular, Anton Lucas, *One Soul, One Struggle: Region and Revolution in Indonesia* (Sydney: Allen and Unwin, 1991).

5. It centered instead on the middle class, which felt a kinship with those from the countryside, based on common nationality as well as self interest (see James Siegel, "The Idea of Indonesia Continues," *Archipel*, no. 64 [June 2002]: 199–229).

6. Anderson, "The Idea of Power in Javanese Culture," 23.

7. The picture was taken on December 29, 1949, and is reproduced, among

other places, in Henri Cartier-Bresson, *Indonésie 1949* (Jakarta: Centre Culturel Français de Jakarta, 2002), 19.

8. Benedict R. O'G. Anderson, "Old State, New Society: Indonesia's New Order in Comparative Historical Perspective," in Anderson, *Language and Power,* 94–120 (this essay was first published in *Journal of Asian Studies,* no. 42 [May 1983]: 477–96); Ruth McVey, "The Beamtenstaat in Indonesia," in *Interpreting Indonesian Politics: Thirteen Contributions to the Debate,* ed. Benedict Anderson and Audrey Kahin (Ithaca, N.Y.: Cornell University Southeast Asia Program, 1982), 84–91.

9. On the "gap," see my "Early Thoughts on the Violence of the 13th and 14th of May, 1998, in Jakarta," *Indonesia* (October 1998) (reprinted in Benedict R. O'G. Anderson, ed., *Violence and the State in Suharto's Indonesia* [Ithaca, N.Y.: Cornell University Southeast Asia Program, 2001]). On the middle class and assimilation, see my "The Idea of Indonesia Continues."

10. This violence is described in several edited volumes, among them Benedict Anderson, *Violence and the State in Suharto's Indonesia*; and Columbijn and Lindblad, *Roots of Violence in Indonesia.*

11. Confusion about political identity was and is not limited to villagers. See the telling account by Pipit Rochijat, "Am I PKI or Non-PKI?," with its accompanying "Afterword" by Benedict R. O'G. Anderson, in *Indonesia,* vol. 40 (1985): 37–56.

12. "But the other liking (the feeling of the sublime) is a pleasure that arises only indirectly; it is produced by the feeling of a momentary inhibition of the vital forces followed immediately by an outpouring of them that is all the stronger. Hence it is an emotion, and so it seems to be seriousness, rather than play, in the imagination's activity. Hence, too, this liking is incompatible with charms, and, since the mind is not just attracted by the object but is alternately always repelled as well, the liking for the sublime contains not so much a positive pleasure as rather admiration and respect, and so should be called a negative pleasure" (Immanuel Kant, *Critique of Judgment,* trans. Werner S. Pluhar [Indianapolis: Hackett Publishing, 1987], 98).

13. Ibid.

14. On the consolidation of power in the experience of the sublime, see Neil Hertz, "A Reading of Longinus" and "The Notion of Blockage in the Sublime," both in *The End of the Line: Essays on Psychoanalysis and the Sublime* (New York: Columbia University Press, 1985).

15. It is, indeed, the blindness of this aggression that explains the role of the government. The regional government is said to have drawn up lists of suspected witches. We have seen how those who were known to the authorities to be the possible targets of aggression were warned to leave. But for the most part the government could no more pinpoint the actors in these incidents than could the N.U.,

which accused the army of instigating the acts against it. Movements without identities are hard to control. We have seen also that there is no evidence from the village that the incidents were "provoked," as the N.U. claimed.

CHAPTER 6

1. On this topic, see Colombijn, "Maling, Maling! The Lynching of Petty Criminals," 299–329, for both his far-reaching analysis and the references cited there.

2. On the role of the police in Indonesia, see the excellent work by Joshua Barker, "State of Fear: Controlling the Criminal Contagion in Suharto's New Order," *Indonesia*, no. 66. (October 1998): 7–45.

3. Siegel, *A New Criminal Type in Jakarta.*

4. On the history of "superstition" in Europe, see Jean-Claude Schmitt, *The Holy Greyhound: Guinefort, Healer of Children since the Thirteenth Century,* trans. Martin Thom (Cambridge: Cambridge University Press, 1983), 14–25.

5. See, particularly, Jean Comaroff, "Consuming Passions: Child Abuse, Fetishism, and 'The New World Order,'" *Culture* 17, no. 1/2 (1997): 7–19.

CHAPTER 7

1. Lévi-Strauss, *Introduction to the Work of Marcel Mauss,* 18; hereafter cited in text.

2. See, e.g., James Siegel, "Dreams, Curing Rites, and Domestic Politics in a Sumatran Society," *Glyph*, no. 3 (1978): 18–32 (reprinted in James Siegel, *The Rope of God,* 2nd ed. [Ann Arbor: University of Michigan Press, 2001]).

3. In this light, witches such as the ones we have examined are not fully realized figures, identical to specific social types, and in that form cannot serve as the enemy. From this point of view, the European witch hunts are anomalous and might be looked at once again. Despite the excellence of the work of Christine Larner and of Robert Muchembled, for instance, they scarcely touch on the sources of the uncanny in Scotland or France, respectively (see Larner, *Witchcraft and Religion: The Politics of Popular Belief,* ed. Alan Macfarlane [New York: Blackwell, 1984]; Larner, *Enemies of God: The Witch-hunt in Scotland* [Baltimore: Johns Hopkins Press, 1981]; Muchembled, *Le Roi et la soriere: L'Europe des buchers, XV–XVIII siecle* [Paris: Desclee, 1993]; and Muchembled, *Sorciéres justice et société aux 16e et 17e siecles* [Paris: Éditions Imago, 1987]).

4. Sigmund Freud, "The Uncanny," trans. James Strachey, in *Studies in Parapsychology,* ed. Philip Rieff (New York: Collier Books, 1977), 54–56 n. 25.

5. Martin Heidegger, *Being and Time,* trans. Joan Stambaugh (Albany: State University of New York Press, 1996), 255–56.

6. Lévi-Strauss, "The Efficacy of Symbols," in Lévi-Strauss, *Structural Anthropology*, 198–99.

7. Emile Benveniste, "The Nature of Pronouns," in Benveniste, *Problems in General Linguistics* (Coral Gables, Fla.: University of Miami Press, 1971), 218.

8. Jacques Derrida, *Monolingualism of the Other*, trans. Patrick Mensah (Stanford, Calif.: Stanford University Press, 1998).

9. Sigmund Freud, "On the Transformation of the Instincts with Special Reference to Anal Eroticism," trans. James Strachey, in Freud, *Character and Culture*, ed. Philip Rieff (New York: Collier Books, 1963), 206.

Cultural Memory | *in the Present*

James Siegel, *Naming the Witch*

J. M. Bernstein, *Against Voluptuous Bodies: Late Modernism and the Meaning of Painting*

Theodore W. Jennings, Jr., *Reading Derrida / Thinking Paul: On Justice*

Richard Rorty, *Take Care of Freedom and Truth Will Take Care of Itself: Interviews with Richard Rorty*, edited and with an Introduction by Eduardo Mendieta

Jacques Derrida, *Paper Machine*

Renaud Barbaras, *Desire and Distance: Introduction to a Phenomenology of Perception*

Jill Bennett, *Empathic Vision: Affect, Trauma, and Contemporary Art*

Ban Wang, *Illuminations from the Past: Trauma, Memory, and History in Modern China*

James Phillips, *Heidegger's Volk: Between National Socialism and Poetry*

Frank Ankersmit, *Sublime Historical Experience*

István Rév, *Retroactive Justice: Prehistory of Post-Communism*

Paola Marrati, *Genesis and Trace: Derrida Reading Husserl and Heidegger*

Krzysztof Ziarek, *The Force of Art*

Marie-José Mondzain, *Image, Icon, Economy: The Byzantine Origins of the Contemporary Imaginary*

Cecilia Sjöholm, *The Antigone Complex: Ethics and the Invention of Feminine Desire*

Jacques Derrida and Elisabeth Roudinesco, *For What Tomorrow . . . : A Dialogue*

Elisabeth Weber, *Questioning Judaism: Interviews by Elisabeth Weber*

Jacques Derrida and Catherine Malabou, *Counterpath: Traveling with Jacques Derrida*

Martin Seel, *Aesthetics of Appearing*

Nanette Salomon, *Shifting Priorities: Gender and Genre in Seventeenth-Century Dutch Painting*

Jacob Taubes, *The Political Theology of Paul*

Jean-Luc Marion, *The Crossing of the Visible*

Eric Michaud, *The Cult of Art in Nazi Germany*

Anne Freadman, *The Machinery of Talk: Charles Peirce and the Sign Hypothesis*

Stanley Cavell, *Emerson's Transcendental Etudes*

Stuart McLean, *The Event and its Terrors: Ireland, Famine, Modernity*

Beate Rössler, ed., *Privacies: Philosophical Evaluations*

Bernard Faure, *Double Exposure: Cutting Across Buddhist and Western Discourses*

Alessia Ricciardi, *The Ends Of Mourning: Psychoanalysis, Literature, Film*

Alain Badiou, *Saint Paul: The Foundation of Universalism*

Gil Anidjar, *The Jew, the Arab: A History of the Enemy*

Jonathan Culler and Kevin Lamb, eds., *Just Being Difficult? Academic Writing in the Public Arena*

Jean-Luc Nancy, *A Finite Thinking*, edited by Simon Sparks

Theodor W. Adorno, *Can One Live after Auschwitz? A Philosophical Reader*, edited by Rolf Tiedemann

Patricia Pisters, *The Matrix of Visual Culture: Working with Deleuze in Film Theory*

Andreas Huyssen, *Present Pasts: Urban Palimpsests and the Politics of Memory*

Talal Asad, *Formations of the Secular: Christianity, Islam, Modernity*

Dorothea von Mücke, *The Rise of the Fantastic Tale*

Marc Redfield, *The Politics of Aesthetics: Nationalism, Gender, Romanticism*

Emmanuel Levinas, *On Escape*

Dan Zahavi, *Husserl's Phenomenology*

Rodolphe Gasché, *The Idea of Form: Rethinking Kant's Aesthetics*

Michael Naas, *Taking on the Tradition: Jacques Derrida and the Legacies of Deconstruction*

Herlinde Pauer-Studer, ed., *Constructions of Practical Reason: Interviews on Moral and Political Philosophy*

Jean-Luc Marion, *Being Given That: Toward a Phenomenology of Givenness*

Theodor W. Adorno and Max Horkheimer, *Dialectic of Enlightenment*

Ian Balfour, *The Rhetoric of Romantic Prophecy*

Martin Stokhof, *World and Life as One: Ethics and Ontology in Wittgenstein's Early Thought*

Gianni Vattimo, *Nietzsche: An Introduction*

Jacques Derrida, *Negotiations: Interventions and Interviews, 1971-1998*, edited by Elizabeth Rottenberg

Brett Levinson, *The Ends of Literature: The Latin American "Boom" in the Neoliberal Marketplace*

Timothy J. Reiss, *Against Autonomy: Cultural Instruments, Mutualities, and the Fictive Imagination*

Hent de Vries and Samuel Weber, editors, *Religion and Media*

Niklas Luhmann, *Theories of Distinction: Re-Describing the Descriptions of Modernity*, edited and Introduction by William Rasch

Johannes Fabian, *Anthropology with an Attitude: Critical Essays*

Michel Henry, *I am the Truth: Toward a Philosophy of Christianity*

Gil Anidjar, *"Our Place in Al-Andalus": Kabbalah, Philosophy, Literature in Arab-Jewish Letters*

Hélène Cixous and Jacques Derrida, *Veils*

F. R. Ankersmit, *Historical Representation*

F. R. Ankersmit, *Political Representation*

Elissa Marder, *Dead Time: Temporal Disorders in the Wake of Modernity (Baudelaire and Flaubert)*

Reinhart Koselleck, *The Practice of Conceptual History: Timing History, Spacing Concepts*

Niklas Luhmann, *The Reality of the Mass Media*

Hubert Damisch, *A Childhood Memory by Piero della Francesca*

Hubert Damisch, *A Theory of /Cloud/: Toward a History of Painting*

Jean-Luc Nancy, *The Speculative Remark: (One of Hegel's bon mots)*

Jean-François Lyotard, *Soundproof Room: Malraux's Anti-Aesthetics*

Jan Patočka, *Plato and Europe*

Hubert Damisch, *Skyline: The Narcissistic City*

Isabel Hoving, *In Praise of New Travelers: Reading Caribbean Migrant Women Writers*

Richard Rand, ed., *Futures: Of Jacques Derrida*

William Rasch, *Niklas Luhmann's Modernity: The Paradoxes of Differentiation*

Jacques Derrida and Anne Dufourmantelle, *Of Hospitality*

Jean-François Lyotard, *The Confession of Augustine*

Kaja Silverman, *World Spectators*

Samuel Weber, *Institution and Interpretation: Expanded Edition*

Jeffrey S. Librett, *The Rhetoric of Cultural Dialogue: Jews and Germans in the Epoch of Emancipation*

Ulrich Baer, *Remnants of Song: Trauma and the Experience of Modernity in Charles Baudelaire and Paul Celan*

Samuel C. Wheeler III, *Deconstruction as Analytic Philosophy*

David S. Ferris, *Silent Urns: Romanticism, Hellenism, Modernity*

Rodolphe Gasché, *Of Minimal Things: Studies on the Notion of Relation*

Sarah Winter, *Freud and the Institution of Psychoanalytic Knowledge*

Samuel Weber, *The Legend of Freud: Expanded Edition*

Aris Fioretos, ed., *The Solid Letter: Readings of Friedrich Hölderlin*

J. Hillis Miller / Manuel Asensi, *Black Holes / J. Hillis Miller; or, Boustrophedonic Reading*

Miryam Sas, *Fault Lines: Cultural Memory and Japanese Surrealism*

Peter Schwenger, *Fantasm and Fiction: On Textual Envisioning*

Didier Maleuvre, *Museum Memories: History, Technology, Art*

Jacques Derrida, *Monolingualism of the Other; or, The Prosthesis of Origin*

Andrew Baruch Wachtel, *Making a Nation, Breaking a Nation: Literature and Cultural Politics in Yugoslavia*

Niklas Luhmann, *Love as Passion: The Codification of Intimacy*

Mieke Bal, editor, *The Practice of Cultural Analysis: Exposing Interdisciplinary Interpretation*

Jacques Derrida and Gianni Vattimo, editors, *Religion*

Jennifer A. Jordan, *Structures of Memory: Understanding Urban Change in Berlin and Beyond*